EXPO Architektur Dokumente

Beiträge zur Weltausstellung EXPO 2000 in Hannover

EXPO Architecture Documents

Contributions for the World Exposition EXPO 2000 in Hanover

Hatje Cantz Verlag

EXPO 2000-Architektur
EXPO 2000 Architecture

Architektur berührt alle Menschen, da ausnahmslos jeder von uns sich in ihr bewegt und mit ihr konfrontiert wird, ob er will oder nicht. Der Architektur kann man sich – anders als anderen Kunstformen – nicht entziehen, man wird von ihr ein Leben lang begleitet. Diese Zwangsläufigkeit macht Architektur zu einem allseits beliebten Diskussionsobjekt.

Weltausstellungen sind – auch und gerade im Zeitalter digitaler Vernetzung – eine einmalige und besondere Möglichkeit, Menschen einander näher zu bringen, sie etwas miteinander erleben zu lassen, miteinander zu feiern und zu lachen. Weltausstellungen gehen alle an, sind für alle Menschen gemacht – sie standen und stehen deshalb im besonderen Interesse der Öffentlichkeit.

Wen wundert es also, daß Architekturen im Zusammenhang mit einer Weltausstellung in einem ganz besonderen Maße – und das mit Recht – im Fokus des öffentlichen Interesses und einer allgemeinen Debattierfreudigkeit stehen? Das war schon immer so und kann bei dieser ersten Weltausstellung in Deutschland, die im Jahr 2000 in Hannover stattfindet, nicht anders sein. Medien nutzen das Ereignis, um über die Baukunst im allgemeinen, über Architektursprache, über »große« Architekten und ihre spezifischen Ausdrucksweisen und natürlich über spezielle Bauwerke der Weltausstellung im besonderen zu berichten. Die Darstellungen variieren so stark wie die Projekte, über die geschrieben wird: mal sachlich, mal emotional, aber immer engagiert.

Dabei haben es die Architekten dieser Weltausstellung sicher nicht einfach. Denn das, was hier im Sinne der Agenda 21 angestrebt wird, nämlich geringer Landverbrauch durch Nutzung eines vorhandenen Messegeländes und möglichst hundertprozentige Nachnutzung auch der neu erschlossenen Flächen, stellt höchste Ansprüche an die Geländeplaner. Sie müssen alle Planungen mit diesen Vorgaben – und natürlich dem gegebenen wirtschaftlichen Rahmen – in Einklang bringen, ganz abgesehen davon, daß von ihnen natürlich erwartet wird, ein perfekt funktionierendes, den praktischen und ästhetischen Ansprüchen der zukünftigen Besucher genügendes Gelände herzurichten.

Dies ist eine Gratwanderung zwischen den Welten (oder: ein Wechselspiel zwischen Kunst und Zweckmäßigkeit)! Daß es gelungen ist, davon berichtet dieses Heft. Es zeigt uns auf eindrucksvolle Weise an unterschiedlichsten Beispielen, daß die Architektur auf dem Weltausstellungsgelände sehenswert ist. Gemeinsam ist es den Geländeplanern und Architekten – in diesen Zeiten, in denen es große Baukunst nach Meinung der Kritiker ohnehin schwer hat – gelungen, herausragende Beispiele moderner Architektur zu realisieren. Das zukünftige Weltausstellungsgelände spiegelt die Vielfalt der heutigen Architektursprache wider, bezieht aber auch sehr selbstbewußt Zwangsvorgaben wirtschaftlicher Gegebenheiten mit ein. Der Besucher, und das ist für die Verantwortlichen für die Vorbereitung und Durchführung der ersten Weltausstellung in Deutschland einer der wichtigsten Aspekte überhaupt, wird schließlich ein homogenes Gelände vorfinden, auf dem er sich wohl fühlt und das ihn zum Verweilen einlädt. Und das ihn – zwangsläufig – zu den unumgänglichen Debattierrunden einladen wird.

Wir freuen uns schon darauf!

Birgit Breuel

Generalkommissarin der Weltausstellung EXPO 2000
Mitglied der Geschäftsführung

Architecture affects everybody, since we all (without exception) move around in it and are confronted by it, whether we like it or not. Unlike other art forms, it is impossible to avoid architecture, it permeates our life. This inevitability makes architecture a universally popular subject for discussion.

World expositions - even (and perhaps particularly) in the age of digital networking - offer a unique and special opportunity for bringing people together, sharing experiences, celebrating and laughing with others. World expositions matter to everybody, are made for everybody - and that's why the public had and has a special interest in them.

It is hardly surprising that architecture in the context of a world exposition should (rightly) attract a very high degree of public attention and stimulate particularly intense discussion. This has always been the case, and for Germany's first world exposition, to take place in the year 2000, it will again prove true. The media are taking this opportunity to report on architecture generally, the language of architecture, the great architects and their specific styles, and, naturally, about specific constructions at the World Exposition itself. The reports usually vary as widely as the projects they deal with - objective, emotional, but always enthusiastic.

This doesn't mean that the architects at the World Exposition have it easy! The goals (in the spirit of Agenda 21) are to minimize land use by utilising existing fairgrounds and ensuring 100% post use (as far as possible) also of newly developed areas. These requirements pose major challenges to the site planners, who have to reconcile all their planning with these demands while, of course, keeping within a given budget framework - quite apart from the fact that they are naturally also expected to create a perfectly functional site which satisfies the practical and aesthetic demands of future visitors.

This involves a tightrope walk between worlds (or a trade-off between art and utility). Its success story is documented in the present volume, with various examples illustrating quite impressively that the architecture on the world exposition site is worth seeing. Together, the site planners and the architects (in an age which the critics argue is a difficult time for great architecture) have succeeded in creating outstanding specimens of modern architecture. The future world exposition site reflects the diversity of style in modern architecture, while at the same time confidently incorporating the requirements dictated by commercial realities. Visitors – and this is one of the most important considerations for those responsible for preparing and running the first world exposition in Germany – will ultimately see a homogenous site which makes them feel comfortable and tempts them to stay.

Yet, it is also a site which will be likely to draw them into the inevitable discussions. And we are already looking forward to these.

Birgit Breuel

Commissioner General of the World Exposition EXPO 2000
Member of the Chief Executive Committee

EXPO 2000: Rückblick und Ausblick

EXPO 2000: Retrospect and Prospect

Andreas Denk und Carl Steckeweh im Gespräch mit/**talking to** Sepp Heckmann

»Unser Motto ist ein Symbol«

»Our Motto is a Symbol«

CARL STECKEWEH: Das Motto »Mensch – Natur – Technik« war im Juni 1990 euphorischer Ausgangspunkt des Unternehmens EXPO 2000. Was ist neun Jahre später, einige Monate vor der Eröffnung, von der damaligen Begeisterung übriggeblieben?

SEPP HECKMANN: Die Euphorie der Bewerbungsphase hat sich bis heute gehalten. Die Thematik und das Ereignis EXPO 2000 haben nach wie vor einen großen Stellenwert und versprechen inhaltlich größte Attraktivität. Wir waren von Anfang an überzeugt, daß ein historischer Moment wie die Weltausstellung ein Wahrzeichen benötigt, einen Kernpunkt, an dem man sich orientieren kann. Die Bestimmung des Mottos »Mensch – Natur – Technik« ist eine solche Leitidee. Sie wird so intensiv verfolgt, daß sich zum ersten Mal in der Geschichte der Weltausstellung ein Großteil aller Länderbeiträge diesem Thema widmen wird.

ANDREAS DENK: Wie kam es damals zur Themenfindung?

HECKMANN: Der Slogan entstand aus der Erkenntnis, daß unsere Welt und wir endlich sind, wenn wir mit derselben Mentalität weiterwirtschaften wie in den letzten 150 Jahren. Wenn uns kein Bewußtseinswandel zu einer Harmonie von Mensch, Natur und Technik gelingt, müssen wir uns über das Ende dieser Entwicklung ernsthafte Sorgen machen. Das Motto soll einen Zeitpunkt, ein Jahr des Umdenkens definieren. Es ist nicht mehr und nicht weniger als ein Symbol, daß wir versuchen müssen, neu zu denken, und daß wir die beklagenswerte, aber notwendige Entwicklung der letzten 150 Jahre mit den Erkenntnissen, die wir heute haben, harmonisch verbinden müssen.

STECKEWEH: Das hört sich recht widersprüchlich nach einer »realen Utopie« an …

CARL STECKEWEH: The motto »Humankind – Nature – Technology« set the euphoric starting signal for EXPO 2000 back in June 1990. Nine years later, some months before the opening, how much of that initial enthusiasm still remains?

SEPP HECKMANN: The euphoria of the candidate phase has stayed with us all the way. Both the theme and actual event of EXPO 2000 still have great importance, and its content promises to have enormous appeal. Right from the start we've been convinced that a historical moment like the World Exposition needs a symbol, a focus you can centre on. The choice of the motto »Humankind – Nature – Technology« provides such a guiding concept. It is being followed up with such commitment that for the first time in the history of the world exposition most of the national contributions deal with this theme.

ANDREAS DENK: How did it come about that this particular theme was chosen?

HECKMANN: The theme arose from the recognition that we and our world will run out of time if we continue to produce with the mentality of the past 150 years. Unless we can create a new awareness leading to a harmony of humankind, nature and technology, we'll have reason for serious concern about where this trend will lead. The motto is intended to define a time, a year of rethinking. It is no more and no less than a symbol that we need to try to change our thinking and that we must bring the regrettable but inevitable trend of the past 150 years into a harmony with the knowledge available to us today.

STECKEWEH: This sounds very much like a contradiction, a »real utopia«…

HECKMANN: I'm not putting any scientific weight into this theme, it's a

HECKMANN: Ich will keine wissenschaftliche Gewichtung in dieses Motto legen. Es ist ein einfacher, pragmatischer Ansatz an der Schwelle, die das Jahr 2000 ist und die symbolischen Charakter für die Menschheit haben wird. Wir wollen darauf hinweisen, daß wir an dieser Schwelle stehen und uns neu zu orientieren und darüber nachzudenken haben, wie wir für unsere Kinder Voraussetzungen für eine Zukunft schaffen können.

DENK: Kann das gelingen? Während des langen Vorlaufs, den das Thema »Mensch – Natur – Technik« in bezug auf die Weltausstellung hatte, hat sich herausgestellt, daß die Inhalte dieser Idee mäßig konkretisierbar und schwer vermittelbar waren. Wie läßt sich Ihrer Meinung nach das schwammige Motto füllen, damit die EXPO 2000 tatsächlich zu einem Teil dieses »Symbols« werden kann?

HECKMANN: Ohne Frage wird die EXPO 2000 in Hannover zu einem Symbol, dazu hat die Diskussion in den letzten Jahren schon zu große Wellen geschlagen. Hätten wir nicht mit diesem symbolhaften Motto begonnen, wäre von anderer Seite ein Vorstoß gekommen, der das Jahr 2000 als Meilenstein des Umdenkens und Neuorganisierens ausgerufen hätte. Und wenn heute Münzen mit der Aufschrift »Mensch – Natur – Technik« geprägt werden und somit das Motto gar nicht mehr EXPO 2000-spezifisch benutzt wird, sondern in vielen Bereichen und Veröffentlichungen als Synonym für eine neue Denkungsart aufgenommen wird, haben wir schon vieles von dem erreicht, was wir wollten.

DENK: »Mensch – Natur – Technik« ist ein Schlagwort, aber kein Inhalt. Wie wollen Sie den Slogan inhaltlich füllen?

HECKMANN: Man braucht für alles eine Überschrift. Das Motto ist eine Metapher, die inhaltlich von der EXPO 2000 in allen Bereichen gefüllt wird. Das fängt mit der Entscheidung für eine Weltausstellung an diesem Standort an: Wir wollten eine EXPO 2000 in neuer Dimension an einem Standort, an dem bereits eine große Struktur vorhanden ist und nicht alles neu gebaut werden muß. Und es geht weiter mit der Nachnutzung all dessen, was für die EXPO 2000 entwickelt wird: Es wird kaum EXPO 2000-spezifisch geplant, sondern unter dem Gesichtspunkt einer Nachnutzung, die sich an den Bedürfnissen der Stadt und der Region orientiert. Das einzige, was nur für die EXPO 2000 entwickelt wird, sind einige Länderpavillons, die jedoch zumeist so geplant und umgesetzt werden, daß sie im Anschluß abgebaut, an anderer Stelle wiederaufgebaut und einer neuen Nutzung zugeführt werden können. Auch für alle Anlagen, die um das Gelände herum geplant sind – wie die Verkehrsinfrastruktur nebst Parkplätzen –, gelten entsprechende ökologische Anforderungen, die auf die Region zugeschnitten sind. Und schließlich wird unsere Gastronomie weitgehend Mehrweg-Geschirr verwenden. Also weg von der Wegwerfgesellschaft, hin zur Wiederverwendung von Ressourcen oder einem Materialeinsatz, der gar keine Entsorgung erforderlich macht. Darüber hinaus betrifft das Motto selbstverständlich auch Inhalte des Themenparkes, in dem in verschiedenen Bereichen aktuelle technologische und wissenschaftliche Erkenntnisse präsentiert werden. »Mensch – Natur – Technik« ist also nicht nur auf einen Bereich der EXPO 2000 zugeschnitten: Die gesamte Weltausstellung unterwirft sich dieser Thematik und arbeitet daran, um in möglichst vielen Bereichen Beispiele für Zukunftsansätze zu geben.

STECKEWEH: Glauben Sie, daß dieser Dreiklang, diese Metapher, die ja durchaus verfängt, überhaupt dargestellt werden kann?

HECKMANN: Die Idee ist schwer vermittelbar. Ihre Inhalte sind einerseits ein-

simple, pragmatic approach to the threshold set by the year 2000 which will have symbolic status for humanity. We're making the statement that we're at this threshold and that we have to reorient and consider how we can create the conditions for a future for our children.

DENK: Can this succeed? Over the long run-up that the theme »Humankind – Nature – Technology« has had for the World Exposition, we've seen only partial success in giving concrete form to the ideas behind the theme, which have been difficult to put across. How do you think this empty formula can be filled so that EXPO 2000 can really become part of this »symbol«?

HECKMANN: EXPO 2000 Hanover will undoubtedly be a symbol, the debate in recent years has already had a great impact. If we hadn't started out with this symbolic theme, other people would have taken the initiative in proclaiming the year 2000 as a crucial time for rethinking and restructuring. And the fact that coins are being struck today with the inscription »Humankind – Nature – Technology«, so that the motto isn't limited any more to EXPO 2000 but is seen in many areas and publications as synonymous with a new way of thinking, shows that we've already achieved a great deal of what we set out to do.

DENK: »Humankind – Nature – Technology« is a formula without content. How do you intend to give it content?

HECKMANN: You need a banner for everything. The motto is a metaphor which will be filled with content in every respect by EXPO 2000. It starts with the decision to hold a world exposition at this venue. We wanted an EXPO 2000 in a new dimension at a site which already had extensive facilities, where everything didn't have to be built from scratch. And this is carried through into the post use of everything developed for EXPO 2000. There's virtually no planning which is restricted specifically to EXPO 2000. Most buildings and facilities are planned for some post use geared to the development of the city and the region. Just a few national pavilions are EXPO-specific, but most of these are planned and implemented so that they can be dismantled afterwards and re-erected at another location for a new use. All the facilities on and around the site – for example, the traffic infrastructure and parking areas – are also subject to ecological requirements tailored to the region. Finally, our catering facilities will largely have reusable crockery. This is a move away from the throw-away mentality of the past towards the recycling of resources or the use of materials which don't require disposal. In addition, the motto naturally also relates to the content of the Theme Park, where various aspects of current technological and scientific knowledge will be presented. »Humankind – Nature – Technology« isn't meant for just one area of EXPO 2000: this theme spans the entire world exposition, aiming at giving examples of future applications in as many fields as possible.

STECKEWEH: While it's very catchy, do you believe that this triad, this metaphor, can be communicated at all?

HECKMANN: The idea is difficult to convey. The content is simple on the one hand, complex on the other. However, we've made a small addition to the EXPO 2000 motto – »Humankind – Nature – Technology – A New World Arising«. This makes our intention very clear.

fach, andererseits komplex. Wir haben aber beim EXPO 2000-Motto eine kleine Ergänzung vorgenommen: »Mensch – Natur – Technik – eine neue Welt entsteht«. Damit wird unsere Absicht bildlich.

STECKEWEH: Sie haben gerade beschrieben, daß von der EXPO 2000 eine Botschaft ausgehen soll. Es gibt viele, die voll und ganz dahinter stehen. Es gibt aber auch nicht wenige Entscheidungsträger in Politik und Wirtschaft, die der Ansicht sind, daß die Zeit für die Umsetzung eines solchen Ansatzes nicht reif ist. Wieweit ist diese Verbildlichung, die »subkutane Unterwanderung«, in die Köpfe der Entscheidungsträger vorgedrungen? Glauben Sie, daß die EXPO 2000 eine angemessene Umsetzung des Mottos leisten kann?

HECKMANN: Die EXPO 2000 wird dies leisten können. Sie wird das Jahrhundertereignis werden. Gerade in bezug auf das Thema »Mensch – Natur – Technik« wird sie ein Meilenstein werden. Selbstverständlich gibt es bei einem solchen Thema Kritiker. Ohne Frage braucht es eine lange Vorbereitungszeit. Und daß es schwierig ist, ein solches Thema kontinuierlich im oberen Bereich der Diskussion zu halten, versteht sich von selbst. Aber im Laufe der nächsten Wochen und Monate werden wir sehen, daß die Zeit *für* die EXPO 2000 läuft: Die Kritiker, die vor zwei bis drei Jahren klagten und unkten, sind heute schon leiser geworden. In der Zwischenzeit ist man in vielen Bereichen, auch in den Unternehmen, intensiv damit beschäftigt, wie man sich in die EXPO 2000 einbringen kann.

DENK: Noch 1998 hatte die EXPO 2000 viele vage Zusagen von verschiedenen Seiten, aber kaum Zusagen für konkrete Projekte. Insbesondere galt dies für einen Hauptwirtschaftsfaktor der Bundesrepublik, die chemische Industrie, die sich mit dem Thema ganz und gar nicht anfreunden konnte. Sehen Sie inzwischen auch bei der Industrie das entsprechende Entgegenkommen?

HECKMANN: Die Industrie ist in der Zwischenzeit in allen wichtigen Bereichen so integriert, daß man heute von konkreten Projekten sprechen kann. Die chemische Industrie beispielsweise wird sich am Themenpark beteiligen, bei dem die Verbindlichkeit unseres Mottos auch in den Verhandlungen mit der Industrie eine wichtige Rolle spielt.

DENK: Stichworte wie »eine EXPO neuen Typs« und »Symbol der EXPO 2000 ist Ihre Idee« subsumieren auch, daß thematisch eine sehr genaue Absprache mit den anderen Teilnehmerländern erfolgen soll. Sie meinen auch, daß externe Projekte stark an das Mutterprojekt angebunden und so die EXPO 2000 in den Bundesländern und auch in anderen Staaten fortsetzen sollen. Was ist von dieser Idee geblieben? Ist es gelungen, die unterschiedlichen Projekte so zusammenzuhalten, daß eine gemeinsame Stoßrichtung erkennbar wird?

HECKMANN: Die Weltausstellung wird genau so umgesetzt, wie es von der Konzeption her gedacht war. Auf der einen Seite muß jedes Land für seinen Beitrag in Hannover eine Begründung einreichen, die geprüft wird. Erst nach der Billigung dieses Konzepts werden die Verhandlungen mit den Ländern über ihre Beteiligung weitergeführt. Die inhaltliche Auseinandersetzung mit der Thematik ist also sichergestellt. Dies gilt auch für die »Weltweiten Projekte«, die wir als Symbolprojekte für zukunftsorientierte Lösungen ins Programm aufgenommen haben, um die EXPO 2000 nicht nur hier in Hannover zu konzentrieren, sondern den Gedanken von »Mensch – Natur – Technik« global zu diskutieren.

STECKEWEH: Auf der einen Seite fördern Sie zentrale Projekte, die auf Hannover bezogen sind, auf der anderen dezentrale Vorhaben, was große Vorteile

STECKEWEH: You've just described that EXPO 2000 is intended to carry a message. There are many who support this entirely. However, there are also quite a few decision-makers in politics and business who feel that such an approach is premature. How far has this dissenting view, this subconscious reservation gained ground among decision-makers? Do you think that EXPO 2000 can bring about implementation of its theme on a reasonable scale?

HECKMANN: EXPO 2000 will do just this. It will be the event of the century. In terms of its theme »Humankind – Nature – Technology« in particular, it will be a milestone. Naturally, with such a theme, there are always critics. Clearly, a lot of preparation is needed. And it goes without saying that it's hard to keep a theme like this constantly to the fore in discussion. But over the weeks and months to come, we'll see that time is on the side of EXPO 2000. The critics who were complaining and scoffing just two or three years ago are all but silenced now. Since then, people in many areas, including the companies, have been working hard on how to place themselves in EXPO 2000.

DENK: Even in 1998 EXPO 2000 had a lot of vague promises from all sorts of people, but virtually no commitments for concrete projects. This was particularly true of a key sector of the German economy, the chemical industry, which wasn´t happy about the theme at all. Do you feel that industry has since become better disposed?

HECKMANN: All the major sectors of industry are now integrated to the point where we can speak of concrete projects. The chemical industry, for example, will participate in the Thematic Area, and the binding nature of our motto is playing a major role in negotiations with the industry as well.

DENK: Slogans like »an EXPO in a new style«, »the symbol of EXPO 2000 – your idea« also imply that close consultation on theme aspects is intended with the other participating nations. You also believe that external projects should be strongly tied to the parent project, continuing the work of EXPO 2000 in the Federal Republic of Germany and in other countries as well. How much of this idea has survived? Have you managed to keep the various projects together so that a common thrust is still apparent?

HECKMANN: The World Exposition will be implemented exactly in accordance with the original concept. Each country has to submit a rationale for its contribution in Hanover for review. Negotiations with countries on participation are only continued after this concept has been approved, and this ensures the focus on the theme. The same goes for the »Worldwide Projects«, which we've included in the programme as symbolic projects for future-oriented solutions in order to ensure that EXPO 2000 isn't clustered here in Hanover but part of a global discussion of the ideas behind »Humankind – Nature – Technology«.

STECKEWEH: You're promoting central projects focused in Hanover and at the same time also decentralized projects, which can be a very good thing. But doesn't this mean you're bringing competitors on board like VW-City at Wolfsburg, which is already being held up as a shining example of »urban entertainment«?

HECKMANN: I don't think we're bringing in competitors. That wasn't the idea. We want the discussion of the theme »Humankind – Nature –

haben kann. Aber holen Sie sich damit nicht unliebsame Konkurrenz ins Boot wie die VW-City in Wolfsburg, die jetzt schon als Musterbeispiel eines »Urban Entertainment« dargestellt wird?

HECKMANN: Ich glaube nicht, daß wir uns Wettbewerber ins Boot holen. Das war auch nicht die Absicht. Wir wollen, daß die Diskussion zum Thema »Mensch – Natur – Technik« weltweit stattfinden kann, und das erreichen wir beispielsweise damit, daß eine ehemals massiv industriell geprägte Region wie Bitterfeld ihr zentrales Thema der Renaturierung und ihre Lösungsansätze darstellen kann. Für viele andere Regionen in der Welt ist dies ein hervorragender Anschauungsunterricht, wie man mit einem solchen Problem umgehen kann.

STECKEWEH: Der Aspekt der Nachnutzung in Verbindung mit dem Primat der Nachhaltigkeit ist Ihrer Auffassung nach in Hannover ideal zu verwirklichen. Es soll keine hinterlassenen Ruinen geben, obwohl man sich bei einigen Länderpavillons fragen muß, was aus ihnen werden soll. Einige Stimmen mutmaßen jedoch, daß ihr größter Kritiker schon jetzt die Deutsche Messe AG in Hannover ist, die mit den übrigbleibenden Bauten etwas anfangen muß …

HECKMANN: Ohne die Messe AG und die bestehende Infrastruktur des Messegeländes hätte es nie eine Weltausstellung gegeben. Insofern war das die Basis. Neben dem Motto »Mensch – Natur – Technik« war es unsere zweite Idee, eine Weltausstellung neuer Dimension zu machen. Es war klar, daß es für eine Weltausstellung im Jahre 2000 nicht ausreichen würde, lediglich nachzuahmen, wie Weltausstellungen in den letzten dreißig Jahren konzipiert wurden. Es ist bekannt, daß die außerordentlich negativen Aspekte im Nachlauf der Veranstaltungen an anderen Expo-Standorten wie beispielsweise Sevilla, wo eine Nachnutzung nicht gegeben war, auch heute noch diskutiert werden. Unsere Basis hingegen ist das weltgrößte vorhandene Messegelände mit seiner Infrastruktur. Wir verfügen also über eine Grundstruktur, die nicht EXPO 2000-spezifisch mit einem Investitionsvolumen von 2,5–3 Milliarden Mark gebaut werden muß, sondern die an die EXPO 2000-Entwicklung so angepaßt werden kann, daß eine hundertprozentige Nachnutzung sicher ist. Das ist eine dieser neuen Dimensionen der EXPO 2000 und war eines der entscheidenden Argumente für das Plazet der Bundesregierung im Jahre 1988.

DENK: Glauben Sie, daß das Anliegen der Agenda 21 nach der EXPO 2000 in einer breiten Öffentlichkeit an Bedeutung gewonnen haben wird?

HECKMANN: Ganz sicher wird es gewinnen, weil sehr viele Gesichtspunkte der EXPO 2000 auf der Agenda 21 beruhen.

DENK: Aber die Agenda 21 ist den meisten Bundesbürgern bislang unbekannt …

HECKMANN: Die EXPO 2000 wird sie transparent machen.

STECKEWEH: Die EXPO 2000 soll eine Art Multiplikatorenwirkung haben, und zwar nicht nur in abstrakt-symbolischen, sondern auch in konkreten Bereichen. Welche neuen Verkehrstechnologien wird man beispielsweise auf der EXPO 2000 anschauen können, und welche Bedeutung wird das Projekt des Transrapid dabei spielen?

HECKMANN: Wir haben im Themenpark eine Sektion unter dem Titel zum Thema »Mobilität«. Es wird eine Reihe von Anregungen geben, wie man den Verkehr in Zukunft gestalten kann, insbesondere, was das Zusammenspiel zwischen öffentlichem und privatem Verkehr angeht. Wichtig ist auch, wie

Technology« to be worldwide, and we're achieving this for example by enabling a former heavily industrial region like Bitterfeld to present its central theme of renaturalization and its various approaches to it. For many other regions in the world this is an outstanding object lesson of how to tackle this kind of problem.

STECKEWEH: You believe that the question of post use combined with the requirement of sustainability can be ideally resolved in Hanover. The aim is to avoid abandoned ruins, even if some national pavilions do raise problems with post use. However, there are voices claiming that your biggest critic is Deutsche Messe AG in Hanover, which will have the job of finding uses for the left-over structures.

HECKMANN: Without Deutsche Messe AG and the existing infrastructure at the fairgrounds the World Exposition would never have been possible. To a large degree, this was the basis for it. Apart from the motto »Humankind – Nature – Technology« our second idea was to create a world exposition with new dimensions. It was clear that it wouldn't be enough for a world exposition in the year 2000 simply to follow the lead of the concepts of world expositions in the past thirty years. We know that the extremely negative aspects following events at other venues – such as Seville, where there was no post-use – are still fuelling debate. By contrast, we had as a basis the world's largest existing fairgrounds, complete with infrastructure. This means that we have a basic structure which doesn't have to be created just for EXPO 2000 with an investment of 2.5–3 billion DM: instead, it can be adapted for the EXPO 2000 development in a way that ensures total subsequent utilization. This is one of the new dimensions at EXPO 2000, and was one of the most important arguments in getting the approval of the German Federal Government back in 1988.

DENK: Do you think that the goals of Agenda 21 will take on new significance for the general public after EXPO 2000?

HECKMANN: They most certainly will, because a lot of aspects of EXPO 2000 are based on Agenda 21.

DENK: But Agenda 21 is still largely an unknown quantity for most Germans …

HECKMANN: EXPO 2000 will make it easy to understand.

STECKEWEH: But EXPO 2000 is supposed to have a sort of multiplier function, not just in abstract and symbolic terms but also in concrete areas. What new transport technologies, for example, will we be able to see at EXPO 2000, and what significance will the Transrapid project have?

HECKMANN: We have a section in the Thematic Area with the heading »Mobility«. There will be numerous impulses on how to design transport of the future, and particularly the interrelationship between public and private transport. Another important question is how to tap energy sources which will make possible more environment-oriented forms of transport. I don't think that the Transrapid will play a major role in this.

DENK: What role will the presentation of innovative architecture play at EXPO 2000? The former EXPO 2000 CEO Theodor Diener once said that the World Exposition has architecture so people have something to photograph …

Energiequellen erschlossen werden, die einen umweltfreundlicheren Verkehr ermöglichen. Ich glaube nicht, daß der Transrapid dort eine große Rolle spielt.

Denk: Welche Rolle wird die Darstellung innovativer Architektur auf der EXPO 2000 spielen? Der ehemalige EXPO 2000-Geschäftsführer Theodor Diener hat einmal gesagt, bei der Weltausstellung sei Architektur dazu da, damit es etwas zu fotografieren gibt ...

Heckmann: Das finde ich zuwenig. Wenn EXPO 2000 und Messe als Bauherr auftreten, müssen sie die heutigen Erkenntnisse und zukunftsorientierte Überlegungen in ihre Planungen integrieren. Das heißt, daß sie zukunftsorientiert bauen: Zunächst muß die inhaltliche Aufgabenstellung für diese Gebäude definiert werden und entsprechenden Ansprüchen genügen. Erst dann kann das fotogene Spektakel hinzukommen. Für die erste Prämisse haben wir bei allen Gebäuden, die bisher geplant worden sind und die im Rahmen der EXPO 2000 realisiert werden, Sorge getragen. Hier kommen völlig neue Konzepte der Energieeinsparung, der Nutzung von natürlichen Ressourcen, der Verwendung von Holz als Rohstoff zur Anwendung – alles Vorhaben, die in dieser Form noch nirgends realisiert worden sind und deshalb beispielgebend wirken sollen.

Steckeweh: Bis heute gibt es nach Aussagen des Investors keine Weiternutzungsmöglichkeit für den Deutschen Pavillon, der das Zentrum der Expo-Plaza bilden wird. Glauben Sie, daß auch die Planung der Plaza ökologisch und betriebswirtschaftlich beispielhaft wird?

Heckmann: Auf dem Gelände der Plaza entstehen keine Expo-Gebäude, sondern Bauten von Investoren, die selbstverständlich eigene Intentionen damit verbinden. Diese Bauten werden nach Investorenart vor allem unter betriebswirtschaftlichen Gesichtspunkten geplant.

Denk: Betriebswirtschaftlichkeit kann aber immer nur ein Segment bei der Beurteilung von Architektur sein. Ökonomie und Nachhaltigkeit im Messebau sind sicherlich interessante und wichtige Themen, aber die Bemühungen um eine Architektur des 21. Jahrhunderts sollten auf breiteren Füßen stehen. Wie bemächtigt sich die EXPO 2000 dieses virulenten Themas?

Heckmann: Ich würde nicht von Messebau sprechen. Wir versuchen, in Hannover beispielgebende Lösungen zu realisieren, die anderswo in die Planung vieler anderer Gebäude hineinwirken. Wir verwirklichen zukunftsorientierte Lösungen in Bereichen, in denen private Bauherrn im Zweifelsfall kaum bereit sind, Risiken auf sich zu nehmen. Wir sind bereit, diese Risiken einzugehen, die für private Auftraggeber untragbar wären, weil sie technisch erst am Beginn des Erprobungsstadiums sind und der Nachweis fehlt, daß sie funktionieren. Damit geben wir neue Anstöße für die gesamte Architektur.

Denk: Ein sinnvolles Projekt in diesem Zusammenhang schien die Entwicklung des Stadtteils Kronsberg im Anschluß an das Messegelände. Einen ähnlichen Versuch gab es bereits bei der Weltausstellung in Lissabon. Das dortige Quartier ist in der Fachpresse sehr unterschiedlich beurteilt worden. Im Falle Kronsberg ist nun schon im Vorfeld von großen finanziellen und konzeptionellen Problemen zu hören. Was wird 2000 dort zu sehen sein?

Heckmann: Der Ortsteil wird wohl nicht im ursprünglichen Umfang realisiert. Man hat den Bedarf überschätzt. Trotzdem wird der Umfang, in dem der Kronsberg bebaut wird, beachtlich sein und die Möglichkeit zu einer weiteren Entwicklung eröffnen. Ich glaube, daß dort eine Reihe interessanter Lösungen zu sehen sein wird. Die EXPO 2000 ist jedoch nicht unmittelbar in dieses eigentlich städtische Projekt involviert. Sie hat lediglich die An-

Heckmann: I don't think that goes far enough. Where EXPO 2000 and Deutsche Messe AG appear as developers, they have an obligation to integrate the latest information and future-oriented thinking into their planning. This means they have to build in a future-oriented way: First, the functions of a building have to be defined, and then the corresponding requirements have to be met. Then you can start talking about the photographic impact. We've taken care of the first aspect in all the buildings planned to date which will be constructed within the context of EXPO 2000. These will exploit completely new concepts in energy conservation, utilization of natural resources, the use of wood as a raw material – all projects which have never before been implemented in this form and which will accordingly serve as examples.

Steckeweh: So far, according to investors, there is no opening for a future use for the German pavilion, which will be the centre of the Expo-Plaza. Do you think that the planning of the Plaza will serve as an ecological and commercial example?

Heckmann: There are no Expo buildings as such being constructed on the Plaza area, these are buildings belonging to investors who naturally have their own plans for them. Investors are primarily planning these buildings on commercial considerations.

Denk: Commercial viability can only ever be one aspect in judging architecture. Economy and sustainability in trade fair construction are certainly interesting and important themes, but the effort to create an architecture of the 21st century should be more broadly based than this. How is EXPO 2000 dealing with this tempestuous question?

Heckmann: I wouldn't limit it to trade fair construction. We're trying to implement exemplary solutions in Hanover which will have an impact on the planning of many other buildings elsewhere. We are implementing future-oriented solutions in areas where private developers will hardly be prepared to accept the risks, in case of doubt. We're prepared to accept risks which would be unacceptable for private clients because they're right at the start of their practical life and lack the proof that they're functional. In this way we're providing new stimulus for architecture as a whole.

Denk: One project that seemed useful in this connection was the development of the Kronsberg section of the city adjoining the fairgrounds. A similar approach was taken at the world exposition in Lisbon. The resulting district has received very varying reviews in the professional journals. In the case of Kronsberg, we're already hearing stories of major financial and conceptual difficulties. What will we be seeing there in the year 2000?

Heckmann: The district won't be implemented on the scale originally intended. We overestimated needs. Even so, the scale of development at Kronsberg will be impressive, and will open up the possibility of further development. I believe that we'll see a whole range of interesting solutions there. However, EXPO 2000 isn't directly involved in the actual urban project. It has simply taken over leasing during the event, because this matches its needs. EXPO 2000 is acting here as a sort of locomotive.

Denk: But Kronsberg was supposed to be a central reference project for EXPO 2000 – which makes it more than just accommodation for

mietung während der Veranstaltung übernommen, weil sie einen entsprechenden Bedarf dafür hat. Die EXPO 2000 dient hier gewissermaßen als Motor.

DENK: Kronsberg sollte jedoch ein zentrales Referenzprojekt der EXPO 2000 werden – und damit mehr als nur Wohnstätte für Expo-Mitarbeiter. Glauben Sie, daß der Stadtteil soviel Attraktivität bekommen wird, daß sich Besucher – wie bei der Stadterneuerungsmaßnahme in Lissabon – vom Messegelände dorthin bewegen?

HECKMANN: Jeder, der mit Architektur und Wohnen beruflich zu tun hat, wird dorthin gehen. Aber das Gesamtvolumen der EXPO 2000 ist so groß, daß die Besucher sich vor allem auf dem Messegelände aufhalten werden und selbst dort tagelang zu tun haben, um alles zu sehen. Aber auch so werden alle von der EXPO 2000 in Hannover mit dem Eindruck zurückkehren, daß sie am Beginn des Aufbruchs in ein neues Zeitalter und am Beginn einer Entwicklung stehen, die jetzt noch nicht genau abzuschätzen ist, die aber – auch mit Wagnissen und Experimenten – eingeleitet werden muß.

Expo employees. Do you think that the district will become attractive enough to draw visitors from the fairgrounds, as happened with the urban renovation measures in Lisbon?

HECKMANN: Anybody professionally concerned with architecture and living environments is going to visit. But the total scale of EXPO 2000 is so large that visitors will primarily stay on the site, and will have their hands full for days trying to see everything. Even so, everybody will come away from EXPO 2000 in Hanover with the impression that they're on the threshold of a new era, at the start of a development which we can't accurately predict yet, but one which – for all its perils and experiments – we have to embark on.

Sepp Heckmann ist Mitglied des Vorstandes der Deutschen Messe AG
sowie verantwortlich für den Bereich Planen und Bauen, Betrieb und Kommunikationstechnik
der EXPO 2000 Hannover GmbH.

Andreas Denk ist Redakteur der Zeitschrift *Der Architekt*.

Carl Steckeweh ist Bundesgeschäftsführer des BDA und Herausgeber von
CENTRUM – Jahrbuch Architektur und Stadt.

Sepp Heckmann is a Member of the Board of Deutsche Messe AG
and also responsible for the devisions planning and construction, operation and
communication technology for EXPO 2000 Hannover GmbH.

Andreas Denk is the editor of the magazine *Der Architekt*.

Carl Steckeweh is the Federal Managing Director of BDA and Editor of
CENTRUM – Jahrbuch Architektur und Stadt.

Ausschnitt aus dem vorhandenen Messegelände
Partial View of Existing Fair Site

Reinhart Wustlich

Technologieentwicklung und Nachhaltigkeit im Bauen. Neuere Bauten der Messe Hannover

Technological Development and Sustainability in Construction. Recent Buildings for the Hanover Trade Fair

Der Begriff des Entwerfens, der den Längsschnitt der Technologieentwicklung einbezieht und auf ihrem gegenwärtigen Stand den reflexiven Begriff der Nachhaltigkeit respektiert, gehört zu den komplexen Definitionen des Bauens. Die Theorie der reflexiven Modernisierung bietet Anlaß für eine »Kehrtwende der Moderne« (Scott Lash), in der das »System« aufhört, immer unerbittlicher die »Lebenswelt« zu zerstören.[1]

Es reicht seit langem nicht mehr aus, das Entwerfen als kleinen Maßstab der Entwicklung auf sich selbst gestellter Gebäude zu verstehen – und die tausendfache, zig-tausendfache Kopie dieses Vorgangs bei anderen Vorhaben und damit den großen Maßstab der Entwicklung zu ignorieren. Das Entwerfen des »Systems«, das die »Lebenswelt« vorausschauend aufbaut, steht zur Disposition: als Antizipation einer zukünftigen Welt, als Rückübersetzung in einen sozial verstehbaren, kulturell geprägten Raum – als Ausdruck einer Gesellschaft, die »sich« entwirft.

Früher Ausdruck dieses reflexiven Gehalts des Entwerfens, das im sozialen Sinne Normen der Tradition überprüft, ist bereits Jean-Paul Sartres existentialistische Auslegung des Begriffs. In der Diktion Sartres ist das Entwerfen eine philosophische Herausforderung: Danach entwirft der Mensch sich in die Zukunft, ist er »nichts anderes als sein Entwurf, ... existiert [er] nur in dem Maße, in dem er sich verwirklicht, er ist also nichts anderes als die Gesamtheit seiner Handlungen, nichts anderes als sein Leben.«[2] Eine solche Bilanz fordert das Entwerfen als Antizipation künftiger »Lebenswelt« heraus, es befragt zugleich das »System«, in dem sich Vorstellungen darüber, wie die Gesellschaft leben will, entwickeln können.

Das Motto der Weltausstellung »Mensch – Natur – Technik« konnte ursprünglich als Anstoß einer existentiellen Auslegung des Entwerfens verstanden werden, einen Ort in die Zukunft zu entwerfen – durch eine »Gesellschaft, die sich entwirft«. Welche Anlässe sollten eine Gesellschaft,

A concept of design that takes account of the breadth of technological developments and respects the reflexive idea of sustainability in its present form belongs to the more complex definitions of construction. The theory of reflexive modernization provides the occasion for a »volte-face of modernism« (Scott Lash), which would put an end to the increasingly relentless destruction of our »habitat« by the »system«.[1]

For a long time now, it has not been adequate to regard design simply as the small-scale development of individual buildings, ignoring the thousandfold, the umpteen-thousandfold, repetition of this process in other projects and thereby overlooking the larger dimension of such developments. What is involved here is a forward-looking design of the system itself, on which the »habitat« is based - in anticipation of a future world; as a reversion to a socially comprehensible, culturally informed space; as an expression of a society that is designing »itself«.

An early expression of the reflexive content of design, which examines the norms of tradition in their social context, can be found in Jean-Paul Sartre's existential interpretation of the concept. According to Sartre, design is a philosophical challenge. In view of the fact that man designs or projects himself into the future, he is »nothing other than his own design; ... [he] exists only to the extent to which he realizes his own self. In other words, he is nothing other than the totality of his actions, nothing other than his own life.«[2] A conclusion of this kind poses a challenge to design in terms of the anticipation of future »habitat«. It also questions the »system« within which concepts may develop of how society wishes to live.

The motto of the World Exposition, »Humankind – Nature – Technology« could originally be understood as an occasion for an existential definition of design: the design or projection of a place into the future - by a »society that designs itself«. What occasions for construction could be

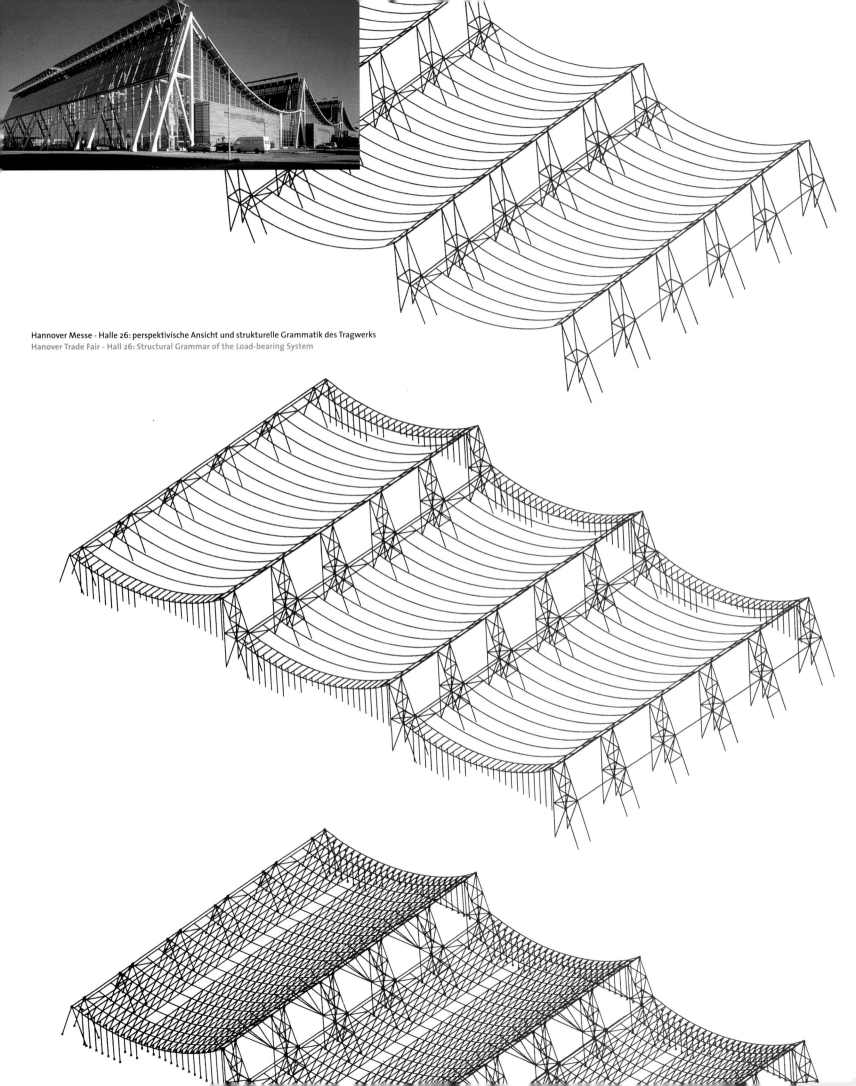

Hannover Messe - Halle 26: perspektivische Ansicht und strukturelle Grammatik des Tragwerks
Hanover Trade Fair - Hall 26: Structural Grammar of the Load-bearing System

einer solch existentiellen Erprobung des Entwerfens näherzukommen, stärker herausfordern als die der Leitprojekte der EXPO 2000, der Erneuerung Berlins, der Internationalen Bauausstellung Emscher Park oder der im Wettbewerb neu ausgeschriebenen HafenCity Hamburgs?

In diesem Sinne meint die Metapher der »Gesellschaft, die sich entwirft«, ein normatives Gegenbild zu den zahllosen Gelegenheiten der faktischen Verhältnisse.

Zugleich gilt es, Marc Augés oder Jürgen Habermas' skeptische Einwände auf das Entwerfen anzuwenden: daß auch dem Entwerfen »Wiederholungen« und »Stereotypen« eigen sind, »die dem Bewußtsein der Handelnden gänzlich oder teilweise entgehen«.[3] Das Entwerfen wird aus der Ausnahmesituation, sich selbst und die Gesellschaft zum Gegenstand reflektierten Verhaltens zu machen[4], in die routinierte Praxis mit all ihren Fallen zurückgeholt. Hier hat es sich mit den Rahmenbedingungen auseinanderzusetzen – zuvorderst mit der, daß die Gesellschaft nicht Gegenstand reflektierten Verhaltens sein will: »Diese Ideologie der Unterkomplexität schwört dem vernünftigen Potential und dem Eigensinn der kulturellen Moderne ab.«[5]

Motiv der modernen Stadt: Außerkraftsetzung von Werken

Die idealistische Vorstellung einer »Gesellschaft, die sich entwirft«, wird immer im Konflikt stehen zu den Befunden der Gesellschaftswissenschaften, die dem Entwerfen gerade diesen gesellschaftlichen Stellenwert nicht zubilligen. »Die Gestalt der Metropole ist ihre Gestaltlosigkeit, wie auch ihr Ziel die ziellose Expansion ist«, sagt bereits Lewis Mumford, der das Paradox der Entwicklung so zusammenfaßt: Die Perspektive der gesellschaftlichen Entwicklung sei die Fortsetzung einer in sozialer Hinsicht rückständigen Zivilisation mit den fortschrittlichsten technischen Mitteln.[6] Eine ähnlich ausgreifende Bilanz war erst wieder von der französischen Zivilisationskritik zu hören, von dem Soziologen Alain Touraine und dem Philosophen Jean-François Lyotard. Angesichts weltweiter Beispiele stellte Lyotard fest, mit dem Leitbild der Megalopolis verwirkliche und verbreite der Westen seinen Nihilismus: Er nennt das »wirtschaftliche Entwicklung«. Die Struktur der Stadt, die sich an den Peripherien breche, definiere er als Reflex auf einen gesellschaftlichen Suchprozeß, der erst in fernerer Linie etwas mit »Gestaltung« zu tun habe: »Das Fragmentarische als das Prinzip der Moderne: die Stadt ist in Bewegung, sich zu formen, indem sie zerlegt, was sie ist.«[7]

Dieser Prozeß werde zum Kainsmal einer Gesellschaft, die keine »Werke« mehr hervorbringe: Zeichen der Communauté désœuvrée.

Jean-François Lyotard, wiewohl er die Communauté désœuvrée kritisiert, die Gesellschaft, die sich nicht entwirft, äußert sich maliziös zu Sartres Position: Er »annexiere« die Dialektik durch den Entwurf. »Letzterer wurde über die Dialektik gestellt, um seinen Anspruch, sich überall zu erheben, herauszustellen. Angesichts des Entwurfs war Passivität banal, beschämend und verlockend wie die Sünde.«[8] Lyotard hat den Gedanken, daß die Gesellschaft sich eher mit der »Außerkraftsetzung von Werken« beschäftigt als mit der Schaffung von Lebensentwürfen, anläßlich einer Analyse von James Joyces Roman *Ulysses*, der in Dublin zu Beginn des Jahrhunderts spielt, als Désœuvrement beschrieben, als einen Sachverhalt, der auch »Entmündigung« einschließe. In dem Roman wird die Stadt, die keine »Werke« mehr hervorbringt, gezeigt als »Lagerraum«, als »Stapelplatz von Tagesresten, über die der Flaneur nachgrübelt, um sich von ihnen zu befreien.«[9] Daß das »Motiv der Stadt« bestimmten Ansprüchen noch nicht – oder nicht mehr – gerecht werde, könne nicht einfach hingenommen werden: »Denn es genügt nicht, es als Historiker oder Soziologe, sozusagen als literarischer

closer to the heart of or represent a greater challenge to a society in respect of its existential attempt at design than major schemes such as the EXPO 2000, the renewal of Berlin, the International Building Exhibition in Emscher Park or the harbour city for Hamburg now advertised in a new competition?

In this sense, the metaphor of a »society that designs itself« suggests a normative counterpart to the innumerable opportunities encountered under real, everyday circumstances.

At the same time, consideration should also be given to the sceptical reservations expressed by Marc Augés and Jürgen Habermas: that even design is subject to »repetitions« and »stereotypes« which »wholly or in part escape the awareness of the persons involved«.[3] Design is thus pulled back from the special situation of making itself and society the object of reflected behaviour[4] and reverts to routine practice with all its inherent pitfalls. At this point, it is necessary for design to come to terms with the prevailing circumstances - first and foremost, with the fact that society does not want to be the object of reflective behaviour: »This ideology of ›undercomplexity‹ renounces the sensible potential and the idiosyncrasy of cultural modernism.«[5]

The Phenomenon of the Modern City: the Invalidation of Achievements

The idealistic concept of a »society that designs itself« will always be at odds with the findings of the social sciences, which do not concede a social status to the process of design. Lewis Mumford defined the form of the metropolis as its formlessness - just as its aim is aimless expansion. Mumford summarized this paradox by saying that the perspective of social development is the continuation of a socially backward civilization, using the most progressive technical means available.[6] A similarly far-reaching conclusion was not heard again until the sociologist Alain Touraine and the philosopher Jean-François Lyotard formulated a French critique of civilization. Citing examples from around the globe, Lyotard came to the conclusion that the Western world is realizing and disseminating its nihilism through the model of the megalopolis and under the name of »economic development«. He went on to define the structure of the city, which breaks down at the periphery, as a reflex action to a process of social searching that has only remotely to do with »design«: »The fragmentary as the principle of modernism: the city is in a state of movement, in a process of forming itself by dismantling what it is.«[7]

This process becomes the stigma of a society that no longer produces great »works« or achievements: it is a symptom of the communauté désœuvrée.

However much he may criticize the communauté désœuvrée - the society that does not design itself - Jean-François Lyotard rejects Sartre's position, arguing that Sartre »annexes« the dialectic through design. »The latter was raised above dialectics in order to formulate the right to elevate itself above everything. Confronted with design, passivity was as banal, shaming and enticing as sin.«[8] It was in the context of an analysis of James Joyce's novel *Ulysses*, set in Dublin at the beginning of the 20th century, that Lyotard described désœuvrement as the phenomenon of society being more concerned with the »invalidation of achievements« than with the creation of designs for life, a condition that also includes an act of »incapacitation«. In Joyce's novel, the city, which no longer produces any »works«, is presented as a »store room«, as a »place where the remains of the day are heaped, over which the stroller ruminates in order to liberate himself from them.«[9] The fact that the »phenomenon of the city« is not yet - or no

Verteidiger der laufenden Urbanisierung abzuhandeln. Wie ich (mit Benjamin) meine, geht es auch und vor allem um die Rückkehr der Einsamkeit, der Wüste und des Müßigwerdens (désœuvrement) inmitten der Gemeinschaft. Die moderne Stadt ist ein Werk, innerhalb dessen die Gemeinschaft und das Individuum durch die Vorherrschaft des Marktwertes um ihr Werk gebracht werden.«[10] Der Begriff des »Müßigwerdens« ist eher einer Ungenauigkeit der Übersetzung zu verdanken: Gemeint ist die Untätigkeit der Gesellschaft, die keine »Werke« mehr hervorbringt.

Eines der Symptome dieses Zustands erscheint in der wiederaufgebrochenen Orientierung an der Architektur des 19. Jahrhunderts, die an Konzepten wie denen der »kritischen Rekonstruktion« innerhalb der zeitgenössischen Architektur demonstriert wird. Sie stellt gerade das Projektive der Architektur, gerade das, was andere Disziplinen beschäftigt, in Frage. »Diese Rückkehr zum Eklektizismus des vergangenen Jahrhunderts verdankt sich, wie damals«, stellt Habermas fest, »kompensatorischen Bedürfnissen. Dieser Traditionalismus ordnet sich dem Muster des politischen Neukonservatismus insofern ein, als er Probleme, die auf einer *anderen* Ebene liegen, in Stilfragen umdefiniert und damit dem öffentlichen Bewußtsein entzieht. Die Fluchtreaktion verbindet sich mit dem Zug zum Affirmativen: alles *übrige* soll bleiben, wie es ist.«[11] Marc Augé hat diese Wendung als Abart des Populismus beschrieben, der nur Klischees bedient: Historisierende Darstellungen »treffen den Geschmack des Publikums und kommen seinem Bedürfnis nach alten Formen entgegen, als verrieten diese alten Formen uns Heutigen, was wir sind, indem sie zeigen, was wir nicht mehr sind.«[12] Das symbolische Beispiel des Abrisses der »Galerie des Machines« der Pariser Weltausstellung von 1889 und der Aufbau des historisierenden Imitats anläßlich der Chicagoer Weltausstellung von 1893 illustriert die Tendenz durch ein historisches Beispiel. Insofern reproduziert die »kritische Rekonstruktion« nur ein systematisches Mißverständnis, die Aufgaben zeitgenössischer Architektur betreffend. Die Debatte um das Berliner Schloß ist ein allgemeines Symptom dieser Entwicklung: Verzicht auf die »Gesellschaft, die sich entwirft«, Retro-Design als »Ersatz« für gesellschaftliche Debatten.

Stilistik – oder Strukturwandel der Ideen

Für die Architektur geht es um eine Neubestimmung, die zwar traditionelle Wurzeln in der Ersten Moderne hat, die sich jedoch zu fortgeschrittenen Konzepten einer Zweiten Moderne entwickelt: zu einer reflexiven Veränderung der Raumauffassung in der Architektur, die ihre Abhängigkeit von Umwelt und Ressourcen neu definiert und die kulturelle Dimension neuer Baukonzepte weiterentwickelt. Ein Anzeichen für diesen Wandel ist, daß er von Architekten getragen wird, die »auf dem Gebiet des Bauens zur technischen Avantgarde gehören, und die offensichtlich ihr Wissen und ihr kreatives Potential nunmehr auch auf solche architektonischen Konzepte richten, deren Schwerpunkt der Einsatz von Solarenergie ist.«[13] Sigfried Giedion sieht, rückblickend bewertet, einen Ausgangspunkt des Auffassungswandels der Ersten Moderne in der Architektur Le Corbusiers: in dem einen, dem unteilbaren Raum, dem Raumkontinuum, bei dem weder die Form selbst noch deren Plastizität zählt, nur Beziehung und Durchdringung: »Die Häuser Le Corbusiers sind weder räumlich noch plastisch: Luft weht durch sie! Luft wird konstituierender Faktor! Es gilt dafür weder Raum noch Plastik, nur Beziehung und Durchdringung! Es gibt nur einen einzigen unteilbaren Raum. Zwischen Innen und Außen fallen die Schalen.«[14]

Zum ersten Mal wird ein – später zeitweise vergessenes – ökologisches Prinzip der Architektur genannt: der dynamisch durchströmte Raum.

longer - in a position to meet certain needs is something that cannot simply be accepted, Lyotard says: »For it is not sufficient just to discuss it as a historian or sociologist, as a literary defender, so to speak, of an ongoing process of urbanization. Like Benjamin, I believe that what is involved here is, in the first instance, is the return of solitude, the wilderness and idleness (désœuvrement) at the heart of the community. The modern city is an entity within which the community and the individual are robbed of their own life achievements through the predominance of market values.«[10] In all likelihood, the concept of leisurely quietude associated with »idleness« can be attributed to the imprecision of translation; what is really meant is the inactivity of a society that no longer produces any »works«.

One of the symptoms of this condition reveals itself in a renewed interest in the architecture of the 19th century, which may be identified in concepts such as »critical reconstruction« in modern architecture. This calls into question the projective nature of architecture: the very aspect with which other disciplines are concerned. »This return to the eclecticism of the previous century is the result, as it was then, of a need for compensation,« Habermas argues. »This traditionalism conforms to the pattern of political neo-conservatism to the extent that it redefines problems that exist on a different plane into questions of style, thus removing them from the realm of public awareness. The escapist reaction is combined with an affirmative tendency: everything else should remain as it is.«[11] Marc Augè has described this development as another form of populism that deals only in clichés: historicist representations »comply with the taste of the public and meet its need for historical forms; as if these old forms would reveal to us modern-day people what we are by showing us what we no longer are.«[12] The symbolic example of the demolition of the Galerie des Machines, erected for the International Exhibition in Paris in 1889, and the reconstruction of a historicist imitation on the occasion of the Chicago World Exposition in 1893 provides a historic illustration of this tendency. As far as the role of modern architecture is concerned, therefore, the process of »critical reconstruction« merely repeats a systematic misapprehension. The debate about the reconstruction of the historic palace in Berlin is symptomatic of this development, signifying the renunciation of a »society that designs itself«; in other words, retroactive design becomes an »ersatz« for social debate.

Stylistics - or the Structural Change of Ideas

Architecture is confronted with a process of reorientation. Rooted though it may be in the tradition of the First Modern Movement, it has proceeded in the meantime to the advanced concepts of a Second Modern Movement: to a reflexive change of attitude towards architectural space that redefines its dependence on the environment and resources and extrapolates the cultural dimension of new building concepts. A sign of this change of attitude may be seen in the fact that it is now upheld by architects who »belong to the technical avant-garde and who are evidently addressing their knowledge and creative skills to architectural concepts that focus on the use of solar energy.«[13] A re-examination of Sigfried Giedion's ideas shows that he saw the beginnings of this change of attitude on the part of the First Modern Movement in the architecture of Le Corbusier; in his concept of a single, indivisible space - the spatial continuum - in which neither the form itself nor its sculptural qualities are important, but only relationships and interpenetration: »Le Corbusier's houses are neither spatial nor plastic: air flows through them! Air becomes a constituent factor! Neither space nor plastic form counts, only relation and interpenetration! There is

Auf der Suche nach dem Gegensatz zu Massivität und Schwere, auf der Suche nach fließender Transparenz, nach der »mariage des contours« der kubistischen Malerei, wird das massive Volumen der traditionellen Bauten aus Stein durchbrochen. Die ehemals monolithischen Wände, die dunklen Gewölbe werden durch hohe Lufträume im Inneren ausgehöhlt, durch breit gelagerte Streifenfenster geschlitzt, durch Fensterwände und unmittelbare Übergänge von Innen und Außen, von Haus und Himmel neu interpretiert. Zum ersten Mal spricht Giedion von der »Entmaterialisierung« der soliden Begrenzungen des Gebäudes (»Warum soll das Haus möglichst leicht und schwebend gemacht werden? Nur dadurch kann einer fatalen Begründung der Monumentalität ein Ende bereitet werden.«) Die mediterrane Romantik, welche die Metapher der Häuser meint, durch welche die Luft ströme, annonciert bereits immaterielle Qualitäten des Raumes – des Klimas und der Energie des Raumes, die später in neuem Sinne bewußt werden.

Der technologische Wandel ermöglicht vierzig Jahre später das turmhohe gläserne Atrium der New Yorker Ford Foundation, 1967 von Kevin Roche und John Dinkeloo gebaut, das die Vorstellung Le Corbusiers in einen Prototyp der nächsten Generation übersetzt: das Haus, das von Luft und Licht durchströmt wird, das sich später mit der »Fassade« des Glasdaches zur Sonne und zum Himmel öffnet. Das große transparente Volumen emanzipiert sich als eigene Qualität der Architektur vom Grundriß wie vom herkömmlichen Verständnis der Funktionen eines Gebäudes. Die hybride Großform, zugleich früher Prototyp für die großen Hallenräume der Architektur der Zweiten Moderne (wie beim Entwurf Francis Solers für das »Centre de conférences internationales«, Quay Branly, Paris 1989 et al.), die sich dem Druck der Metropole aussetzen. Das Atrium, das zugleich die Funktionen des Gebäudes »symbolisch vereint« (Paul Goldberger), wird in der hektischen Atmosphäre der Metropole zum ersten Mal durch ein schützendes, transparentes Volumen begründet, das äußere Einflüsse, das den Druck der großen Stadt zurückweist – als Motiv eines eigenen klimatischen Raumes und einer transparenten Abgeschiedenheit, in der die Gemeinschaft der Foundation wie »mit dem Rücken zur Welt« lebt und arbeitet, um an ein Bild von Cees Nooteboom zu erinnern. Das Gebäude gibt sich ein neues Thema, das neue Thema gibt sich eine neue »Form«.

Wiederum zwanzig Jahre später, beim Bau des UNESCO Workshop-Gebäudes in Vesima (Punta Nave/Genua 1989) bezieht sich Renzo Piano mit der Beschreibung der flutenden Transparenz des Raumes erneut auf Le Corbusier: »Das Gebäude ist ein Gebilde aus Raum, Sonne und Natur, wie Le Corbusier es definiert hat, es ist aber mit Hilfe von modernsten elektronischen Kommunikationsmitteln mit der ganzen Welt verbunden.«[15]

Wieder gibt es einen thematischen Anlaß, dem das Gebäude als Experiment gewidmet wird, das sich eine eigene Form sucht: Es bietet nicht nur ein »Interieur mit bestehenden und zukünftigen Werken« (Topoi), wie es bereits Constantin Brancusi formuliert hatte, sondern inkorporiert die Bedingungen des Klimaeinflusses und des Gebrauchs natürlichen Lichts in der Architektur als eigenes Thema des Bauens. Die Weiterentwicklung gegenüber Le Corbusiers intuitivem Gebäude-Umwelt-Verständnis liest sich bei Piano so, daß er die idealisierte Auffassung des Gebäudes im Luftstrom als »Druck äußerer Bedingungen« interpretiert, denen das Gebäude ausgesetzt ist – und auf den es zu reagieren vermag (»the pressure the outside exerts on the inside«[16]). Hier ist es das Gebäude, das unter Kontrolle hält, was ihm Lebendigkeit verleiht: das alles überströmende Sonnenlicht. Der Laborbau definiert sich architektonisch vom Sonnenlicht her, setzt aber auch raffinierte Technik ein, um dessen schädlichen Einfluß zu mindern. Das Dach, die fünfte Fassade, besteht aus Glas und ist mit sensorgesteuerten Jalousien

only a single indivisible space. The shells fall away between interior and exterior.«[14]

For the first time, an ecological principle of architecture is described (which was later forgotten from time to time), namely the principle of dynamic, continuously flowing space.

In search of an alternative to mass and weight, in search of a flowing quality of transparency, of the »mariage des contours« of Cubist painting, the massive volumes of traditional stone structures are dissolved. The once monolithic walls and dark vaults are given an entirely new interpretation: they are hollowed out internally to accommodate tall, airy spaces, and they are slit open with broad, horizontal window bands and glazed walls that afford direct transitions from inside to outside, from building to sky. For the first time, Giedion speaks of a »dematerialization« of the solid enclosure of a building. »Why should the house be made as light as possible, so that it would seem to hover in the air?« he asks; and his answer is that only in this way can one put an end to a disastrous urge towards monumentality. The Mediterranean romanticism implicit to the metaphor of the house through which air streams anticipates the idea of the immaterial qualities of space – the indoor climate and the energy requirements of a space which will subsequently impress themselves on our awareness in a new sense.

Forty years later, in 1967, technological change enabled Kevin Roche and John Dinkeloo to realize the towering glazed atrium of the Ford Foundation in New York. This structure translates Le Corbusier's concept into a prototype for the next generation: buildings through which light and air stream and which will later open themselves to the sun and the sky in the form of a glass roof or fifth »facade«. The large transparent volume becomes a distinctive kind of architecture, emancipating itself from the ground plan as indeed it does from the conventional functional concepts of a building. The large-scale hybrid form was also an early prototype for the huge hall spaces of the architecture of the Second Modern Movement, as may be seen, for example, in Francis Soler's design for the Centre de Conférence Internationales, Quay Branly, Paris, 1989. Structures of this kind are exposed to the pressures of the metropolis. In this hectic environment, the atrium - which also «symbolically unites» the various functions of the building (Paul Goldberger) - is justified for the first time as a protective, transparent enclosure that keeps external influences and the pressures of the big city at bay. It establishes the motif of an independent climatic space, transparent yet removed from the outside world; and within this space, the community of the Ford Foundation lives and works, turning its back on the world, in a sense - to use an image created by Cees Nooteboom. The building adopts a new theme; and the new theme leads to a new »form«.

Twenty years later, in his description of the flowing spatial transparency of the UNESCO workshop building in Vesima (Punta Nave, Genoa, 1989), Renzo Piano again refers to Le Corbusier: »The building is a composition of space, sun and nature, as Le Corbusier defined it. But it is linked with the entire world by means of state-of-the-art electronic communications media.«[15]

In its experimental context, this building is also dedicated to a specific theme and seeks its own form: it provides not only an »interior with existing works (topoi) and others to be created in the future«, as Constantin Brancusi once formulated it. The workshop also incorporates the conditions that permit the manipulation of indoor climate and the use of natural light in architecture as an independent constructional theme. The extrapolation

Hannover Messe – Halle 26 im Gelände
Hanover Trade Fair – Hall 26 in its Site Context

ausgestattet, die auf unterschiedliche Lichtintensität reagieren und mittels kalkulierter Verzögerung das Licht langsam in seinem Verlauf um das Gebäude herum spürbar machen. Das Sichtbarmachen, die langsame, kaum merkliche Bewegung der Filterelemente in Reaktion auf den wechselnden Sonnenlichteinfall – ist der Indikator für den Druck der Außenbedingungen. Das belebende Element – Tageslicht, Sonnenlicht – wird kontrolliert gefiltert eingelassen. Damit wandelt sich zugleich der Charakter der Form. Ein Zuviel verkehrte die positiven Bedingungen ins Gegenteil (Blendwirkung, Treibhauseffekt): »Die Arbeit in diesen Räumen evoziert eine ganz besondere Form der Sammlung und Konzentration, die verbunden ist mit dem Gefühl, in einem unmittelbaren Kontakt mit der Natur, dem Klima und den Jahreszeiten zu stehen. Die Architektur hat hier etwas Immaterielles eingefangen.«[17]

Anders als bei traditionellen Gebäuden und städtischen Strukturen, die auf die »monolithische« Masse der Gebäude als starre Begrenzung zwischen der Innen- und Außenwelt setzen, werden Gebäudekonzepte der Zweiten Moderne als »reaktive Gebäude« verstanden, eine Entwicklung, die auch bei gebauten Beispielen auf dem Expo-Gelände eine Entsprechung findet.

Ein Rückblick auf die Jahre 1996 bis 1990 zeigt einige Bauten im Bestand der Hannover Messe und erfolgt deshalb, um die Tradition des Ortes als Entstehungsort eindrucksvoller Bauwerke mit zukunftsweisender Architektur zu zeigen.[18] Wesentlich ist dabei die Tendenz, vom sparsamen Umgang mit den Ressourcen stufenweise auf den behutsamen Umgang mit Energie, sodann auf den gezielten Einsatz von Umweltenergien umzuschalten und auf dem Weg fortzuschreiten, Umweltenergien neu zu interpretieren, sie intensiv zur Wärmegewinnung, zur Kühlung, zur natürlichen Lüftung, Belichtung, schließlich zu neuen Formen der Stromgewinnung zu nutzen, bei denen Solarenergie letztlich auch gestaltprägend und ästhetisch wirksam wird.[19] Auf dem Gelände der Deutschen Messe AG sind in den neunziger Jahren innovative Bauten geschaffen worden, die nicht nur besondere Messehallen und ein charakteristisches Tagungszentrum umfassen, sondern auch als Vorgriff, als Antizipation baukultureller Entwicklung im Hinblick auf die EXPO 2000 wahrzunehmen sind. Die gezeigten Bauwerke stehen selbst für avancierte Ausprägungen des Bauens im Rahmen der Technologieentwicklung, die sich mehr und mehr dem Ziel der Nachhaltigkeit im Bauen öffnet.

of Le Corbusier's intuitive understanding of building and the environment is evident in Piano's interpretation. The idealized notion of a building enveloped by a stream of air is interpreted here as a structure subject to »the pressure of outward conditions«, to which it is also capable of reacting (»the pressure the outside exerts on the inside«[16]). In this case, it is the building that keeps under control the phenomenon that lends it life and vigour, namely the sunlight in which everything is bathed. Although the laboratory-workshop is defined architecturally in terms of sunlight, the structure activates a range of sophisticated technology to reduce the harmful effects of the sun. The roof, the fifth façade, consists of glass and is equipped with sensor-controlled blinds that react to different intensities of light. With a calculated delay, this installation allows the sun to be experienced as it moves round the building. The process by which the slow, scarcely noticeable reaction of the filtering elements to the changing incidence of sunlight is made perceptible becomes the indicator of the pressure of outward conditions. The animating element - daylight or sunlight - is admitted in a controlled, filtered manner. In this way, the character of the form changes, too. An excess of sunlight - resulting in glare and a hothouse atmosphere - would reverse the positive conditions: »Work in these spaces leads to a quite special form of composure and concentration, combined with the feeling of being in direct contact with nature, the weather and the seasons. Here, the architecture has captured an immaterial quality.«[17]

In contrast to traditional buildings and urban structures, where the »monolithic« mass of the object imposes a rigid boundary between internal and external worlds, the architectural concepts of the Second Modern Movement may be regarded as an expression of »reactive building« – a development that may be recognized in the structures on the Expo site.

A survey extending back from 1996 to 1990 and showing some of the existing buildings on the Hanover Trade Fair site illustrates the tradition of the fair as a location for impressive buildings and future-looking architecture.[18] One important phenomenon in this respect is a clearly recognizable trend in the use of resources. It manifests itself in a step by step progression from the economic use of basic resources to the restrained use of energy and a deliberate shift to the exploitation of environmentally friendly forms of energy. This will ultimately lead to a new approach, in which environmentally sustainable forms of energy will be intensively exploited for heat gains, cooling, natural ventilation, lighting and finally for new forms of power generation. In this respect, solar energy becomes become a key factor in terms of design and aesthetics.[19] In the 1990s, a number of innovative buildings were realized on the site of the Deutsche

Beispiel Messe Hannover: Halle 26 (1996)

Im Sommer 1994 beauftragte die Deutsche Messe AG, Hannover, die Münchner Architekten Herzog + Partner damit, ein Konzept für ihr Gesamtareal zu entwickeln, auf dem der Welt größte Industrie- und Kommunikationsmessen stattfinden. Es sollte eine Vision davon entstehen, wie künftige Hallenbauten unter Einbeziehung des Bestands aussehen könnten. Die unmittelbar bevorstehende Realisierung der Halle 26 war als Lösungskonzept aufzuzeigen. Neue architektonische Qualitäten sollten entstehen, die sich am Leitmotiv der EXPO 2000 orientierten: »Mensch – Natur – Technik«. Mit der Halle 26 wurde ein eindrucksvolles Bauwerk mit zukunftsweisender Architektur geschaffen, ein innovativer Bau, der nicht nur einer besonderen Messehalle Gestalt gab, sondern auch als Vorgriff auf die EXPO 2000 wahrzunehmen war.

Die spezielle Aufgabe der Halle 26 bestand darin, bei einer Größe von 25.000 bis 30.000 Quadratmetern den Typus einer neuartigen Querschnittsgeometrie zu entwickeln, deren Profil der Dynamik des Raumklimas und der natürlichen Belichtung entgegenkommt. Das Konzept der Architekten hebt eine Reihe von Merkmalen hervor: Es sollte die Form eines Tragwerks entwickelt werden, das für große Spannweiten prädestiniert war – ein Hängedach wurde gewählt. Die Querschnittsgeometrie sicherte einerseits die in weiten Bereichen funktional benötigte Raumhöhe, andererseits ist sie durch die Ausbildung von Hochpunkten charakterisiert, die zur natürlichen Entlüftung erforderlich sind, da sie thermischen Auftrieb ermöglichen. Große Bereiche der Fassaden und der Dachflächen wurden so ausgebildet, daß sie den Einlaß von Tageslicht unterstützen, zugleich aber die direkte solare Einstrahlung reduzieren. Ein Hallentypus wurde entwickelt, der mit hoher Wirkung Umweltenergien einfängt. Er enthält zwei Grundrißzonen. Zum einen weiträumige, stützenlose, frei disponierbare Ausstellungsbereiche unter dem leichten, zugbeanspruchten Hängedach aus Stahl, auf dem eine Holzdecke aufliegt; zum anderen schmale Bereiche zwischen den Ausstellungsflächen und an ihrem Rand, Zonen, in denen die Stahlpylone zur Aufnahme der Kräfte der Konstruktion stehen.

Die programmatischen wie die konstruktiven Ideen für die Halle 26 gehen über traditionelle Hallentypen hinaus: Die Begründung eines neu ver-

Halle 4: Hauptstruktur des Tragwerks
Hall 4: Main Load-bearing Structure

Messe AG. These include not only special trade fair halls and a distinctive Congress Centre, but also structures in anticipation of and forming part of the architectural programme for the EXPO 2000. The buildings described here represent advanced forms of construction in terms of technological developments. These, in turn, are opening up more and more perspectives for durability and sustainability in building.

Hanover Trade Fair: Hall 26 (1996)

In the summer of 1994, the Deutsche Messe AG in Hanover commissioned the Munich architects Herzog + Partner to draw up a concept for the entire site on which the world's largest industrial and communication fairs are held. The proposals were to take account of existing developments on the site and at the same time create a vision of how hall structures should look in the future. Hall 26, which was scheduled for immediate construction, was to provide a conceptual solution. New architectural qualities were to be realized, oriented to the leitmotif of the EXPO 2000: »Humankind –

Halle 4 als transparenter Platzrand bei Nacht
Hall 4, forming a transparent wall to the square at night

Halle 4: perspektivische Ansicht
Hall 4: Interior View

Halle 4: begehbare Dachstruktur
Hall 4: Accessible Roof Structure

standenen Programms, das gewandelte Verständnis der Technik, die skulpturale Geste der Form – und die Neugier konstruktiven Entwerfens teilen sich in Konturen mit, in denen die Funktion des Längsschnitts eine neue Eigenständigkeit gewinnt – als Raum klimatischer Dynamik, als Raum natürlichen Lichts, als Raum von Reflexionen.

Mit der Halle 26 kommt ein expressiver, dynamischer Ausdruck in die Beziehung von Konstruktion und Erscheinung. Veränderungen in der energetischen und klimatischen Auffassung der Ganzheit des Baukörpers lassen sich im veränderten Längsschnitt ablesen. Die dynamische Korrespondenz von Konstruktion und Hallenvolumen ist sinnlich ablesbar, hat für den Betrachter Erlebniswert: Der konstruktive Typus, der die gedanklichen Prinzipien verdeutlicht, wird in der Ausbauphase nicht hinter Schichten und Hüllen verborgen, er bleibt klar und attraktiv erhalten. Gestalterische Prinzipien des Structural engineering sind anschaulich: Vielschichtigkeit, Komplexität, gleichwohl große Klarheit prägen dieses Gebäude als Entwurf der reflexiven Moderne.

Beispiel Messe Hannover: Halle 4 (1996)

Parallel zur Halle 26 beauftragte die Deutsche Messe AG, Hannover, die Hamburger Architekten gmp von Gerkan, Marg und Partner, ein Konzept für das östlich der »grünen Mitte« gelegene Areal der Halle 4 zu entwickeln.

Völlige Stützenfreiheit, Tagesbelichtung und Leichtigkeit charakterisieren die grundrißliche und konstruktive Konzeption dieser Halle, die die Platzwand abschließt. Die eingeschossige Hallenfläche mit den Maßen von 185,6 x 116 Metern wird durch die Kombination von achtzehn 122 Meter weit spannenden Stahlbinderkonstruktionen in Verbindung mit Trapezblechdächern mit linsenförmigen, begehbaren Hohlkörpern und aufgesattelten Oberlichtdächern überdacht. Die Montage erfolgte im Rhythmus der gestaffelten Konstruktion von Unterbau, Scheiben, Bindern und Trapezblechen abschnittsweise im Abstand der Binder von 10,8 Metern: Vorfabrikation in der Fabrik und Montageschritte vor Ort waren zeitlich minimiert. Während die neue Halle an den Längsseiten geschlossen ist, bleibt sie an den Stirnseiten in ganzer Höhe optisch geöffnet und durchsichtig verglast. Transparenz und Übersichtlichkeit vermitteln das Messegeschehen durch die Schauseite.

»Es gibt keine pure Konstruktion und keine pure Technik. Beide bedürfen einer Form, um zu sein – einer Form, die erfunden und entworfen werden muß. Jede Baukonstruktion ist ein Gefüge, das sinnvolle Prinzipien der

Nature – Technology«. Hall 26 proved to be an impressive structure with forward-looking architecture. It is an innovative building that not only represents a new model form for a trade fair hall; it can also be seen to anticipate other developments for the EXPO 2000. The design of Hall 26, which has an area of 25,000-30,000 square metres, was expected to fulfil special conditions. A hall type with a new cross-sectional geometry was to be created, the outline of which would respond to the dynamics of the internal climate and the needs of natural lighting. The architectural concept accentuates a whole series of distinctive features. A load-bearing structure was to be developed in a form suited to covering large spans. For this reason, a suspended roof structure was chosen. The cross-sectional geometry provides the functional clear height required over large areas of the hall. At the same time, it is distinguished by the upward curving forms of the roof and the articulation of the crests. These elements of the construction also facilitate thermal uplift and therefore form an essential part of the natural ventilation system. Large areas of the façades and the roof were designed to allow the ingress of daylight while reducing insolation. A hall type was developed that effectively exploits environmentally friendly forms of energy. In its layout, it contains two kinds of zones: the broad, column-free, functionally flexible exhibition areas covered by a lightweight, tensile, suspended steel roof structure with a timber decking; and secondly, the narrow strips at the edges of the hall and between the exhibition areas, where the steel load-bearing pylons are located.

The programmatic and structural ideas implemented in Hall 26 go far beyond those of traditional hall types. The logic of the new concept underlying the brief, a changed understanding of technology, and the sculptural gesture of the form - plus the sense of innovative inquiry informing the structural design - communicate themselves through the outline of the hall. In its functionally motivated longitudinal section, the structure acquires a new independent status: as a space of climatic dynamics, as a space of natural light, and as a space for reflection.

Hall 26 exhibits a strikingly new dynamic expression in the relationship between structure and outward appearance. Changes that have occurred in the energy and indoor climate concepts of buildings in the course of time are reflected in the modified longitudinal section. The dynamic correspondence between the structure and the three-dimensional volume of the hall is sensuously legible. For the observer, it is an experi-

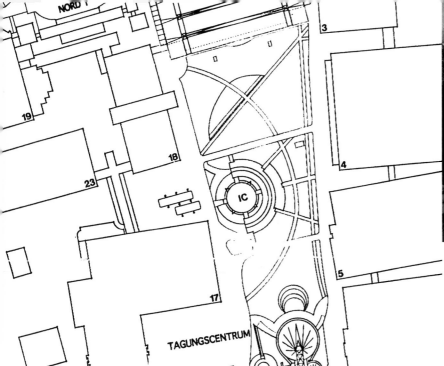

Halle 2 (Europahalle): Lageplan und Perspektive des Eingangsbereichs
Hall 2 (Europahalle): Site Plan and View of Entrance Area

Lastabtragung, der Steifigkeit und der Widerstandsfähigkeit material-
gebunden in Form umsetzt. Diese Form kann plump und mit viel Material-
verbrauch durchaus ihren Dienst leisten, man kann sie verkleiden und ver-
stecken. Man kann aber auch subtile Konstruktionen erdenken, die Material
sparen und ästhetische Anmut ausstrahlen. Solche Gefüge leiten sich
immer aus einem konstruktiven Sinn her. Damit vereinen sich Sinnfälligkeit,
Ökonomie und Ökologie mit der Ästhetik zu einem fast unerschöpflichen
Gestaltrepertoire, ohne irgendeinen Stil zu bemühen, nur die Logik.«[20]

Ausstellungsarchitektur wird als komplexes Gesamtsystem erfahrbar,
das die strukturelle und ästhetische Integration des Entwerfens demonstriert: als Zusammenwirken von Structural engineering und Architektur. Es
zeigt sich, daß »qualitätvolle umweltorientierte Planung mit der Auseinandersetzung und Einbindung von spezifischen lokalen Gegebenheiten und
Anforderungen viel mehr zu tun hat als mit schematischen, normativen Set-
zungen, die schnell zu Nivellierung und ästhetischer Verarmung führen können.«[21]

Beispiel Messe Hannover: Halle 2 (Europahalle, 1992)

Nach einem gutachterlichen Wettbewerb beauftragte die Deutsche Messe
AG, Hannover, im August 1991 die Hannoveraner Architekten Bertram Bünemann Partner GmbH damit, ein Konzept für das Entree des Messegeländes
am nördlichen Eingang zu schaffen. Die dem Tagungszentrum gegen-
überliegende Halle 2 sollte die alte, mehrgeschossige Halle an diesem
Standort ersetzen und etwa 15.000 Quadratmeter eingeschossige, stützenfreie Ausstellungsfläche bereitstellen. Neben der Erfüllung der funktionalen
Anforderungen, einen hochtechnisierten Ausstellungsbereich mit Eingangshalle zu schaffen, galt es, ein gemeinsames Foyer auch für die große, bereits
bestehende Halle 1 zu gestalten. Ziel war es, eine Architektursprache zu finden, die Foyer und Neubau aus der baulichen Struktur der damals vorhandenen Messehallen heraushob. Die neue Halle 2 sollte zugleich ein spannungs-

ence in itself. The structural form, designed to articulate the conceptual
principles, was not concealed during the fitting out stage beneath masking
layers and cladding. It remains clearly and attractively visible. The design
principles underlying the structural engineering are evident: characterized
by its polyvalency, complexity and yet great clarity, the building is an
example of reflexive modernism.

Hanover Trade Fair: Hall 4 (1996)

Parallel to Hall 26, the Deutsche Messe AG in Hanover commissioned the
Hamburg architects von Gerkan, Marg und Partner (gmp) to draw up a concept for Hall 4 on the area to the east of the «green centre» of the site.

In its layout and structural concept, the hall, which closes a gap in the
surrounding development at this point, is distinguished by the absence of
intermediate columns, by an effective system of daylighting and by its
lightweight appearance. The roof over the single-storey structure,
185.6 x 116 metres in size, consists of trapezoidal-section ribbed sheet
metal bays fixed between wide-span steel girders at 10.8-metre centres.
Over the top of the girders are skylight strips. The sheet metal bays have a
hollow lenticular cross-section and are accessible for maintenance purposes. The assembly followed the rhythm of the staggered construction
sequence: substructure, slabs, girders and sheet roofing, which was executed bay by bay between the girders. The period required for prefabrica-
tion at works and for the various stages of the assembly on site was
reduced to a minimum. Although the long faces of the new hall are closed,
the end walls are clad over their full height with transparent glazing,
thereby opening the interior visually to the outside world. Trade fair events
are communicated through these show faces by virtue of the transparency
and clarity of the structure.

»Pure structure and pure technology do not exist. Both need form in
order to exist – a form which has to be found and designed,« Meinhard
von Gerkan wrote. Every piece of construction is a structure that translates
the logical principles of load transmission, rigidity and stability into material form. The form may be crude and require great quantities of materials
to perform its required function; or it may be clad and concealed. But it is
also possible to design subtle forms of construction that are aesthetically
pleasing and economical in the use of materials. Objects of this kind
always embody a structural purpose, thereby uniting symbolic content,
economic and ecological considerations and aesthetics to create an almost
inexhaustible repertoire of design forms, without striving for any specific
style – only logic.[20]

Exhibition architecture may thus be experienced as a complex universal system that demonstrates how structural and aesthetic aspects can be
integrated in the design process: a collaboration between structural engi-

volles Gegenüber zu dem anspruchsvollen und erfolgreichen Tagungszentrum TCM der Messe bilden.

Die konzeptionellen Überlegungen entwickelten sich zu einem dreischiffigen Hallentypus, dessen Form sich als besonders geeignet erwies, die vielfältigen Anforderungen aus dem Raumprogramm und der städtebaulichen Situation zu erfüllen. Das mittlere Schiff mit dem Hauptausstellungsbereich wird bogenförmig in einer Länge von 120 Metern und einer Breite von 100 Metern überspannt. Die zentrale Ausstellungsfläche von 12.000 Quadratmetern ermöglicht neben der Realisierung aller konventionellen Messe- und Ausstellungskonzepte auch Großveranstaltungen mit unterschiedlichsten Inhalten und raumtechnischen Anforderungen. Die dreigeschossigen, schlanken Seitenschiffe beinhalten die erforderlichen Flächen für das übrige Raumprogramm, für die Eingangshalle, die Restaurants und Veranstaltungsbüros, die Technikräume und weitere Ausstellungsflächen.

Das westliche Seitenschiff ist als transparente, 200 Meter lange Halle nach Norden vorgeschoben, es beinhaltet die Eingangshalle und das gemeinsame Foyer der Hallen 1 und 2. Die prägnante Flügelform der Seitenschiffe und der Bogen des Hauptschiffes bilden mit ihren zeichenhaften Dimensionen das gewünschte Gegenüber für das Tagungszentrum. Die leichte, transparentklare Architektur macht das Messegeschehen zum Eingangsbereich und zur »grünen Mitte« hin gleichermaßen von innen und außen erlebbar.

neering and architecture. It also goes to show that »qualitative, environmentally oriented planning has much more to do with the reflection and integration of specific local conditions and needs than with any programmatic, normative precepts, which can quickly lead to uniformity and aesthetic impoverishment.«[21]

Hanover Trade Fair, Hall 2 (Europahalle), 1992

In August 1991, following an investigatory competition, the Deutsche Messe AG, Hanover, commissioned the Hanover architects Bertram Bünemann Partner GmbH to draw up a concept for the entrance situation to the trade fair site at the northern point of access. Situated opposite the Congress Centre, Hall 2 was to replace the old multistorey hall located at this point with a roughly 15,000-square-metre single-storey column-free exhibition area. In addition to complying with the functional conditions of the brief, which required an exhibition building with an entrance hall and all necessary technical facilities, a common foyer was to be created that would also serve the large existing Hall 1. The aim of the design was to find an architectural language that would give prominence to the foyer and the new structure against the background of the trade fair halls existing at that time. The new hall, Hall 2, was also to form an exciting counterpoint to the striking and successful trade fair Congress Centre (TCM).

Conceptual ideas led to the design of a three-bay hall type, the form of which was ideally suited to accommodating the complex spatial pro-

Halle 2: Transparenz der Halle als landschaftsprägendes Element
Halle 2: The Transparency of the Hall as an Element of the Landscape Design

Halle 2: Eingangsbereich
Hall 2: Entrance Area

Halle 2: überspannter Raum
Hall 2: Curved Roof Spanning the Width of the Hall Space

Aus städtebaulichen Gründen wurde die größere der beiden möglichen Spannweiten überbrückt, um eine breit ausladende Kontur als architektonisches Pendant zum Tagungszentrum TCM zu verwirklichen. Die acht Pylone tragen die vier großen Dreigurtbinder und die seitlichen Auskragungen. Die im Werk vorgefertigten Dreigurtelemente wurden auf der Baustelle zusammengeschweißt, mit Überhöhung eingebaut und an mehrgliedrigen Tragstangen abgehängt, die über die Pylonköpfe und die auskragenden Binderenden (»Schwingen«) doppelt geführt werden. Zugpfahlgruppen verankern sie im Baugrund. Die Fachwerkpfetten und die Trapezbleche wurden zeitversetzt verlegt.

Die transparente Fassadenhülle besteht aus vorgefertigten Stahlrahmen mit einer Größe der Felder bis zu 6 x 3,6 Metern, die an der Tragstruktur befestigt wurden. Differenzierte Verglasungssysteme und Metallpaneele bilden die Ausfachung. Innenliegende Sonnenschutzrollos regeln die Licht- und die solare Energiezufuhr. Oberlichtbänder über den Haupttraggliedern, den Dreigurtbindern, akzentuieren die Dachflächen. Die Architekturidee wird ergänzt durch eine sensible Lichtplanung, deren Leuchten ein ruhiges, gleichmäßiges Raster an der Hallendachkonstruktion bilden: einen Lichthimmel über der Ausstellungshalle.

Beispiel Messe Hannover: Tagungszentrum TCM (1989–1990)

Nach einem Wettbewerb (1986) beauftragte die Deutsche Messe AG, Hannover, die Hannoveraner Architekten Storch und Ehlers mit der Planung des Tagungszentrums der Messe. Obwohl von der Vorstellung geprägt, das Tagungszentrum spielerisch, gleichsam luftig, wie mühelos in die »grüne Mitte« der Messe einzufügen, zeigt der Entwurf dennoch kein willkürliches Formenspielwerk, so lautet die Erläuterung der Architekten. Es folgt vielmehr äußeren – aus der Situation abgeleiteten – und inneren – selbst gegebenen – Bedingungen. Am Übergang zur Informationsgesellschaft werden ausstellungsbegleitende Fachtagungen für Messen besonders wichtig. Das Tagungszentrum folgt der Philosophie der Messe, den vielerlei Veranstaltungen ein humanes Umfeld zu schaffen, dem Menschen Technik nahezubringen, demnach dazu beizutragen, den Gegensatz zwischen Natur und Technik zu überwinden.

Die Klarheit des räumlichen Gefüges, so die Architekten, wurde zur selbstgegebenen Grundbedingung. Sie erleichtert es dem Gastgeber, mühe-

gramme and the urban planning needs in this situation. The middle bay, containing the main exhibition areas, is covered by an arched roof 100 metres wide and spanning a distance of 120 metres. The central exhibition area, roughly 12,000 square metres in extent, can accommodate not only all conventional types of trade fairs and exhibitions, but also a wide range of large-scale events of varied content and with different spatial and technical requirements. The narrow three-storey side bays provide the requisite space for other functions - entrance hall, restaurants, events offices, services rooms and further exhibition areas.

The side bay to the west is extended northwards in the form of a transparent hall with an overall length of 200 metres. It houses the entrance hall and the joint foyer for Halls 1 and 2. The symbolic dimensions and the striking wing-like form of the side bays together with the curving arch of the main bay suspended between them provide the desired counterpoint to the Congress Centre. The clear, lightweight, transparent architecture allows the events of the trade fair to be experienced from inside and outside, both in the entrance area and from the central landscaped open space.

Tagungszentrum TCM
Congress Centre TCM

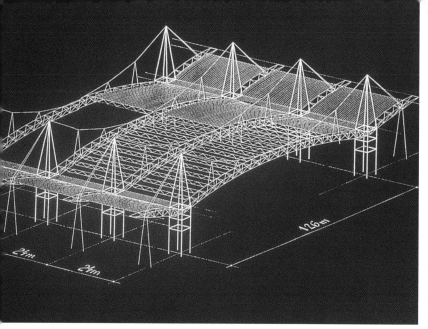

Halle 2: strukturelle Grammatik des Tragwerks
Hall 2: Structural Grammar of the Load-bearing System

There were two main options for the length of the roof span. Urban planning considerations led to a choice of the longer span in order to achieve a broad, sweeping line as an architectural pendant to the conference centre. The four large triangular trussed girders and the cantilevered structures at the sides are supported by eight pylons. The girders, prefabricated at works and welded together on site, were erected in a hogged form and suspended from multiple supporting rods, which are run double over the heads of the pylons and the cantilevered ends of the girders (»rocker beams«). The suspension members are anchored to groups of tension piles in the ground. The trussed purlins and the trapezoidal-section ribbed sheet-metal roofing were assembled in a staggered working sequence.

The transparent facade consists of prefabricated steel framing, the bays of which are up to 6 x 3.6 metres in size. The framing is fixed to the load-bearing structure. Various glazing systems and metal panels were used as infill elements. Internal sunblinds control the ingress of light and solar energy. The roof surface is articulated by skylight strips over the main structural members - the triangular trusses. The architectural concept was complemented by a sensitive lighting design, with the light fittings forming a calm, regular grid against the background of the roof structure - like an illuminated sky over the exhibition hall.

Hanover Trade Fair: Congress Centre (TCM), 1989-1990

Following a competition held in 1986, the Deutsche Messe AG, Hanover, entrusted the Hanover architects Storch and Ehlers with the planning of the Fair Congress Centre. Although dominated by the concept of making the centre a playful, airy structure set effortlessly in the landscaped middle of the site, the design is by no means a random play of forms, according to the description of the architects. It was governed by external conditions imposed by the location and by internal, self-defined constraints.

At a time when we are witnessing the transition to an information society, specialist conferences organized parallel to trade fairs are becoming increasingly important. The conference centre adheres to the philosophy of the trade fair as a whole, seeking to provide a friendly, attractive environment for the many different events to be held here, to bring people closer to technology, and at the same time to help overcome the opposition between technology and nature.

According to the architects, the clarity of the spatial structure was a fundamental condition they themselves specified. This allows the host

los und souverän sein Ziel zu verwirklichen, Menschen zu erreichen, an die Ausstellungen heranzuführen, schnell und treffend zu informieren. Sowohl der Ausstellung von Produkten als auch der Vermittlung von Wissen zur Entwicklung der Technik und ihrer Anwendungsmöglichkeiten kommt große Bedeutung zu. Wissenstransfer manifestiert sich in ausstellungsbegleitenden Fachtagungen. Das Tagungszentrum entwickelt sich an der Aufgabe, Tagungsräume und Ausstellungsflächen unter einem Dach zur Verfügung zu stellen. Darüber hinaus wurde die Leitidee entwickelt, in der »grünen Mitte« der Messe ein sympathisches Umfeld für Tagungen und Ausstellungen zu schaffen.

Das Bauwerk teilt sich mit, ist informativ, entspricht dem Wunsch nach vertiefter Information. Die Grundbedingungen des Programms, so die Architekten, sind in einem für den Ort und Zweck typischen und einprägsamen Bauwerk zur Gestalt verschmolzen. Aus dem Boden wachsendes Gezweig leichter Stahlgerippe, brückenähnliche Fachwerke und zeltartig angebrachte Abspannungen formen eine Kontur, aus deren Anblick unschwer zu erkennen ist, welche Aufgabe ihnen zukommt. Das Wesen des Gebäudes und seiner Teile ist ablesbar, auf ein auf Repräsentation abzielendes Image wurde verzichtet.

Tagungszentrum TCM, Detailansichten
Congress Centre TCM, Detailed Views

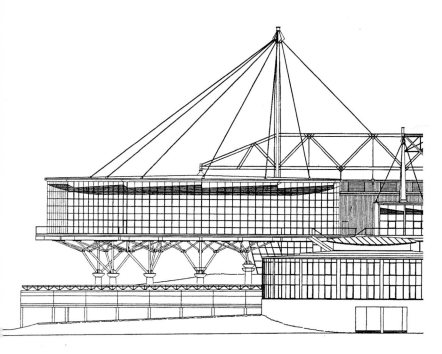

Teilansicht des Tagungszentrums TCM
Part View of the Congress Centre TCM

Nachnutzung als Leitprinzip für eine ressourcenschonende Planung

Zu den Rahmenbedingungen, die eine experimentelle, ungewöhnliche Architektur besonders herausfordern, gehört die Diskussion über die Nachnutzung des Weltausstellungsgeländes. Die normative Kraft des zukünftig Faktischen, die Funktion eines »normalen«, »alltäglichen« Stadtquartiers prägt das Layout des Masterplans. »Man darf nicht einen ganzen Stadtteil bauen, um ihn hinterher zu einer Ruinenlandschaft verfallen zu lassen, wie es in Sevilla geschehen ist. Darum hat man in Hannover, wie schon in Lissabon, so geplant, daß das Weltausstellungsgelände hinterher ein Bestandteil der Stadt ist. Natürlich muß auf dem Kronsberg kein neues Gewerbegebiet entstehen. Es werden aber neue Gewerbeflächen benötigt, viel mehr, als dort zur Verfügung stehen. Es ist nicht auszuschließen, daß dadurch andere Gewerbeflächen leerstehen, aber vielleicht ermöglicht diese Fluktuation Entwicklungen, durch die alte Gewerbegebiete saniert werden. Das 100 Hektar große Messegelände wurde neu strukturiert und in wesentlichen Teilen neu bebaut, diese Gebäude sind in das Konzept der Deutschen Messe AG eingebunden.« Eine Weltausstellung, so Hubertus von Bothmer, »ist auch ein Spiegel der momentanen gesellschaftlichen Realität. ... Natürlich müssen sich die Träger der Weltausstellung, Bund, Land und Stadt, für dieses Weltereignis engagieren. Aber ein Gebäude wie die Arena darf keine öffentlichen Subventionen bekommen, sondern muß durch die späteren Betreiber finanziert werden. Wenn dabei mittelmäßige Architektur herauskommt, wird das zwar nicht meinem Anspruch gerecht, ist aber Spiegelbild der gesellschaftlichen Situation.«[22]

Und doch ist es eine Herausforderung und keineswegs beliebig, welche Bilder die Architektur in ihren Leitprojekten präsentiert. »Die alten Bilder sind Ab-bilder von etwas, die neuen sind Projektionen, Vor-bilder für etwas, das es nicht gibt, aber geben könnte. Die alten Bilder sind ›Fiktionen‹, ›Simulationen‹, die neuen sind Konkretisationen von Möglichkeiten. Die alten Bilder sind einer abstrahierenden, zurücktretenden ›Imagination‹, die neuen einer konkretisierenden, projizierenden ›Einbildungskraft‹ zu verdanken. Wir denken also nicht etwa imaginativ magisch, sondern im Gegenteil

organization to reach people easily and confidently, to draw them into the exhibitions and to provide them quickly with relevant information. Great importance is attached to the display of products as well as to the communication of information and knowledge on the development of technology and the scope for its application. The desired transfer of knowledge also occurs in the specialist conferences accompanying the exhibitions. The centre is designed to provide conference spaces and exhibition areas beneath a single roof. As part of the basic concept, a pleasant ambiance was to be created for these activities at the heart of the trade fair site.

The structure communicates itself spontaneously to visitors. It is informative and reflects a desire for deeper insight. The basic conditions of the brief, according to the architects, were fused together in a form that is in keeping with the purpose and location and that is also strikingly memorable. Consisting of lightweight branching structures in steel that seem to grow like trees from the ground, together with trussed bridging members and tent-like stays, the centre has a form that quickly reveals the function it is designed to fulfil. The character of the building and its various elements is clearly legible. There is no attempt to create a special image as a means of self-representation.

Scope for Subsequent Use as a Guiding Principle of Planning to Conserve Resources

Among the constraints that present a special challenge to experimental, unusual architecture in the present context is the question of the subsequent use of the World Exposition site. The normative force of future circumstances - the function of a »normal«, »everyday« urban district - was fundamental in drawing up the master plan. »One may not build an entire urban district, only to let it fall into ruin afterwards, as was the case in Seville. For that reason, in Hanover, as in Lisbon, the planning proposed that the site should become an integral part of the city after the World Exposition. A new commercial zone does not have to be created on the Kronsberg, of course. But new commercial areas will be required - far more than are available there. One cannot preclude the possibility that other commercial areas will become redundant as a result, but perhaps these fluctuations will inspire developments that will lead to the rehabilitation of the old commercial districts. The trade fair site, covering an area of nearly 250 acres, has been restructured and redeveloped to a large extent. These buildings form part of the concept of the Deutsche Messe AG.« A world exposition, according to Hubertus von Bothmer, »is also a reflection of the social reality at a particular moment in time. ... Of course those responsible for staging the world exposition - the federal and state governments and the city council - have to demonstrate their commitment to an international event of this kind. But a building like the arena structure should not receive public subsidies. It should be financed by those who will subsequently operate it. If this results in mediocre architecture, it will not meet my expectations, but it will be a reflection of the social situation.«[22]

Nevertheless, the undertaking represents a great challenge, and it is by no means unimportant what architectural images the leading projects present. »The old images are re-presentations of something; the new images are projections, models, foretokens of something that does not yet exist, but that might exist. The old images are ›fictions‹ ›simulations‹, the new ones are the concretization of possibilities. The old images are a generalizing, receding ›imagination‹; the new ones are the product of a reifying, projecting ›power of imagination‹. We do no think in an imaginatively magical way; on the contrary, our thinking is conceptually designing.«[23]

einbildend entwerfend.«[23] Die Absicht des Entwurfs ist es, die Stadt als Projektion zu konstituieren, die »theoretischen Raum« zuläßt. »Die Absicht dieses projektiven Raums ist nicht, Politik und Wirtschaft herzustellen und zu lenken, sondern dem intersubjektiven Netz angesichts der allgemeinen Entropie ... einen Sinn zu geben; kurz, Theorie nicht mehr als Entdecken der Wahrheit, sondern als Projizieren von Bedeutung zu begreifen.«[24]

Über den Status von »Werken« von Bedeutung äußert sich Jürgen Habermas, wenn er an Adornos Unterscheidung anknüpft, das »in sich« funktionelle Kunstwerk stehe dem für »äußere Zwecke« funktionalen Gebilde gegenüber.[25] Die moderne Architektur befinde sich in einer paradoxen Situation. »*Auf der einen Seite* war Architektur stets zweckgebundene Kunst. Anders als Musik, Malerei und Lyrik, kann sie sich aus praktischen Bewandtniszusammenhängen so schwer lösen wie die literarisch anspruchsvolle Prosa von der Praxis der Umgangssprache. ... *Auf der anderen Seite* steht die Architektur unter Gesetzen der kulturellen Moderne – sie unterliegt, wie die Kunst überhaupt, dem Zwang zur radikalen Autonomisierung, zur Ausdifferenzierung eines Bereichs genuin ästhetischer Erfahrungen, den eine von den Imperativen des Alltags, von Routinen des Handelns und Konventionen der Wahrnehmung freigesetzte Subjektivität im Umgang mit ihrer eigenen Spontaneität erkunden kann.«[26]

Dr. Reinhart Wustlich ist Stadtplaner und Publizist; er ist Herausgeber von *CENTRUM – Jahrbuch Architektur und Stadt*.

The aim of the design is to constitute the city as a projection that admits of »theoretical space«. »The aim of this projective space is not to generate and manipulate a political and economic climate, but to invest the intersubjective network with meaning, in view of the general state of entropy... In brief, theory is no longer to be understood as the discovery of the truth, but as a projection of meaning.«[24]

Jürgen Habermas discusses the status of significant «achievements» when he refers to a distinction drawn by Adorno: namely that works of art with their own »innate« function are opposed to things whose function serves »extraneous purposes«.[25] Modern architecture is in a paradoxical situation today, Habermas argues. »On the one hand, architecture has always been a form of art with a specific purpose. Unlike music, painting and poetry, it is as difficult for architecture to escape from practical applications as it is for demanding literary prose to escape the usage of everyday speech... On the other hand, architecture also obeys the laws of cultural modernism. Like art in general, it is subject to an irresistible process of radical autonomization, the segregation of a realm of genuine aesthetic experience, which can be explored by a subjectivity liberated from everyday imperatives, from behavioural routine and the conventions of perception, in the context of its own spontaneous actions.«[26]

Dr. Reinhart Wustlich is an urban planner and editor (*CENTRUM – Jahrbuch Architektur und Stadt*).

Anmerkungen

1   Scott Lash, »Reflexivität und ihre Doppelungen: Struktur, Ästhetik und Gemeinschaft«, in: Ulrich Beck, Anthony Giddens, Scott Lash, *Reflexive Modernisierung. Eine Kontroverse*, Frankfurt/M. 1996, S. 198
2   Jean-Paul Sartre, *Drei Essays*, Frankfurt/M. und Berlin 1962, S. 11
3   Marc Augé, *Orte und Nicht-Orte. Vorüberlegungen zu einer Ethnologie der Einsamkeit*, Frankfurt/M. 1994, S. 48
4   Ebd., S. 49
5   Jürgen Habermas, »Moderne und postmoderne Architektur«, in: ders., *Die Neue Unübersichtlichkeit*, Frankfurt/M. 1985, S. 27
6   Lewis Mumford, *Die Stadt. Geschichte und Ausblick*, München 1979 (*The City in History*, 1961)
7   Jean-François Lyotard, »Die Philosophie in der Zone. La Philosophie dans la zone«, in: ders., *Moralités postmodernes*, Paris 1993
8   Jean-François Lyotard, »Wörter: Sartre«, in: ders., *Kindheitslektüren*, Wien 1995, S. 120
9   Jean-François Lyotard, »Rückkehr: Joyce«, ebd., S. 17
10 Ebd., S. 26
11 Habermas 1985, S. 26
12 Augé 1994, S. 34
13 Thomas Herzog, »Vorwort des Herausgebers«, in: *Solar Energy in Architecture and Urban Planning*, München und New York 1996, S. 16
14 Sigfried Giedion, *Bauen in Frankreich, Bauen in Eisen, Bauen in Eisenbeton*, Leipzig 1928; als Reprint: *Building in France. Building in Iron. Building in Ferroconcrete*, hg. von The Getty Center for the History of Art and the Humanities, Santa Monica 1995, S. 168
15 Renzo Piano, *Out of the Blue. Renzo Piano Building Workshop*, Ostfildern-Ruit 1997, S. 172
16 Herzog 1996, S. 120
17 Piano 1997, S. 168
18 Deutsche Messe AG als Bauherr der dokumentierten Beispiele
19 Herzog 1996, S. 14
20 Meinhard von Gerkan, in: von Gerkan, Marg und Partner, *Architektur 1991–1995*, Basel, Boston und Berlin 1995
21 Herzog 1996, S. 15
22 Hubertus von Bothmer, »Mittelmäßige Architektur für eine mittelmäßige Gesellschaft, ein Gespräch« in: *deutsche bauzeitung*, 38, 23, Oktober 1998, S. 40
23 Vilém Flusser, »Vom Projizieren«, in: ders., *Vom Subjekt zum Projekt. Menschwerdung*, Frankfurt/M. 1998, S. 25
24 Ders., »Städte entwerfen«, ebd., S. 57
25 Habermas 1985, S. 21
26 Ebd.

Notes

1   Scott Lash, »Reflexivität und ihre Doppelungen: Struktur, Ästhetik und Gemeinschaft«, in: Ulrich Beck, Anthony Giddens, Scott Lash, *Reflexive Modernisierung. Eine Kontroverse*, Frankfurt-on-Main 1996, p. 198
2   Jean-Paul Sartre, Drei Essays, Frankfurt-on-Main and Berlin, 1962, p. 11
3   Marc Augè, *Orte und Nicht-Orte. Vorüberlegungen zu einer Ethnologie der Einsamkeit*, Frankfurt-on-Main 1994, p. 48
4   Ibid., p. 49
5   Jürgen Habermas, »Moderne und postmoderne Architektur«, in: Habermas, *Die neue Unübersichtlichkeit*, Frankfurt-on-Main 1985, p.27
6   Lewis Mumford, *Die Stadt, Geschichte und Ausblick*, Munich 1979 (*The City in History*, 1961)
7   Jean-François Lyotard, »Die Philosophie in der Zone. La Philosophie dans la zone«, in: Lyotard, *Moralitès postmodernes*, Paris 1993
8   Jean-François Lyotard, »Wörter: Sartre«, in: Lyotard, *Kindheitslektüren*, Vienna 1995, p. 120
9   Jean-François Lyotard, »Rückkehr: Joyce«, ibid, p. 17
10   Ibid., p. 26
11 Habermas, see note 5, p. 26
12 Augè, see note 3, p. 34
13 Thomas Herzog, *Solar Energy in Architecture and Urban Planning*, Munich, New York 1996, p. 16
14 Sigfried Giedion, *Bauen in Frankreich, Bauen in Eisen, Bauen in Eisenbeton*, Leipzig 1928; reprinted as *Building in France. Building in Iron. Building in Ferroconcrete*, ed. The Getty Center for the History of Art and the Humanities, Santa Monica 1995, p. 168
15 Renzo Piano, *Out of the Blue. Renzo Piano Building Workshop*, Ostfildern-Ruit 1997, p. 172
16 Herzog, see note 13, p. 120
17 Piano, see note 15, p. 168
18 Deutsche Messe AG, as the client for the examples documented here
19 Herzog, see note 13, p. 120
20 Meinhard von Gerkan, in: von Gerkan, Marg und Partner, *Architektur 1991-1995*, Basle, Boston and Berlin 1995
21 Herzog, see note 13, p. 120
22 Hubertus von Bothmer, »Mittelmäßige Architektur für eine mittelmäßige Gesellschaft, ein Gespräch«, in: *deutsche bauzeitung* 10/1998, 38/23, p. 40
23 Vilém Flusser, »Vom Projizieren«, in: Flusser, *Vom Subjekt zum Projekt. Menschwerdung*, Frankfurt-on-Main 1998, p. 25
24 Flusser, »Städte entwerfen«, ibid, p. 57
25 Habermas, see note 5, p. 21
26 Ibid.

Hubertus von Bothmer

Planung für die Weltausstellung: eine besondere Herausforderung

Planning for the World Exposition: A Special Challenge

Am 14. Juni 1990 erhielt die Bundesrepublik Deutschland auf der Vollversammlung des »Bureau International des Expositions« (Internationale Organisation für Ausstellungswesen B.I.E.) in Paris den Zuschlag, erstmals eine Weltausstellung auszurichten. Als Veranstaltungsort hatte sich Hannover beworben. Nach erheblichen politischen Diskussionen Anfang der neunziger Jahre wurde Mitte 1994 endlich die EXPO 2000 Hannover GmbH, die Gesellschaft zur Vorbereitung und Durchführung dieser Weltausstellung, gegründet. Sie suchte Ende 1994 einen Leiter für den Bereich Planen und Bauen. Die Wahl fiel auf mich, und so habe ich im Februar 1995 die Verantwortung für die Planung und Realisierung sämtlicher Baumaßnahmen auf dem Weltausstellungsgelände übernommen.

Seither dreht sich meine Welt mindestens dreimal so schnell wie zuvor. Es ist unbeschreiblich aufregend, an einer derartigen Aufgabe verantwortlich mitzuwirken. Es sind nicht nur die zahlreichen Kontakte und Begegnungen mit interessanten Kollegen und Planern aus aller Welt, die an dieser Aufgabe faszinieren. Die Komplexität des ganzen Vorhabens, das Fehlen jeglicher Vorerfahrungen mit Weltausstellungen in Deutschland, der Erwartungsdruck einer ganzen Nation und die unerbittlich näherrückende Deadline des Eröffnungstages machen diese Arbeit – wenn sich ein solcher Vergleich überhaupt anstellen ließe – nur mit der Vorbereitung von Olympischen Spielen vergleichbar.

Eine Weltausstellung stellt höchste Ansprüche an Städtebau und Architektur. Seit der ersten Weltausstellung 1851 in London sind Weltausstellungen immer auch Weltschauen der internationalen Baukunst und Bautechnologie gewesen und haben architektonische Impulse gesetzt. Ob Joseph Paxtons Kristallpalast auf der Londoner Weltausstellung 1851, die Rotunde mit der damals größten Kuppel der Welt in Wien 1873, der Deutsche Pavillon von Ludwig Mies van der Rohe in Barcelona 1929 oder der Philips-Pavillon

At the plenary session of the »Bureau International des Expositions« (BIE) in Paris on 14 June 1990, the Federal Republic of Germany was for the first time awarded the contract to stage a world exposition, and it was Hanover which was the German candidate for the venue. After extensive political debate at the start of the nineties, the EXPO 2000 Hannover Corporation, the corporation for the organization and realization of the World Exposition EXPO 2000 in Hanover, was finally formed in mid-1994. At the end of 1994, the corporation was looking for a director for the Planning and Construction Department, and I was selected. In February 1995, I assumed responsibility for planning and implementing all construction activities on the world exposition site.

Since then, my world has been spinning at least three times as fast as it used to. To play an executive role in such an activity is incredibly exciting. Not only are there numerous fascinating contacts and meetings with interesting colleagues and planners from all over the world, there is also the challenge of the complexity of the entire project, the absence of any prior experience with world expositions in Germany, the pressure of an entire nation's expectations and the remorseless deadline set by the approaching opening date. All these factors make it a project which can only be compared – to the extent that any comparison is possible – with the preparations for the staging of the Olympic Games.

A world exposition demands the utmost in terms of urban planning and architecture. Ever since the first world exposition in London in 1851, world expositions have always been global showcases for international architecture and construction technology, and have provided new inspiration for architecture. Joseph Paxton's Crystal Palace at the London World Exposition of 1851, the Rotunda in 1873 in Vienna (in its day, the largest dome in the world), the German Pavilion by Ludwig Mies van der Rohe in 1929 in

Das gesamte Weltausstellungsgelände 1995 und 1998
The Whole Exposition Site 1995 and 1998

von Le Corbusier 1958 in Brüssel – kaum ein Land ließ sich die einmalige Chance entgehen, die eigene Baukultur in einem Pavillon zu demonstrieren.

Die besondere Herausforderung zu Beginn der Planungen zur EXPO 2000 bestand darin, ohne existierende Organisationsstruktur und mit einer sehr heterogenen Zusammensetzung der Anteilseigner – Bundesrepublik Deutschland, Land Niedersachsen, Stadt und Landkreis Hannover und die Beteiligungsgesellschaft der deutschen Wirtschaft – die notwendigen Planungsprozesse so zu initiieren, daß die Ergebnisse dem hohen Anspruch einer Weltausstellung gerecht werden würden. Nicht nur die Frage, was und wo gebaut werden sollte, sondern auch das Auftreiben der für die Realisierung der Projekte notwendigen Geldmittel war zumeist nicht abschließend geklärt. Diese Phase liegt heute hinter uns – inzwischen gibt es den Masterplan Planen und Bauen und ein Budget für die eigenen Projekte der EXPO 2000.

Der zweite Aspekt besonderer Herausforderung ist der Umfang und die Komplexität eines solchen Großprojekts. Der erste Masterplan für die weit über 200 Hektar große Fläche, die zu beplanen war, wurde bereits 1994 vorgelegt. Und dennoch waren in den beiden darauffolgenden Jahren 1995 und 1996 umfangreiche Diskussionen zur städtebaulichen Struktur des Weltausstellungsgeländes notwendig. Obwohl die Form der einzelnen Wettbewerbe (eingeladener und offener Wettbewerb, Wettbewerbe nach Auswahlverfahren und Gutachten) immer wieder zu öffentlicher Diskussion Anlaß gegeben hat, zeigten die Ergebnisse der durchgeführten städtebaulichen, landschaftsplanerischen und architektonischen Wettbewerbe, daß die Durchführung von Wettbewerben dennoch die beste Möglichkeit war, zu qualitativ hochwertigen Planungen zu kommen.

Der dritte Aspekt der besonderen Herausforderung ist die Inhomogenität der Geländestruktur: Das Weltausstellungsgelände (160 Hektar) bestand zu rund zwei Dritteln aus dem bestehenden Messegelände und zu etwa einem Drittel aus einem unbebauten und neu zu entwickelnden Geländeteil. Um hier ein einheitliches visuelles Erscheinungsbild zu gewährleisten, wurde ein Gestaltungskreis unter Leitung von Eberhard Stauß (Inhaber des Büros für Gestaltung in München) mit der fachlichen Beratung des Bauherren EXPO 2000 beauftragt. Mit seiner fachlichen Kompetenz für die Bereiche Städtebau, Landschaftsplanung, Architektur und Design berät der Gestaltungskreis die Weltausstellungsgesellschaft bei allen Einzelplanungen.

Der vierte und möglicherweise wichtigste Aspekt ist der Anspruch, die Weltausstellungsgebäude langfristig – möglichst ohne große Umbauten – nutzen zu können. Dies läßt sich nicht erreichen, indem man die Pavillons nach dem Ende der Weltausstellung für eine dauerhafte Nutzung vermarktet. Die baukonstruktiven Anforderungen sind für eine langfristige Nutzung in der Regel ganz andere als für vergleichsweise kurzfristig zu nutzende Ausstellungsbauten. Deswegen müssen die Nutzungen für die Zwecke der Weltausstellung und spätere Nutzungen in der Planung und Realisierung der einzelnen Projekte von Anfang an zusammengedacht werden. Da dies aber zu erheblich höheren Baukosten führt, ist es notwendig, die Gebäude durch den Weltausstellungsnutzer und einen Investor für die Langfristnutzung zu finanzieren. Zu welchen fatalen Diskussionen und Irritationen hinsichtlich der Rolle des eigentlichen Bauherrn eines Weltausstellungspavillons dies führen kann, konnte am Beispiel des Deutschen Pavillons intensiv erlebt werden. Aber nur das Festhalten an dem Konzept, Weltausstellungsnutzung und Langfristnutzung in einem Gebäude zu harmonisieren, hat dazu geführt, daß Bauinvestitionen in Milliardenhöhe eben nicht als »Ex-und-Hopp«-Architektur für fünf Monate Weltausstellung, sondern dau-

Barcelona, and the Philips Pavilion by Le Corbusier in 1958 in Brussels – many countries have seized the unique opportunity to display their architectural tradition in a pavilion.

The particular challenge at the start of planning for EXPO 2000 was how to initiate the planning process without any existing organizational structure and with a highly heterogeneous group of shareholders – the German Federal Government, the government of Lower Saxony, the city and regional administrations of Hanover and the Corporation of German Industry, the Beteiligungsgesellschaft der deutschen Wirtschaft, and to do so in a way that the results would match the high standards of a world exposition. Besides the question what should be built and where, the problem of raising the necessary funding for the project was also generally left without a final resolution. Having left this phase behind us, we now have a master plan for Planning and Construction and a budget for EXPO 2000's own projects.

Another aspect of this challenge is the scale and complexity of a major project like this. The first master plan for the area covering well over 200 hectares was submitted in 1994, but even so extensive discussion was needed over the next two years to determine the planning structure of the world exposition site. Although the form of the individual competitions (open and by invitation, with selection process and expert appraisal) repeatedly prompted public discussion, the results of the urban engineering, landscaping and architectural competitions showed that competitions were the best way of ensuring high-quality planning.

A third aspect of this challenge is the diversity of the site. The world exposition site (160 hectares) consisted of the existing fairgrounds (two-thirds) and an undeveloped area (the remaining one-third). To ensure a uniform visual image, a design group headed by Eberhard Stauß (proprietor of the Munich Büro für Gestaltung) was formed to provide expert guidance to the EXPO 2000 Corporation in its capacity as a developer. The design circle with its expertise in urban planning, landscaping, architecture and design advises the World Exposition company on all individual planning.

The fourth (and arguably most important) aspect is the need to be able to use the World Exposition buildings in the long term, if possible without any major conversion work. This cannot be done only by looking for permanent occupants for the pavilions after the close of the World Exposition. The structural requirements for long-term use are generally very different to those for exhibition structures with their comparatively short period of utilization. This is why world exposition and subsequent uses need to be considered side by side right from the start in the planning and implementation process of individual projects. As this results in substantially increased construction costs, it is necessary to obtain financing for buildings from both the world exposition tenant and an investor for long-term use. The German Pavilion provided a vivid example of the tense discussion, alarms and irritations that may come with being the actual developer of a world exposition pavilion. However, firm adherence to the concept of uniting world exposition and long-term use within a particular building was the only way of ensuring that investment in construction running into billions would produce buildings that provide long-term capacities and not just temporary structures for the five months of the World Exposition. The arena, a hotel, a cinema, a discotheque, a university (covering two buildings) and a sporting equipment store are just a few examples of post exhibition use. Only in this way, the World Exposition´s very demand for sustainability could be satisfied.

The fifth and most attractive challenge is advising and assisting the

erhaft genutzt werden. Die Arena, ein Hotel, ein Kino, eine Diskothek, eine Fachhochschule in zwei Gebäuden und ein Sportartikelmarkt sind nur einige Beispiele für Nachnutzungen. Nur so können wir dem Anspruch der Nachhaltigkeit einer Weltausstellung gerecht werden.

Die fünfte und schönste Herausforderung aber ist die Beratung und Betreuung der Pavillonprojekte der eingeladenen Staaten. Die Entwürfe der bisher vorgelegten Projekte versprechen hohes Besucherinteresse. Auch im Zeitalter der Informations- und Kommunikationsgesellschaft unterliegen Weltausstellungen kaum der Konkurrenz digitaler Angebote; kein Internet kann den sinnlichen Gesamteindruck von Architektur – das Zusammenspiel von Volumen, Materialien, Räumen und Licht – ersetzen. Die Weltreise zu Fuß, in der die Kontinente und ihre Baukultur nur ein paar Schritte voneinander entfernt liegen, ermöglicht nur eine Weltausstellung.

Die EXPO 2000 Hannover GmbH baut bis auf die temporären Eingänge und Gastronomiegebäude selbst keine Hochbauten, da die Deutsche Messe AG ihre Hallenbauten selbst verantwortet, die Plaza weitestgehend von Investoren realisiert wird und die beiden Pavillongelände durch die Nationenpavillons bebaut werden. Wir tragen die Verantwortung für die städtebauliche Struktur des Gesamtgeländes sowie für die Qualität der Landschaftsplanung. So haben wir in den ersten Monaten unserer gemeinsamen Arbeit mit dem Gestaltungskreis die Leitlinien zur Struktur des Gesamtgeländes ebenso erarbeitet wie zum Konzept der Freiraumplanung und vor allem zur Homogenisierung des bestehenden Messegeländes und seiner Bebauung mit dem neu entwickelten Kronsberg.

Das Gesamtbild des Weltausstellungsgeländes ist durch die Vielzahl der öffentlichen Einrichtungen in den Freianlagen geprägt: durch die einzelnen Bauten, das Beleuchtungskonzept, die Beschilderungen, Werbeträger, Kioske und die Vielzahl der Außenmöbel. Unser erklärtes Ziel ist es, hier keine Reizüberflutung zu erzeugen und zu hinterlassen.

Die architektonischen Projekte, die auf diesem komplexen und heterogenen Hintergrund realisiert worden sind und in diesem Band der *EXPO Architektur Dokumente* vorgestellt werden, können sich sehen lassen. Auch die architektonischen Projekte der Nationenpavillons sind äußerst vielversprechend. In ihnen zeigt sich der eigentliche Sinn einer Weltausstellung.

Die neuen Hallen, die Entwürfe der Nationenpavillons und das qualitativ hochwertige Erscheinungsbild der Gartenanlagen werden im Jahr 2000 Bühne sein für die Weltausstellung, für Events des Kultur- und Ereignisprogramms, für den Themenpark als Beitrag der EXPO 2000 Hannover GmbH, für Veranstaltungen der Nationen und, last but not least, für ein Treffen der Völker dieser Welt.

Hubertus von Bothmer ist Bereichsleiter Planen und Bauen der EXPO 2000 Hannover GmbH.

pavilion projects of the nations invited. The designs for the projects presented so far promise a high level of visitor interest. Even in the age of the communication and information society, world expositions are virtually immune to digital competition: no Internet site can replace the overall sensual impact of architecture, the interplay of volumes, materials, space and light. Only a world exposition can make you feel like a real globetrotter, with just a few steps separating continents and their architecture.

EXPO 2000 Hannover Corporation itself is not erecting any buildings, apart from temporary entrance and catering structures, as Deutsche Messe AG is managing its own exhibition halls, the Plaza is largely being implemented by investors, and the two pavilion areas are being developed by respective national pavilions. We are responsible for the urban engineering of the site as a whole and for the quality of the landscaping. In the first few months of our collaboration with the design group, we drew up the guidelines for the structure of the overall site, the concept for open-air site planning and, above all, for integrating the existing fairgrounds and its structures into the newly developed Kronsberg village.

The overall picture of the world exposition site is determined by a large number of public facilities in the open-air zones, individual buildings, lighting, signs, advertising surfaces, kiosks and variety of street furniture. Our stated goal is to avoid creating a flood of distractions (and leaving them for later users).

The architectural projects implemented in this complex and heterogeneous framework are impressively featured in this volume of *EXPO Architecture Documents*. The architectural projects for the national pavilions are extremely promising. They are, indeed, the true purpose of a world exposition.

The new halls, the designs for the national pavilions and the attractive gardens will provide the setting for the EXPO 2000 World Exposition, for the culture and events program, for the Thematic Area as the contribution of EXPO 2000 Hannover GmbH, for national events and – last but not least – for a meeting between the peoples of the world.

Hubertus von Bothmer is the Director of Planning and Construction of the EXPO 2000 Hannover GmbH.

Adelbert Reif im Gespräch mit/talking to Albert Speer

Im Zeichen der Qualität des öffentlichen Raumes
The Mark of Quality in Public Areas

ADELBERT REIF: Herr Professor Speer, wie alle Weltausstellungen seit der ersten 1851 im Londoner Kristallpalast will auch die EXPO 2000 »ein Spiegel der gesellschaftlichen, politischen und industriellen Entwicklung« der einzelnen Länder sein. Was bedeutet dieser Anspruch für die Planung in Hannover?

ALBERT SPEER: Unsere Aufgabe der Entwicklung des Geländes für die Weltausstellung besteht darin, die vorgesehenen Aktivitäten auf der gegebenen Fläche zu koordinieren. Unser Anspruch ist es, für diese Weltausstellung nichts zu bauen, was nicht hinterher auch gebraucht wird. Wir bemühen uns also um eine nachhaltige Entwicklung ganz im Sinne des Mottos der EXPO 2000 »Mensch – Natur – Technik« und orientieren uns an den Inhalten der Agenda 21, dem Aktionsprogramm der Umweltkonferenz von Rio de Janeiro 1992, so daß wir am Ende der EXPO 2000 ein Gelände haben, das hervorragend für die Aufgaben der Region Hannover im nächsten Jahrtausend gerüstet ist.

REIF: Könnten Sie die wesentlichen Vorgaben erläutern, die der von Ihnen gepflegte Masterplan beinhaltet?

SPEER: Der Masterplan für die EXPO 2000 bildet die Grundlage für alle Investitionen sowie für die gesamte Infrastruktur, die auf dem Expo-Gelände und in seinem engeren Umfeld entsteht. Da sich im Laufe der fortschreitenden Arbeiten diese Vorgaben ständig verändern, haben wir davon Abstand genommen, einen traditionellen Masterplan auszuarbeiten, sondern wir reden vom »Masterplanning«. Das heißt: Wir haben ein organisatorisches System entwickelt, in dem alle an der Entwicklung der EXPO 2000 beteiligten Akteure halbjährlich einen neuen Masterplan vorgelegt bekommen. Dabei ist das 1994 gemeinsam mit Arnaboldi und Cavadini entwickelte städteplanerische Grundgerüst stabil und unverändert geblieben. Verändert

ADELBERT REIF: Professor Speer, like all world expositions since the first in the Crystal Palace, London, in 1851, EXPO 2000 also wishes to mirror the social, political and industrial development of the individual nations. What does this aim mean for the planning in Hanover?

ALBERT SPEER: Our task of developing the site for the World Exposition consists of coordinating the intended activities within the available space. Our aim is to build nothing for this World Exposition which will not also be put to a post use. We are therefore striving to achieve sustainable development which fully reflects the EXPO 2000 motto »Humankind – Nature – Technology«, and our output is informed by the contents of Agenda 21, the action programme of the environment summit held in Rio de Janeiro in 1992, so that ultimately, at the end of EXPO 2000, we will have a site which is ideally equipped for the activities and tasks of the Hanover region in the next millennium.

REIF: Could you describe the main principles contained in the masterplan for which you have been responsible?

SPEER: The EXPO 2000 masterplan forms the basis for all of the investments as well as for the complete infrastructure which is being created on the Expo site and in the immediate vicinity. As these requirements are constantly changing during the ongoing work process, we have refrained from preparing a traditional masterplan, but rather talk in terms of «masterplanning». Thus we have developed an organizational system by means of which all of the agents involved in the development of EXPO 2000 receive a new masterplan every six months. Yet, the basic structure of the urban planning framework developed in 1994 together with Arnaboldi and Cavadini has remained stable and unchanged. Many details have changed, however. The mas-

haben sich viele Einzelheiten. Der Masterplan wird in einer zweitägigen Diskussion mit allen erörtert und dann als der jeweils gültige Masterplan verabschiedet. Eine solche Vorgehensweise war notwendig, weil das Gelände der EXPO 2000 von seinen Ausmaßen her einer Stadt gleichkommt und sich die Vorgaben, Inhalte und Ziele ständig verändern, teilweise durch unsere Arbeit selbst und teilweise durch Einflüsse von außen.

REIF: Traten dadurch besondere Probleme bei der Realisierung des Masterplans auf?

SPEER: Im Gegenteil. Diese Art der Organisation minimiert mögliche Probleme, die bei einer so gewaltigen Aufgabe ständig auftreten, haben doch die Beteiligten alle sechs Monate die Gelegenheit, ihre unterschiedlichen Ansprüche zu koordinieren.

Die grundsätzlichen Prinzipien wie die generelle Erschließung des Geländes, die Neuordnung des Messegeländes mit Grünzonen, die Allee der Vereinigten Bäume oder die Lage der Plaza, die im ursprünglichen Masterplan festgeschrieben waren, sind natürlich in ihm verblieben. Aber die Fülle an Details, die sich fortlaufend verändern, kann jeweils in den neuen Plan eingearbeitet werden.

REIF: Wo haben im Fortgang Ihrer Arbeit wichtige Veränderungen stattgefunden?

SPEER: Zwei Beispiele mögen das verdeutlichen. Zum einen wurde für den gesamten südlichen Pavillonbereich ein landschaftsplanerischer Wettbewerb ausgeschrieben, der auf unseren stadtplanerischen Rahmenbedingungen aufbaute und den wir auch als Büro AS&P vorbereiteten und durchführten. Dieser Wettbewerb wurde von dem Landschaftsplaner Kamel Louafi, Berlin, gewonnen und brachte viele hervorragende Ideen, an die die ursprüngliche Planung nicht gedacht hatte. Die Verwirklichung eines Teils dieser neuen Ideen führte zu Veränderungen im ganzen Eingangsbereich Süd und in der Grünzone bis hin zur Plaza.

Das zweite Beispiel: Das Expo-Gelände ist so groß, daß es kein Fußgänger an einem Tage erlaufen kann. Aus diesem Grunde erwies es sich als notwendig, ein internes Bewegungsmittel zu entwickeln. Unsere Vorstellungen liefen auf eine Art Seilbahn hinaus, die auf einer anderen Ebene über das Gelände führt. Diese Seil-, Gondel- oder Einschienenbahn ist in ihrer Trassenführung immer wieder anders gedacht worden, abhängig von den jeweils vorgeschlagenen Systemen. Es kommt aber noch eine ganz andere Komponente hinzu, nämlich eine wirtschaftliche. Die Seilbahn muß sich selbst tragen, sie wird nicht aus dem Budget der EXPO 2000 finanziert. Die Verhandlungen mit Unternehmern, die solche Seilbahnen bauen, wurden demnach ständig überlagert von unseren Überlegungen, was unter Aspekten wie etwa der Ankunft der Besucher, ihrer Führung durch das Gelände und so weiter städtebaulich sinnvoll ist.

Mittlerweile ist nun definitiv beschlossen worden, daß wir eine Gondelbahn bekommen, die ein weltweit renommiertes Südtiroler Unternehmen bauen und betreiben wird. Jetzt geht es darum zu entscheiden, wo oder wie die Stützen dieser Seilbahn plaziert werden sollen, damit sie nicht im Wege stehen und möglicherweise das ästhetische Gesamtbild der EXPO 2000 beeinträchtigen. Auch müssen die Stationen, an denen die Besucher ein- und aussteigen, gestaltet werden. All dies sind Fragen, die wiederum einen direkten Einfluß auf den Masterplan haben.

REIF: Nun wurde der Anspruch der Nachnutzung, den Ihre Konzeption für Hannover in den Mittelpunkt stellt, bereits bei früheren Weltausstellungen erhoben ...

terplan is usually reviewed in a two-day discussion with all parties and then adopted as the currently valid masterplan. It was necessary to adopt such an approach because, in terms of its dimensions, the Expo site is equivalent to a town, and because the requirements, contents and aims are constantly changing, partly as a result of our work itself and partly in consequence of outside influences.

REIF: Have any particular problems arisen in consequence during the implementation of the masterplan?

SPEER: On the contrary. This form of organization minimizes the potential problems which constantly occur with such a monumental undertaking, because all parties involved are given an opportunity every six months to coordinate their various demands. The basic principles, such as the general development of the site, the reorganization of the trade fair grounds with green areas, the United Trees Avenue or the location of the Plaza, which were prescribed in the original masterplan, have of course been retained. But the numerous details that are constantly changing can be incorporated in each case into the new plan.

REIF: Where have significant changes taken place during the process of your work?

SPEER: I can quote two examples to illustrate this. On the one hand, a landscape planning competition was announced for the complete southern Pavilion Area, on the basis of our urban planning framework conditions. The competition was prepared and carried out by our AS&P office and was won by the landscape architect Kamel Louafi, from Berlin. It produced many outstanding ideas which had not been thought of during the original planning. The realization of some of these new ideas led to changes in the complete Southern Entrance Area and in the green area extending as far as the Plaza.

The second example relates to the size of the Expo site, which is so big that a pedestrian cannot cover it all in one day. Consequently, it became necessary to develop an internal means of transport. Our concept targeted a form of overhead cable rail system traversing the site at a different level. The route of this cable car, gondola or monorail system has been constantly reconsidered, depending upon the various types of system proposed. However, a quite different element also has to be taken into consideration, namely the economic factor. The overhead rail system must be self-financing, as it will not be paid for out of the EXPO 2000 budget. The negotiations with companies who build such overhead rail systems were thus constantly influenced by our considerations about what would be worthwhile from the urban planning viewpoint in terms of the arrival of visitors, their route through the site, and similar aspects. It has now been definitively decided that we shall have a gondola rail system, which will be constructed and operated by a world-famous company from the South Tirol. The issue now at hand is deciding where or how the supports for this overhead rail system are to be located, so that they are not in the way and possibly detract from the overall aesthetic impression of EXPO 2000. Stations have to be designed for the visitors to board and leave the gondolas. All these aspects have a direct influence on the masterplan.

REIF: The principle of post use, on which your concept for Hanover focuses, has already been raised at previous world expositions.

Wettbewerb Masterplan EXPO 2000/Messe/Kronsberg, 1. Preis
Architekten: Michele Arnaboldi, Raffaele Cavadini, Locarno, und
Guido Hager, Zürich
1992 wurde der internationale stadt- und landschaftsplanerische
Ideenwettbewerb Weltausstellung EXPO 2000 in Verbindung mit
dem Strukturkonzept Messe/Kronsberg durchgeführt. Aus fast 60
Planungsteams mit Stadtplanern, Architekten und Landschaftsarchitekten waren 16 Gruppen von einem Planungsbeirat zur Teilnahme
aufgefordert worden. Die Aufgabe bestand darin, unter kritischer
Prüfung der bis dahin vorliegenden Aussagen ein stadt- und land-
schaftsplanerisches Konzept für den Gesamtbereich Messe/Krons-
berg zu entwickeln, in das sich im Jahre 2000 ein Weltausstellungsgelände als Zwischennutzung einfügen können lassen würde.
Gefordert waren
– ein Konzept für das Weltausstellungsgelände unter Einbeziehung
des Messegeländes,
– die Entwicklung eines Wohngebiets am Kronsberg einschließlich
des Expo-Quartiers,
– Vorschläge für die Gestaltung des Landschaftsraumes
Messe/Kronsberg,
– Aussagen zur Nachnutzung des Weltausstellungsgeländes.

Competition Masterplan EXPO 2000/Messe/Kronsberg 1. Price
Architects: Michele Arnaboldi, H. Cavadini, Lorcarno and
Guido Hager, Zürich
In 1992 a competition was carried out in the international and
landscape a Architecture for the EXPO 2000 in connection with the
structure of Messe/Kronsberg. Out of 60 planner teams with urban
planners, architects and landscape architects 16 teams were named
by a jury to take part. The task was to develop / an urban and landscape concept for the whole/ Messe/Kronsberg site where an exposition site could be inserted / added in between. It was about for .
– concept for the exposition site incl. the Messe site
– development of a residential area on Kronsberg incl. Expo camp
– suggestions on landscape architecture Messe/Kronsberg
– statements on utilizability after the exposition.

SPEER: Die Vorgaben in Hannover sind für eine Weltausstellung insoweit neu, als sie erstmals zu über siebzig Prozent auf einem schon genutzten Gelände, dem alten und neuen Messegelände, stattfindet. Dies ist ganz im Sinne der Kriterien einer nachhaltigen Nutzung. Von Anfang an haben wir neue Formen erfunden und auch für die Pavillons Gebäudetypen entwickelt, die nach Beendigung der Ausstellung nicht mehr abgerissen werden, wie es in der Vergangenheit geschah, sondern weiter verwendbar sind. So bleibt alles, was rings um die Expo-Plaza gebaut wird, erhalten – ausgenommen die Pavillons auf der Westseite des Messegeländes, das zukünftig als Freigelände für die Messe genutzt wird.

Für die Gebäude rings um die Plaza gilt: Bei der Arena ist der Zweck ein-deutig bestimmt. Sie wird für Veranstaltungen verschiedenster Art genutzt werden. Zwei große Gebäude werden die Kunst- und Musikabteilung der Fachhochschule von Niedersachsen aufnehmen. Für den Deutschen Pavillon hat der Investor bis jetzt noch nicht über die Nachnutzung entschieden. Der Bertelsmann Verlag, der auf dem Platz ebenfalls mit einem großen Gebäude vertreten ist, will dieses auch nach der EXPO 2000 weiter betreiben. Des weiteren entsteht ein Hotel sowie ein Bereich mit verschiedenen Unterhal-tungseinrichtungen, die ebenfalls zum zukünftigen festen Bestand gehören sollen. Der einzige Bau auf der Plaza, der wieder abgebaut, aber keineswegs verschrottet wird, ist der Pavillon der Kirchen. Dieser Pavillon, entworfen von dem Hamburger Architekten Meinhard von Gerkan, wird komplett demon-tiert und auf dem Gelände eines Klosters in der Nähe von Mühlhausen, Thüringen, wieder aufgebaut.

REIF: Sehen Sie dennoch die Gefahr, daß sich diese Plaza – ähnlich wie die Zentren der meisten deutschen Trabantenstädte – nach dem Ende der EXPO 2000 ohne pulsierendes Leben präsentieren könnte?

SPEER: Diese Frage läßt sich nur sehr schwer beantworten, und jede Antwort wird mit vielen unbekannten Aspekten behaftet sein. Mit Sicherheit läßt sich aber folgendes sagen: Es wird unterschiedlich frequentierte Bereiche geben. Die Hannover Messe ist wie jede andere Messe auch ein Bereich, in dem nicht ständig Betriebsamkeit herrscht. Das Leben dort ist nun einmal ausschließlich an den direkten Messebetrieb gebunden. Der ganze Ostbereich aber, das Gelände mit den Gebäuden an der Plaza und das daran im Süden angrenzende Gelände mit den Pavillons, ist so konzipiert worden, daß dort ständig Leben sein wird, sich Gewerbe ansiedeln wird, Dienstlei-stungen vorhanden sind und in der Arena kulturelle Veranstaltungen statt-finden. Überdies ist das Ganze durch eine neue S-Bahnlinie erschlossen. Vor

SPEER: The requirements for Hanover are new for a world exposition to the extent that for the first time the exposition is being held on a site of which about seventy per cent is already being used for the so-called old and new trade fair grounds. This is completely in line with the criteria for sustainability and post use. Right from the start we invented new forms and even developed new types of building for the pavilions so that these no longer need to be demolished after the event – as was the case in the past –, but rather will continue to be usable. For example, everything which is being built around the Expo-Plaza will be retained, with the exception of the pavilions on the western side of the fairgrounds, which will make way for an open space for trade fairs.

As far as the buildings around the Plaza are concerned, the pur-pose of the Arena is clearly determined. It will be used to hold events of various types. Two large buildings will accommodate the art and music departments of the Lower Saxony College of Technology. The investor has not yet decided on the subsequent use for the German Pavilion. The Bertelsman publishing group is also represented on the square, with a large building which it also intends to use after EXPO 2000. There will also be a hotel and an area with entertainment facili-ties which will be permanent features for the future. The only building on the Plaza which will be removed, but in no way demolished, is the pavilion of the churches. This pavilion, designed by the Hamburg architect Meinhard von Gerkan, will be completely dismantled and reconstructed on the grounds of a monastery near Mühlhausen in Thuringia.

REIF: Nevertheless are you not afraid that this Plaza – just like the cen-tres of most German satellite towns – might lose its pulse of life after EXPO 2000 has ended?

SPEER: This is a very difficult question to answer, and any answer will be tainted by many imponderables. However, it is certainly possible to say that areas will have different frequency levels. Just like any other trade fair, the Hanover Trade Fair is also not constantly full of activity. After all, its life is exclusively associated with the direct support of trade fairs. However, the whole eastern area consisting of the build-ings on the Plaza and the site with the pavilions bordering to the south, has been designed in such a way that there will be constant life, so that businesses will set up there, service industries will be

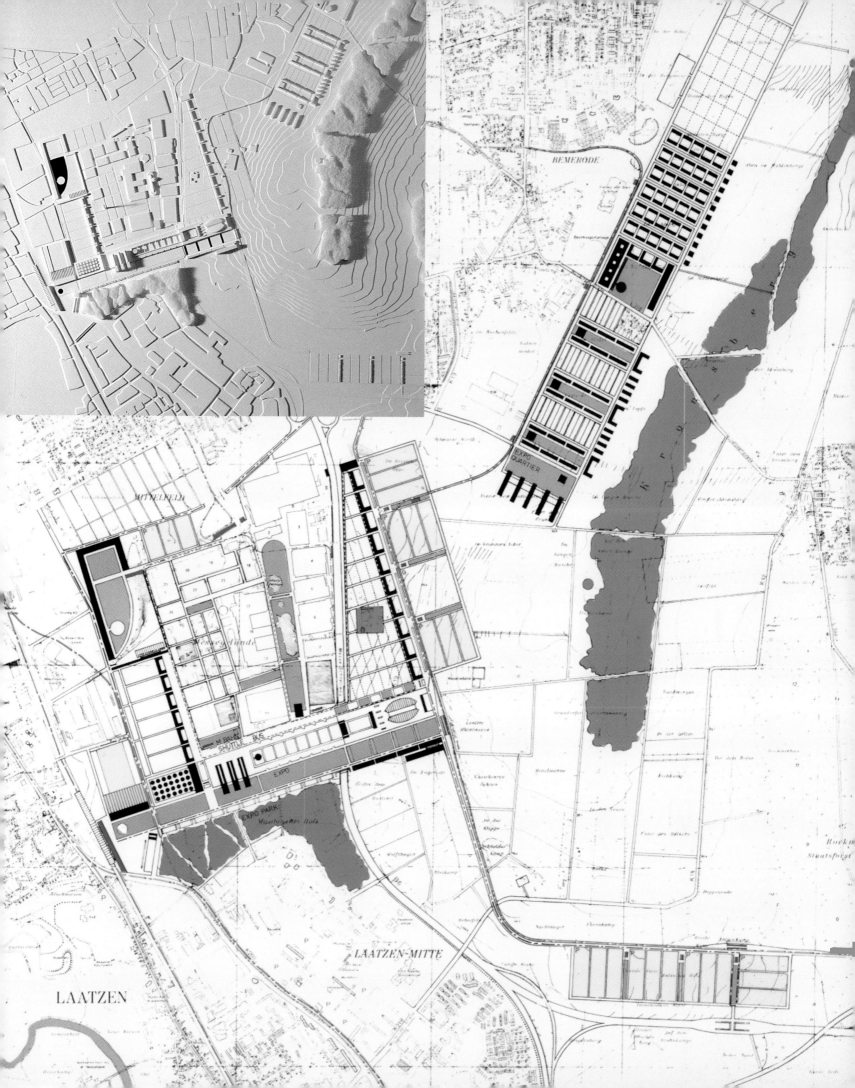

BEMERODE

EXPO QUARTIER

MITTELFELD

M. BAHN
SHUTTLE BUS
EXPO

EXPO PARK

LAATZEN-MITTE

LAATZEN

Fortschreibung des Masterplans durch AS&P Albert Speer und Partner GmbH, Zwischenstand 11/96
Auftraggeber: EXPO 2000 Hannover GmbH
Plangebiet: 160 ha

Masterplan continued by AS&P / as of 11/96
Client: EXPO 2000 Hannover GmbH
Planning Site: 160 ha

diesem Hintergrund sehe ich durchaus eine große Chance, daß sich hier auch nach der EXPO 2000 ein vielfältiges Leben etablieren kann.

REIF: Was zeichnet die EXPO 2000 in Hannover in städtebaulich-planerischer Sicht aus im Vergleich zu den vorangegangenen Expo-Veranstaltungen?

SPEER: Zunächst einmal hat die EXPO 2000 von Anfang an größten Wert auf die Qualität des öffentlichen Raumes gelegt. Und in der Tat bekommen wir öffentliche Räume von einer äußerst hohen Qualität, wobei wir nicht der Versuchung nachgegeben haben, in Hinblick auf die in Hannover nicht gerade günstigen klimatischen Bedingungen alles zu überdachen. Ferner ist die EXPO 2000 in ihrer Grundstruktur eine städtische EXPO. Die Besucher werden über Straßen und Plätze laufen. Es wäre von daher falsch zu versuchen, über das Ganze gewissermaßen einen »Deckel« zu stülpen. Wir hoffen natürlich, daß wir im Jahr 2000 einen prachtvollen Sommer haben und daß dann diese öffentlichen Räume, die ja die Ergänzung zu den Hallen bilden und sich als Rückzugs- oder Erholungsorte für die Besucher verstehen, wirklich angenommen werden. Alle diese Straßen, Plätze und Grünräume sind mit einem enormen Aufwand gestaltet und gleichzeitig ein wesentlicher Teil der Nachhaltigkeit der EXPO 2000, denn sie werden sich erst richtig über die nächsten zwanzig bis dreißig Jahre entwickeln.

REIF: Worin besteht das inhaltliche Kernstück der EXPO 2000?

SPEER: Inhaltlich gliedert sich die EXPO 2000 in drei wesentliche Elemente: Da ist einmal der große Themenpark, den wir jetzt zu einem Großteil in den etwas älteren Hallen im Zentrum des Messegeländes untergebracht haben und der sich auf einer Fläche von über hunderttausend Quadratmetern mit den Zukunftsproblemen der Menschheit auseinandersetzt. Hier werden Themen wie »Gesundheit«, »Mobilität« oder »Zukunft der Arbeit« an realen und virtuellen Beispielen demonstriert. Dieser Themenpark stellt zweifellos eine Attraktion dar, die es in dieser Größenordnung und mit der Zielrichtung »Mensch – Natur – Technik im nächsten Jahrtausend« noch nicht gegeben hat.

Das zweite besteht im traditionellen Element jeder Weltausstellung: den Beiträgen der einzelnen Länder und internationalen Organisationen. Wir werden sehr schöne Pavillons bekommen, wobei sich alle Aussteller dem Thema »Mensch – Natur – Technik« zuordnen und es aus ihrer jeweiligen Sicht behandeln.

Und drittens schließlich wird die EXPO 2000 ein außergewöhnliches Kulturprogramm bieten, das von Pop bis Klassik reicht. Jeden Tag wird auf dem Gelände der EXPO 2000 eine andere Veranstaltung, besonders auch in den Abendstunden, angeboten werden.

REIF: Die EXPO 2000 soll durch »Weltweite Projekte« ergänzt werden. Was ist darunter zu verstehen?

SPEER: »Weltweite Projekte« heißt, daß die EXPO 2000 über mehrere Ausschreibungsverfahren Veranstalter, Organisatoren und Investoren in aller Welt aufgerufen hat, Projekte zu benennen, die im Sinne der EXPO 2000 nachhaltige Entwicklungen an anderen Orten aufzeigen. Diese Projekte sind zum Teil von der EXPO 2000 mitgefördert worden, zum Teil bekamen sie

available, and cultural events can take place in the Arena. Furthermore, the whole area is connected to a new rapid transit railway line. Against this background, I certainly see a good chance that varied activities will provide a lively atmosphere here after EXPO 2000.

REIF: How does EXPO 2000 Hanover compare with previous EXPOs in terms of urban engineering and planning?

SPEER: First, EXPO 2000 from the very start put great value on the quality of public open spaces. And indeed, we shall have public areas of extremely high quality, even though, faced with the rather unfavourable climatic conditions in Hanover, we have not surrendered to the temptation to roof over everything. Furthermore, the EXPO 2000 is an urban EXPO in terms of its basic structure. The visitors will walk along streets and squares. It would therefore be wrong to place a kind of »lid« over the whole thing. We hope, of course, that we shall have a glorious summer in the year 2000, and that there will then be a really positive response to these public areas, which after all form a complement to the halls and are intended as retreats or leisure areas for the visitors. All the streets and squares and green areas have been created with enormous effort and are simultaneously an important element of EXPO 2000's post-use concept, as they will only really reach their full bloom over the next twenty or thirty years.

REIF: What is the key content of EXPO 2000?

SPEER: In terms of content, EXPO 2000 can be divided into three prime elements. On the one hand, there is the great Thematic Area, which we have largely accommodated in the somewhat older halls at the centre of the trade fair site, and which is addressing the problems of the future of humankind in a space of more than one hundred thousand square metres. This is where themes such as »Health«, »Mobility« or »The Future of Work« will be demonstrated by means of actual and virtual examples. This Thematic Area unquestionably will offer an attraction yet unknown on this scale under the motto »Humankind – Nature – Technology« in the next millennium.

The second element consists of the traditional element of all world expositions: the presentations of the individual countries and international organizations. We will have some very beautiful pavilions, with all exhibitors addressing the theme »Humankind – Nature – Technology« and tackling it from their own viewpoint.

Finally, as the third element, EXPO 2000 will offer an extremely unusual cultural programme, ranging from pop to classic. Each day a different event will be offered on the Expo site, especially in the evening.

REIF: EXPO 2000 is to be complemented by «Worldwide Projects». What does that mean?

SPEER: »Worldwide Projects« means that, in the scope of several public bids for applications, EXPO 2000 has called upon promoters, organizers and investors throughout the world to nominate projects which

EXPO 2000 HANNOVER
MASTERPLAN Planen + Bauen 11/96

13	Hallennummerierung		EXPO-Grünflächen
T	Themenpark		Wald
A	Ausstellungshallen		Wasserflächen
V	Veranstaltungsstätten		Parkplätze (Pflaster)
P	Partnerpräsentation		Parkplätze (Schotterrasen)
J	Jokerhalle		Zaun des EXPO-Geländes / Fluchttore
S	Serviceflächen		Bahnhof / ÖPNV-Haltestelle
	Hallen		Skywalk
	Hallen - Neubau		Internes Verkehrsmittel
	Flächen für Pavillons		Besuchereingänge
	Sonderbauten		

0   100m   200m   300m   400m

Stand: 12.12.1996

AS&

auch nur das Prädikat eines externen Projekts der EXPO 2000 und können damit für ihre Region werben.

Wir gehen davon aus, daß viele der internationalen Besucher nicht nur nach Hannover kommen, sondern auch andere Regionen und Orte in Deutschland besuchen werden, um sich über die dortige Entwicklung zu informieren. Ich denke hier besonders an die »Chemie-Region« um Bitterfeld und an das Städtedreieck Dessau – Bitterfeld/Wolfen – Wittenberg, das als Korrespondenzregion der EXPO 2000 registriert worden ist. In der vierhundert Quadratkilometer großen Region mit fast 500.000 Einwohnern werden exemplarische Projekte realisiert, die dem Strukturwandel dieser alten Industrieregion auch über das Jahr 2000 hinaus ein besonderes Profil geben werden. Ein auf ihre Struktur zugeschnittenes vergleichbares Projekt hat die Region Rhein-Main entwickelt, und wir hoffen sehr, daß es bis zum Beginn der EXPO 2000 möglich sein wird, daß in Tokio ein Reisender zur EXPO 2000 ins Flugzeug steigt und sein Gepäck am neuen Intercity-Bahnhof in Hannover in Empfang nehmen kann. Logistische Innovationen dieser Art sind ein wesentlicher Beitrag für die Zukunft des Messestandorts Hannover.

REIF: Sie sind Mitglied des Gestaltungskreises, der mit der Geschäftsführung der EXPO 2000 und der Deutschen Messe AG, der Stadt Hannover und den Professoren Meinhard von Gerkan sowie Thomas Herzog und dem Büro von Professor Kienast aus Zürich besetzt ist. Worin besteht die Aufgabe dieser Einrichtung?

SPEER: Ich gehöre dem Gestaltungskreis seit seiner Gründung an. Der Gestaltungskreis hat es sich zur Aufgabe gesetzt, alle Architekturen sowie die Gestaltung der Freiräume auf dem Expo-Gelände als ein »Rat der Weisen«, eine Art »kritisches Kontrollgremium« zu begleiten. Jedes Projekt der EXPO 2000 wird dem Gestaltungskreis von den verantwortlichen Architekten persönlich vorgetragen, der Gestaltungskreis diskutiert darüber und gibt seinen Kommentar dazu ab. Ein Großteil der einheitlichen Gesamtqualität ist zweifellos stark beeinflußt durch die Arbeit des Gestaltungskreises, der seit vier Jahren jeden Monat zusammentritt. Das ist nicht zuletzt ein Verdienst von Ursula Wangler, die den Kreis leitet.

REIF: Wie wird sich nun das Gesamtgelände der Weltausstellung den Besuchern darbieten?

SPEER: Das Messegelände in Hannover sah ursprünglich aus wie alle gewachsenen Messegelände, nämlich relativ ungeordnet. Mit den Planungen für die Weltausstellung EXPO 2000 ist erreicht worden, daß sich dieses Gelände in großen Teilen verändert und ganz neu präsentiert. Das gilt insbesondere für die Qualität der Außenräume, die der erst kürzlich verstorbene Züricher Gartenbauprofessor Kienast gestaltet hat, und es gilt auch für die Qualität der neu entstandenen Hallen.

Ein wesentlicher Faktor darüber hinaus ist, daß die gesamte technische Infrastruktur auf dem Gelände der Weltausstellung und im weiteren Umfeld eine entscheidende Verbesserung erfährt. Deshalb sprechen wir auch immer von einer »Vornutzung« dieser Einrichtungen durch die EXPO 2000, die ja nur fünf Monate dauert, während die gebauten Anlagen eine Lebensdauer von vierzig bis fünfzig Jahren haben.

REIF: Vor welche besonderen Herausforderungen sahen Sie sich während Ihrer bisherigen Arbeit an der EXPO 2000 gestellt?

SPEER: Als außergewöhnliche Herausforderungen würde ich zwei Dinge bezeichnen. Der Hauptplatz der EXPO 2000 ist die Plaza. Sie liegt außerhalb des bisherigen und auch des künftigen Messegeländes. Die Plaza wird be-

demonstrate sustainable development at other locations, in line with the EXPO 2000 motto. Some of these projects have been co-promoted by EXPO 2000, others were simply accorded the status of an EXPO 2000 worldwide project, allowing them to publicize their regions. We assume that many of the international visitors will not only come to Hanover, but that they will also visit other regions and places in Germany in order to learn about the developments there. I am thinking in particular of the »chemical industry region« around Bitterfeld here, and the triangle of the towns Dessau – Bitterfeld/Wolfen – Wittenberg, which has been registered as an EXPO 2000 partner region. In this region, which covers four hundred square kilometres and has 500 000 inhabitants, exemplary projects are being implemented which characterize the structural change this former industrial region is undergoing well beyond the year 2000. Another region, the Rhine-Main region, has developed a logistics project tailored to its structure. We very much hope that by the start of EXPO 2000 it will be possible for travellers to EXPO 2000 to board their aircraft in Tokyo and collect their baggage at the new Intercity railway station in Hanover. Logistical innovations of this type are an important contribution to the future of the Hanover trade fair site.

REIF: You are a member of the design circle which comprises the directors of EXPO 2000, of the Deutsche Messe AG and of the city of Hanover as well as Professors Meinhard von Gerkan and Thomas Herzog and the office of Professor Kienast from Zurich. What are the tasks of this circle?

SPEER: I have been part of this design circle since its inception. The circle has set itself the task of acting as an advisory council, a sort of »critical review body«, for all architects as well as the designers of the open spaces on the Expo site. Each EXPO 2000 project is presented personally to the design circle by the architects responsible; the members of the design circle discuss and comment upon the project. Without doubt a large proportion of the overall holistic quality is strongly influenced by the work of the design circle, which has met every month for four years. Much of the credit for this is due to Ursula Wangler, who chairs the circle.

REIF: How will the World Exposition site as a whole appear to the visitor?

SPEER: The trade fair site in Hanover originally looked like all evolved trade fair sites, in other words relatively disorganized. The planning for the World Exposition EXPO 2000 has managed to a large extent to present a changed and completely new look for the site. This applies in particular to the qualities of the open air areas, which were designed by the Zurich garden designer Professor Kienast, who sadly passed away recently, and it is also true for the quality of the new halls.

An important additional factor is the decisive improvement of the whole technical infrastructure on the site of the World Exposition and in the area beyond. Thus we can speak of a pre-use of these facilities by EXPO 2000, which only lasts five months, whereas the building structures have a working life of forty to fifty years.

REIF: What were the special challenges which you were confronted with in your EXPO 2000 work to date?

baut mit verschiedenen Gebäuden, unter anderem mit einer 14.000 Besucher fassenden Arena sowie gegenüberliegend dem Deutschen Pavillon. Sämtliche Gebäude rings um die Plaza mit einem Kostenvolumen von rund 800 Millionen Mark werden von privaten Investoren finanziert. Ein wesentliches Kernstück der EXPO 2000 ist demnach nicht die Messe, sondern ein Platz, um den herum Privatinvestoren in Kooperation mit zehn verschiedenen Architekten Gebäude für unterschiedliche Nutzungsvorhaben errichten.

Die Herausforderung an uns bestand darin, daß wir einen Gestaltungsrahmen entwickelt haben, der den Architekten nicht vorschreibt, was sie im einzelnen tun müssen, der aber dennoch versucht, aus städtebaulicher, ganzheitlicher Sicht einen Rahmen festzuschreiben, in dem sich die einzelnen Architekturen bewegen. Wir haben alle diese Architekten und Investoren bis heute betreut, um zu erreichen, daß sowohl die Gestaltung des gesamten Platzes, für die der Landschaftsarchitekt Professor Hinnerk Wehberg aus Hamburg verantwortlich zeichnet, wie auch die Gebäude eine Einheit bilden und nach Abschluß der EXPO 2000 weiterhin attraktiv sind, vom Publikum angenommen werden und benutzbar bleiben.

REIF: Inwieweit werden die Planungen der EXPO 2000 Einfluß auf die Stadtentwicklung von Hannover nehmen?

SPEER: Wir müssen einen kurzen Blick auf die Vergangenheit werfen. Die Idee zu einer EXPO in Hannover ist entstanden, als die Berliner Mauer noch existierte und die innerdeutsche Grenze unweit von Hannover verlief. Ein Teil von Niedersachsen lag mithin im sogenannten »Zonenrandgebiet«. Mit der Entscheidung für eine EXPO und mit der Festlegung eines Termins sollte ein Anlaß gegeben werden, die Infrastruktur von Hannover und seiner Umgebung entscheidend zu verbessern. Das ist inzwischen weitgehend geschehen, anderes befindet sich noch im Bau.

So wird der Flughafen Hannover erweitert und eine direkte S-Bahnlinie zwischen dem Flughafen und der Messe geschaffen. Der neue Intercity-Bahnhof Messe existiert bereits, und es ist eine neue Stadtbahnlinie aus der Innenstadt heraus über den Kronsberg gebaut worden. In der Region Hannover ist mit einem Investitionsvolumen von über 3,5 Milliarden Mark eine hochwertige, auf das Jahr 2010 ausgerichtete Infrastruktur entstanden. Außerdem baut die Stadt Hannover auf dem Kronsberg 3.000 Wohnungen, die zum Teil von den circa 20.000 Beschäftigten der EXPO 2000 genutzt werden. Diese Investitionen erfolgten außerhalb des EXPO 2000-Budgets und zeigen, in welch großem Umfang Mittel zur Verbesserung des Standortes Region Hannover bereitgestellt wurden.

REIF: Wie bewerten Sie diese Projekte als Modelle für mögliche Entwicklungen in anderen Regionen Deutschlands? Welche Vorbildfunktion haben sie?

SPEER: Als Stadtplaner vertrete ich grundsätzlich die Ansicht, daß es immer von Vorteil ist, wenn Regionen sich um Großereignisse von Weltbedeutung bewerben. Allein durch ihre Bewerbung geht schon ein Ideenschub durch die Politik und alle beteiligten Gruppen. Nehmen wir die Fußballweltmeisterschaft in Deutschland im Jahre 2006: Sie bietet Anlaß, in einem Dutzend deutscher Städte die maroden Fußballstadien zu sanieren. Das sind Aufgaben, die ohnehin anstehen, wie ja auch in Hannover der Ausbau der Infrastruktur schon seit langem ganz oben auf der Prioritätenliste vermerkt ist. Jetzt aber, mit einem festen Termin, geschieht das, was sich sonst über zwanzig Jahre erstreckt hätte, innerhalb von sechs Jahren. Feste Termine halte ich für ungeheuer wichtig, denn nur durch sie lassen sich Politik, Verwaltung, Investoren und andere Beteiligte dazu bewegen, tatsächlich im

SPEER: I would say that there were two exceptional challenges. EXPO 2000's central focus is the Plaza. Its location is outside the previous and also the future fairgrounds. This Plaza will have different buildings, including an arena to seat 14 000 spectators, and the German pavilion on the opposite side. All the buildings around the Plaza cost approximately 8000 million DM and are financed by private investors. A core area of EXPO 2000, therefore, is not the trade fair but the Plaza, a square in which private investors, in co-operation with ten different architects are constructing buildings for different uses. The challenge to us was that we have developed a design frame which does not prescribe to the architects what they must do in each case, but which nevertheless attempts to provide a holistic architectural framework in which the individual architectures can move and act. We have provided back-up support to all these architects and investors to date, in order to ensure that both the design of the overall square, for which the landscape architect Professor Hinnerk Wehberg from Hamburg is responsible, and also the buildings, constitute a unit, will continue to be attractive after the completion of EXPO 2000 and will be appealing to and used by the general public.

REIF: To what extent does the EXPO 2000 planning influence the urban development of Hanover?

SPEER: To answer this we must briefly look back into the past. The idea to hold EXPO 2000 in Hanover developed at a time when the Berlin wall was still standing, and the inner-German frontier was situated not far from Hanover. Part of Lower Saxony was in the so called east-west border region. The decision to hold an EXPO there and the dates chosen were to be an opportunity decisively to improve the infrastructure of Hanover and its hinterland. This work has been largely completed, and building is still going on.

Hanover Airport, for example, is being expanded and a direct urban rail line built between the airport and the fairgrounds. The new Intercity Trade Fair Station has also been finished in the meantime, and a new local transport line has been built from downtown Hanover via the Kronsberg area. In the Hanover Region, investments of over DM 3.5 billion have been used to create a high-quality infrastructure geared to the year 2010. In addition, the City of Hanover is building 3000 housing units on the Kronsberg estate, part of which will be used by the some 20 000 people working during EXPO 2000. These investments were made outside of the EXPO 2000 budget and show the large extent to which funds have been made available to upgrade the Hanover region as a locality for business and life.

REIF: To what extent do you consider these projects to be models for possible developments in other regions of Germany? What is their model function?

SPEER: As an urban planner I am basically of the opinion that when regions take part in competitions to stage large scale events of global importance benefits always ensure. The competition alone is an enormous impulse for ideas trickling down to politics and all groupings involved. Let us take the Soccer World Cup in Germany in the year 2006 as an example. It will be an opportunity to rehabilitate derelict football stadiums in a dozen German cities. These are tasks which have to be tackled anyway. As in Hanover, the redevelopment of infrastructure has been high on the priority list for a long time. But now, with a

EXPO 2000 Hannover – Masterplan Planen und Bauen 07/99,
AS&P Albert Speer & Partner.

EXPO 2000 Hanover - Masterplan Planning and Building 07/99,
AS&P Albert Speer & Partner.

Rahmen einer bestimmten Zeitspanne tätig zu werden. Am Beispiel Hannover erweist sich das erneut.

REIF: Welche Auswirkungen wird die EXPO 2000 auf Berlin haben, das ja nun die neue alte Hauptstadt Deutschlands ist?

SPEER: Der größte Teil der Expo-Besucher aus dem Ausland dürfte selbstverständlich auch nach Berlin reisen. Berlin hat übrigens einen Kooperationsvertrag mit der EXPO 2000 abgeschlossen, denn Hannover und seine Region verfügen gar nicht über genügend Hotelbetten, um alle Gäste unterbringen zu können. Die neue ICE-Strecke zwischen Berlin und Hannover ist fertiggestellt. Innerhalb von zwei Stunden sind die Reisenden entweder in Hannover oder in Berlin. Mit ähnlichen Auswirkungen der EXPO 2000 auf Hamburg und Frankfurt ist ebenfalls zu rechnen, wenn auch vermutlich in einem etwas geringeren Maße.

REIF: Im Prinzip stellt sich aber doch die Frage, ob die Idee der EXPO im Zeitalter der elektronischen Medien nicht überholt ist. Und wenn schon »EXPO«: Wäre nicht eine ganz andere Ausstellungskonzeption erforderlich, eine, die die seit 1851 herrschende Tradition endgültig verabschiedet?

SPEER: Das ist ein Thema, das uns bei unserer Konzeption für Hannover immer wieder beschäftigt hat und weiterhin beschäftigt. Selbstverständlich kann sich heute jeder im Internet holen, was er will. Ungeachtet dessen bin ich der Überzeugung, daß die Menschen auch im nächsten Jahrtausend nicht nur etwas abstrakt sehen, sondern es auch individuell erleben und erfahren wollen. Darauf beruhen ja die Erfolge von Freizeitparks und großen Sportveranstaltungen. Gerade weil die Animationen im eigenen Heim so abstrakt geworden sind, nimmt das Bedürfnis zu, sich zu besonderen Anlässen irgendwohin zu begeben.

Die EXPO 2000 in Hannover ist solch ein besonderer Anlaß. Sie bietet ja nicht nur Länderausstellungen, vielmehr besteht sie aus einem Themenpark, in dem auf einer Fläche von 100.000 Quadratmetern die Zukunftsvisionen der Menschheit in allen Lebensbereichen dargestellt werden. Diese Vielfältigkeit wird noch durch ein Kulturprogramm ergänzt, das von Pop, Rock über Zirkus bis hin zur klassischen Musik alle möglichen künstlerischen Sparten umfaßt. Die Menschen werden nach Hannover kommen, um unterschiedliche Kulturen und Sichtweisen durch persönliche Inaugenscheinnahme kennenzulernen.

Der deutschen Wirtschaft bietet die EXPO 2000 auf jeden Fall eine einmalige Chance. Insbesondere die großen Unternehmen erhalten die Möglichkeit, sich mit ihren Produkten und Leistungen vor Millionen Besuchern zu präsentieren, verbunden mit der Gelegenheit, neue Kontakte für den Export und für Kooperationen zu knüpfen. Aus diesem Grund halte ich solche Ausstellungen keineswegs für überflüssig und auch nicht durch die modernen Medien ersetzbar.

Prof. Albert Speer ist Mitglied des Gestaltungskreises der EXPO 2000 und betreut den Masterplan des Geländes, die Planung der Messehalle 12 und die Supervision der Neubauten an der Expo-Plaza.

Adelbert Reif ist Publizist.

set deadline in front us, work is taking place in six years which would otherwise have stretched over twenty years. I consider fixed deadlines to be enormously important, because they are the only thing that move politics, administrations, investors and other agents involved to actually becoming active within a specific time period. Hanover is just another example.

REIF: What impact will EXPO 2000 have on Berlin, which has now become Germany's new old capital?

SPEER: The majority of Expo visitors from abroad will probably also travel to Berlin. You may know that Berlin has entered into a cooperation contract with EXPO 2000, because Hanover and its hinterland do not have enough hotel beds to accommodate all guests. The new ICE rapid rail track between Berlin and Hanover has been completed. Travellers can reach Hanover or Berlin within two hours. EXPO 2000 is expected to have a similar impact on Hamburg and Frankfurt, although probably to a lesser extent.

REIF: In principle, however, the question remains of whether the idea of an EXPO is not outdated in this era of electronic media. And if an EXPO has to take place, would it not have been better to adopt a completely different exhibition concept, one which finally takes farewell from the traditions reigning since 1851.

SPEER: That is a topic which has repeatedly concerned us in our design work for Hanover, and continues to do so. Of course, nowadays people can get all the information they want from the internet. Nevertheless, I am convinced that even in the coming century people will not be contented to simply see things in the abstract but will also want to experience them for themselves. This is the basis for the success of the leisure parks and large sporting events. Because animations in the home have become so abstract, there is a growing need to go and experience special occasions.

EXPO 2000 in Hanover is such a special event. It offers not just country presentations, but also and especially, a Thematic Area in which the visions of humankind for the future in all spheres of life will be presented on an area stretching over a hundred thousand square meters. These diverse attractions are rounded off by a culture programme which ranges from pop, rock, circus to classical music, and all other spheres of art. People will come to Hanover in order personally to see and learn about different cultures and attitudes.

In all events EXPO 2000 offers the German economy a unique opportunity. Particularly the large companies will have an opportunity to present themselves and their products and services to millions of visitors, combined with an opportunity to make new contacts for export and cooperation. For this reason, I consider events of this type to be in no way superfluous, nor can they be replaced by the modern media.

Prof. Albert Speer is a member of the design circle EXPO 2000. He is in charge of the masterplan, the planning of Hall 12 and also supervising the new buildings on the Expo-Plaza.

Adelbert Reif is a journalist.

EXPO 2000 HANNOVER
MASTERPLAN Planen + Bauen 07/99

13	Hallennummerierung
T	Themenpark
A	Ausstellungshallen - Nationen
V	Veranstaltungsstätten
P	Partnerpräsentation
S	Serviceflächen

Hallen - Bestand
Flächen für Pavillons
D Baufeldbezeichnung, hier Baufeld D
Vollständige Bezeichnung: Baufeld West/Ost D
Besucherservice / MSK / Verwaltung
Nebengebäude
Lagerflächen

Besuchereingänge
Grünflächen
Wald
Wasserflächen
Parkplätze (Pflaster)
Parkplätze (Schotterrasen)
Zaun des EXPO-Geländes / Rettungstor
Zaun / Ver-/ Entsorgungstor/Feuerwehrzufahrt
Bahnhof / ÖPNV-Haltestelle
Skywalk
Internes Transportmittel
Erdölbohrung

0   100m   200m   300m   400m

Stand: Juli 1999

AS&P

Kamel Louafi

»Panta rhei«. Die Gärten im Wandel
»Panta rhei«. The Evolving Gardens

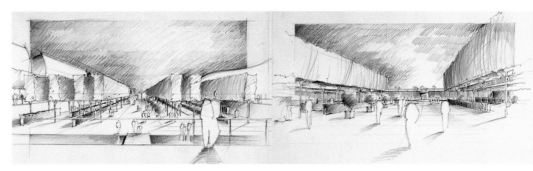

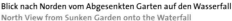

Blick nach Süden vom Belvedere auf den Abgesenkten Garten
South View from Bevedere onto Sunken Garden

Blick nach Norden vom Abgesenkten Garten auf den Wasserfall
North View from Sunken Garden onto the Waterfall

Das Millennium ist eigentlich nur ein weiterer Jahreswechsel – und doch mehr. Es ist ein chronometrischer Markstein zweitausendjähriger, christlich gerechneter Zeit: die Bewußtseinsschwelle zwischen Bestandsaufnahme und Vorausschau. Es ist ein Zustand dazwischen: am Ende des einen und Anfang des anderen; deutlich geprägt vom Bewußtsein des Wandels mit dem perspektivisch fragenden Blick in das soeben beginnende Jahrtausend – der in der Ambivalenz zwischen Verheißung des Unbekannten und den archaischen Ängsten davor gefangen ist.

Die Weltausstellung ist der (Bei-)Spielort. Zum Ende des Jahrtausends begegnet uns hier, unter dem Brennglas betrachtet, die unauflösliche Trinität »Natur – Mensch – Technik«, aus der sich die großen, fast übergroßen Themen einer Zukunft formulieren. Es ist unsere Entscheidung, diesen mit der einfachen und doch vielfältigen Metapher des »Flusses« zu antworten. Dieser ist ein Symbol des Wandels und Quelle des Lebens. Er ist hervorragender Ort der Evolution, Anziehungspunkt der Kultur und bei aller Stetigkeit in seinem Fluß der Träger der Entwicklung. Die Festschreibungen rigider Ordnungen, die Halt und Kontinuität vermitteln sollten – sie müssen sich bewegen und gehen so langsam über in ein Bewußtsein steter Veränderung und Umwälzung, das eine souveräne – aber nicht überhebliche – Freiheit auszeichnet. Hier ist nichts von Bestand, alles fließt und unterliegt ständigem Wechsel. Und dennoch: Im ganzen ist alles beständig, Wechsel nur eine Form. Entstehen und werden heißt, anders zu sein als sonst, und vergehen, nicht mehr so sein wie zuvor.

Im Bild des Flusses finden archaische Legenden vom Zweistromland (Turmbau zu Babel) ebenso Platz wie Computersimulationen (virtuelle Realitäten) oder die aktuellen Erscheinungen einer Kommunikation ohne Grenzen (Internet). Flüsse bedeuten die Kraft der Verwandlung von Bergen zu Stränden ebenso wie den geistreichen Willen dazu.

In reality, the millennium is no more than the turn of another year; and nevertheless, it is something more. It marks a chronometric boundary in the 2000-year Christian calendar, a threshold of awareness between a stocktaking backward glance and an act of looking into the future. It is an in-between state, at the end of one period and the beginning of another; and it is characterized by an awareness of change, with a perspectively questioning glance into the new millennium, caught ambivalently between unknown promise and archaic fears.

The World Exposition site is a model location. Here, at the end of the millennium, as if beneath a magnifying glass, we find the indissoluble trinity of nature, man and technology - the material from which the major, sometimes seemingly overwhelming, themes of the future will be formulated. We may respond to them with the simple yet manifold metaphor of the »stream«. The stream is the source of life and a symbol of change; it is an outstanding location for evolution and a point of attraction for cultural activity; and in view of its constantly flowing state, it is a vehicle for ongoing development. The establishment of a rigid order - meant to convey a sense of stability and continuity - should contain a potential for movement and gradual transformation, so that an awareness of constant change and upheaval may manifest itself in a sovereign, though not arrogant, expression of freedom. There is nothing of permanence here. Everything is in a state of flux and subject to a constant process of change. And nevertheless, overall, everything remains steady. Change is only a form. Genesis and growth mean being in a different state from what is usual; and decay implies that something is no longer as it was before.

The image of the stream may embrace archaic legends, from Mesopotamia, for example, between the Rivers Tigris and Euphrates - the building of the Tower of Babel - as well as computer simulations (virtual realities) or

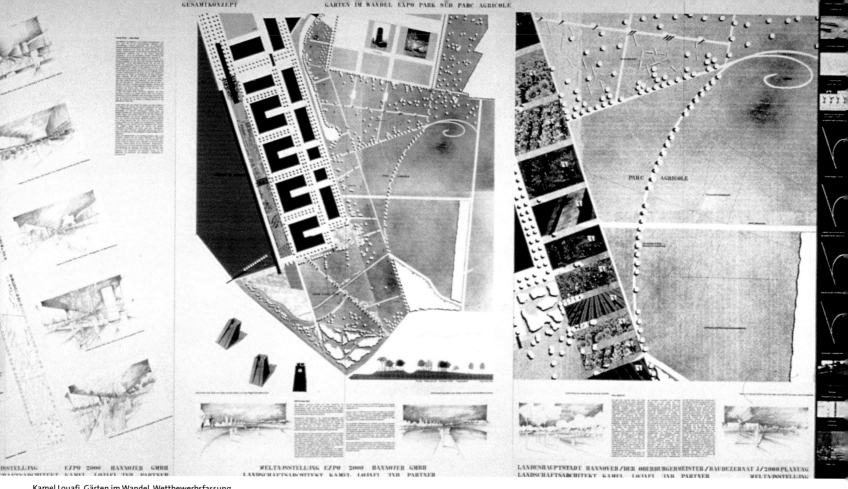

Kamel Louafi, Gärten im Wandel, Wettbewerbsfassung
Kamel Louafi, Evolving Gardens, Competition Version

Flüsse liefern auch das Wasser für Gärten, und diese wiederum sind Ausdruck der Kulturen; sie sind eine Visitenkarte. Der Garten einer Weltausstellung bietet daher idealerweise in seinem großzügigen und dennoch differenzierten Gelände Raum für Neugier und Erfahrung – des Eigenen ebenso wie des Anderen. Die positive Utopie eines solchen Gartens ist die eines blühenden, entwicklungsfähigen und dennoch beständig nutzbaren Stückes Land. Der ressourcenschonende, effiziente Einsatz von Material und Technik beweist dabei Sinn nicht nur für Verantwortung, sondern ebenso für die Eleganz des gestalterischen Prozesses. Schließlich ist ohne Technik auch die Gestaltung eines Gartens nicht denkbar. Gärten ebenso wie Technik sind Resultat menschlicher Produktion und Kultur oder auch »Kultivierung«, Land-Wirte erste Ökonomen. Dauerhafte Nutzung der Erde ist daher auch gebunden an den intelligenten Einsatz der Mittel für ihre Gestaltung.

»Anders als beispielsweise in der Hochbauarchitektur oder in der Fotografie erlauben uns die meisten Elemente im Repertoire unserer Arbeit als Landschaftsarchitekten aufgrund ihrer Substanz, ihres Wachstums, ihrer Farben, Dichte et cetera, Räume, Orte zu gestalten, die sich permanent verändern. Habitus, Farben, die vier Jahreszeiten – all dies gibt uns die Chance, auch bei einer reduzierten Gestaltung vielfältig zu sein. Gestaltelemente wie l´Indecision de Frontière, der Schatten, aber auch die Strenge der Geometrie, die Inszenierung der Leere, der Gegensatz des Künstlichen und Natürlichen lassen uns die Möglichkeit, die Sehnsucht, das Imaginäre zu artikulieren/zu kompensieren.«

Die Gärten im Wandel

Von intensiv zu extensiv, von dunkel zu hell, von »tief unten« nach »hoch oben«, von laut bis leise, von geschnitten-gestaltet zu landschaftlich-natür-

modern phenomena such as unlimited communication (Internet). Streams represent the power to transform mountains into beaches, as well as the intellectual will to do so.

Streams also supply the water for gardens, which are, in turn, an expression of various cultures: their visiting cards, so to speak. Forming part of an extensive and varied site, therefore, the garden of a world exhibition is a space for curiosity, investigation and experience - one's own as well as that of others. The positive utopia such a garden represents is that of a blossoming piece of land capable of development, but in constant use. The sustainable use of materials and technology to conserve resources demonstrates not only a sense of responsibility, but a feeling for the elegance of the design process. But the shaping of a garden is inconceivable without technology. Gardens, like technology, are the outcome of human production and (horti)culture or »cultivation«: husbandry as the first form of economy. The permanent use of the earth is, therefore, dependent on an intelligent application of the means of shaping it.

»In view of their substance, growth, colours, density, etc., most of the elements of our repertoire as landscape architects allow us to shape spaces and places that will be subject to a permanent process of change - in contrast to the architectural design of buildings, or photography, say. Habitus, colours, the four seasons - all these elements give us an opportunity to achieve diversity even in a limited design. Design factors such as »l'indecision de frontiére« (the undefined border) and shadow, as well as strict geometric order, the organization of space, and the contrast between artificial and natural phenomena afford us scope to articulate imaginary concepts.«

43

lich erfolgt die Metamorphose eines Gartens von der Plaza in die Landschaft hinein.

Einleitung ist ein breiter Übergangsweg, der von der Expo-Plaza auf die Piazza führt, einen großzügig bemessenen, seiner Erinnerung nach städtischen Freiraum. Seitlich markieren schwarze Kiefern den Übergang zu und den Beginn der Gärten im Wandel. Im Schwarzen Garten werden große Felsblöcke zu Geröll und schließlich zu Flußkieseln in schmalen Rinnen zwischen den Steinplatten des Platzes. Unbearbeitete Steine werden zu Quadern, auf denen Platz genommen und das Geschehen der Weltausstellung in Ruhe beobachtet werden kann.

Am südlichen Rand schließt die geräumige Piazza mit einem Belvedere ab. Die Brüstung eröffnet den Blick über den tieferliegenden Garten. Von der Höhe der Piazza fällt hier ein Wasserfall in 3,5 Meter Tiefe: die Quelle des Flusses.

Zum Fuß des Wasserfalls gelangt man durch einen Einstieg: die Himmelstreppe oder über seitliche Rampen. Wasserfall und kubisch geschnittene Linden produzieren eine frisch-schattige Atmosphäre. Der Formschnitt der Bäume geht über in natürlichen Wuchs, das dichte Blätterdach der geschnittenen Pflanzen weicht dem lichten Blattwerk freiwachsender Bäume. Zwischen den Alleen zeigen während der Weltausstellung Orangenbäume und Zypressen in Pflanzkübeln klassische Gartenkunst.

Der optischen Verwandlung folgen akustische Installationen. Mobiles oder andere leichte Kunstobjekte erzeugen im Klanggarten leise Töne. Sie werden ergänzt durch die Geräusche des gegenüberliegend an den Hauptweg angrenzenden Wasserspiels.

In diesem Teil der Gärten im Wandel ist die strenge Baumachse Bambus und Birkenflächen gewichen. Ein geschwungener Weg führt durch das Gelände weiter in Richtung Süden. Die Sukzession wird zu ihren Ursprüngen zurückverfolgt. Man gelangt zum Gräsergarten mit Gräsern in verschiedenen Farben und Höhen und schließlich zu den Sanddünen, die ihre natürliche Dynamik zeigen.

In den »Fluß« des Grünfingers sind einzelne »Schleusen« integriert: offene Räume. Der Mediterrane Garten und der Sandgarten zeigen Natur und Elemente, Maschinenraum und Jardin des Illusions die Entwicklung

Der Schwarze Garten
Black Garden

The Evolving Gardens

From intensive to extensive, from dark to light, from far below to high above, from loud to quiet, from trimmed, controlled nature to natural park - the garden undergoes a metamorphosis from the plaza into the landscape. The prelude to this is a broad transitional path, leading from the Expo-Plaza to the piazza, a generously dimensioned open space with urban connotations. To the sides, black pines mark the beginning of the Evolving Gardens. In the Black Garden, large rocks crumble into a scree and are ultimately reduced to river gravel in narrow channels between the stone paving slabs. Large rough-hewn blocks of stone provide seats from which people can observe the events of the world exhibition in peace.

On its southern edge, the broad piazza is closed by a belvedere. Over a balustrade, a view opens to a garden at a lower level. At this point, a cascade of water falls 3.5 metres from the level of the piazza. Here is the source of the stream. Access to the foot of the waterfall is via a flight of steps or via ramps at the side. The waterfall and lime trees cut to a cubic form create a fresh, shady atmosphere. The shaped trees give way to others with natural growth; the dense canopy formed by the trimmed vegetation yields to the open foliage of freely growing trees. During the world exposition, orange trees and cypresses in tubs between the avenues will provide a touch of classical horticulture.

The visual transition is followed by acoustic installations. In the tonal garden, mobiles or other lightweight art objects produce soft sounds. These are complemented by the sounds of the playing water along the main path opposite.

In this section of the Evolving Gardens, the strict axial arrangement of the trees yields to areas of bamboo and birch. A curving path leads towards the south. The sequence of plantings reverts back to its origins. Visitors come to areas planted with grasses of various heights and colours, and finally to the sand dunes with their own natural dynamics.

Integrated into the stream of the »Green Finger« are individual spatial »locks«: open spaces between different realms of the gardens. The Mediterranean Garden and the Sand Garden contain natural vegetation and horticultural elements; the Machine House and the Jardin des Illusions illustrate the development of the tools used in their transformation (the history of technology). Modern communicational media are used in the Jardin des Illusions to project virtual images of imaginary gardens. Illusion and reality, the tangible and intangible, are juxtaposed here, revealing their ever greater proximity to each other in the age of cyberspace. The force of attraction exerted by this constant process of technical development is contrasted with the permanence of a tea house in a bamboo garden.

der Werkzeuge ihrer Transformation (Geschichte der Technologie). Moderne Kommunikationsmedien projizieren im Jardin des Illusions virtuelle Bilder möglicher Gärten. Illusion und Realität, das Faßbare und das Unfaßbare stehen hier dicht beieinander, verdeutlichen ihre immer stärkere Annäherung aneinander im Zeitalter des Cyberspace. Dem Sog dieses ständigen technischen Fortschritts steht das Beständige eines Teepavillons am Bambusgarten gegenüber.

Im Geschehen der Weltausstellung dienen die Schleusen in den Gärten im Wandel als Orte der Ruhe und Kontemplation. Außen sind die Wände der Schleusen farblich einheitlich verputzt, die Unterschiedlichkeit und Eigenständigkeit nach innen werden durch die Geometrie, die Öffnungen, farbige Wandgestaltung und die Inhalte betont.

Im Innenbereich des Patio verweisen die Gestaltelemente Wasser, Mosaik, Schattenrelief und Farbkomposition auf die maurische Kultur. Präziser,

During the World Exposition, the lock-like spaces in the Evolving Gardens will serve as oases of peace and contemplation. On the outside, the walls of the locks are rendered and have a uniform coloration. Internally, the various spaces are articulated by means of their geometry and openings, by the coloured wall designs and the actual contents to achieve an individual character and independent quality.

Within the »patio«, various design elements - water, mosaics, reliefs and the shadows they cast, as well as the coloration - make allusion to Moorish culture. More precisely, here at the end of the millennium, the patio is a reference to the »Medersa«, the school of translation in 14th-century Toledo, which stood for a universal culture and tolerance between different religions and races. The design is thus an act of homage to the age of discovery in science, mathematics and horticulture; but it is also an expression of hope in the future.

Blick in den Abgesenkten Garten
View of Sunken Garden

am Ende des Millenniums ist der Patio eine Referenz an die »Medersa«, jene Übersetzerschule im spanischen Toledo des 14. Jahrhunderts, die eine universelle Kultur und die Toleranz zwischen unterschiedlichen Religionen und Rassen vertrat – eine Hommage an die Zeit der Entdeckungen in der Wissenschaft, der Mathematik, Gartenkultur und zugleich eine Hoffnung für die Zukunft.

Was wären wir ohne Illusion? Sie begleitet uns in unseren Träumen und Hoffnungen, in der Kindheit, in der Liebe, in der Literatur, in der Wissenschaft, in der Arbeit, auf der Straße, in den Bergen, in den »eigenen vier Wänden« oder auch in der Wüste – manchmal gleich einer Verschmelzung des Realen und Irrealen – ob wir schwarz, weiß, gelb, rot, Nomaden, Städter, »Wolkenkratzerbewohner«, arm, reich, Kind oder erwachsen sind. Im Pavillon der Illusion nehmen Spiegelreflexionen und die Überlagerung von Bildern dieses Thema ausschnittweise in Form der Reflexion des Selbst (und des Anderen), des Lichtes und der Reproduktion imaginierter Bilder auf.

Die reale Umsetzung des Imaginierten wird angesprochen mit dem Maschinenhaus. Eine schieferne Schultafel mit eingravierten mathematischen Zeichnungen verweist auf die Bedeutung von Logik, Rationalisierung und den Prozeß der Mechanisierung. Die Wände des Maschinenhauses besitzen kleine Fensteröffnungen, zwischen denen Räder montiert sind, die sich gekoppelt an Klanginstallationen im Inneren des Hauses bewegen – beide sonnenenergetisch angetrieben. Die Räder sind gleichzeitig Referenz

What would we be without illusion? It is part of our dreams and hopes, of our childhood, of love, literature and science; it accompanies us in our work, in the street, in the mountains, within »our own four walls« and even in the wilderness - sometimes like a union of reality and unreality - whether we be black, white, yellow or red, nomads, city dwellers or the residents of skyscrapers, whether we be rich or poor, children or adults. In the Pavilion of Illusion, this theme is taken up in a series of mirror reflections, overlaid images of oneself and others, of light and the reproduction of imaginary pictures in an excerpt-like manner.

The translation of the imaginary into reality is addressed in the Machine House, where a slate blackboard with mathematical drawings engraved in it indicates the importance of logic, rationalization and the process of mechanization. In the walls of this building are small window openings, between which are moving wheels linked to sound installations within the room. Both are powered by solar energy. The wheels are also a reference to wind-powered irrigation technology among other things. The black and khaki coloration internally makes allusion to industry.

In contrast to the incessant movement of the technology in the Machine House, the Tea House is a place of stillness, peace and contemplation. The red coloration and the interior design are a reference to Asia, to the horticulture and philosophy of life of a continent that is often associated with a different concept of nature (a metaphor?).

an zum Beispiel windgetriebene Bewässerungstechniken. Die Farbgebung des Inneren in Schwarz und Khaki verweist auf die Industrie.

Gegenüber der unablässigen Bewegung der Technik im Maschinenhaus vermittelt das Teehaus den Ort der Pause, der Ruhe und der Kontemplation. Farbgebung in Rot und Innenraumgestaltung nehmen Bezug auf den asiatischen Kontinent, ein Bezug auf die Gartenkultur, die Lebensphilosophie eines Kontinents, die oft in Zusammenhang mit einem anderen Beispiel für den Umgang mit der Natur (eine Metapher?) gebracht wird.

Das Sandhaus im Sandgarten steht für meine Jugendheimat, für die Erfahrung der Faszination und Schönheit der Leere, Stille und Größe (ein Drittel unserer Erde ist Wüste). Das Bild der Dünen wird durch die schmalen vertikalen und die horizontalen Öffnungen beziehungsweise Schlitze in Kniehöhe vermittelt, durch die der umgebende Sandgarten nur ausschnittweise zu sehen ist. Die Umgebung wird für einen Moment lang ausgeblendet, sichtbar ist nur die Düne. Die Farbe, der Boden, die Strukturen, die inszenierte Perspektive vermitteln das Gefühl, sich an einen anderen Ort zu versetzen, zu empfinden.

Tennenwege kreuzen den »Grünfinger« an verschiedenen Stellen und stellen Querverbindungen zwischen der Servicezone und den Ausstellungspavillons her. Abschluß des Gartens und Beginn des Parks bildet ein Obsthain. Anschließend folgt die Querung des Hauptwegs vom Eingang Süd.

Expo-Park Süd

Die Differenz zwischen Garten und Park verdeutlicht ein Wasserkanal, der sich entlang des Eingangsbereichs bis zur Kalsaunequelle zieht. Der Kanal nimmt die Tradition eines »Landschaftspark-Aha's« auf, so daß dem Besucher vom Eingang Süd der freie Blick in die offene Landschaft möglich ist. Die Neugier auf das kommende Erlebnis wird geweckt. Wasserkanal, Wassergarten, Kai, Regenrückhaltebecken und künstliche Anhöhe bilden das Hauptgerüst des Expo-Parks Süd und erlauben dem Besucher die Dimension des Parks, die inszenierte Weite und im Rückblick die Gärten im Wandel zu erfahren. Der Damm mit pyramidalen Bäumen und Vogelscheuchen-Skulpturen bildet die Kulisse zur im Hintergrund liegenden, künstlich angelegten Wald- und Wiesenlandschaft.

Die Himmelstürme auf der künstlichen Anhöhe eröffnen in einem Zusammenspiel mit den Lichtungen, Sichtachsen und dichterer Waldstruktur den Ausblick auf die Exposition und den Parc Agricole. Das lineare Element – der Wasserkanal – kontrastiert den natürlichen Wasseraustritt der Kalsaunequelle und ihrer Gräben. Die Integration der traditionellen Entwässerung der Äcker geht einher mit deren Wiedervernässung zum Zwecke der Anlage von Feuchtgrünland; »artificiel« und »naturel« begegnen sich.

Der Expo-Park Süd besitzt einen landschaftlichen und zugleich sehr geformten Charakter. Prägend sind die künstliche Anhöhe, das durch sie seitlich aufgefangene Regenrückhaltebecken und die auf der Basis von Sichtbe-

The Sand House in the Sand Garden stands for my childhood home, for the sense of fascination and beauty of emptiness, stillness and vastness. (A third of the land area of our earth is desert.) A picture of the dunes is afforded by narrow vertical openings and knee-high horizontal slits, through which parts of the Sand Garden can be glimpsed. For a moment, the surroundings are faded out. All that remains visible is the sand dune. As a result of the colours, the ground, the textures and the staged perspective, the observer has a sense of being translated to a different place.

Sand paths intersect the Green Finger at various points, establishing cross-links between the service zone and the exhibition pavilions. Marking the end of the garden and the beginning of the park is an orchard. Finally, the visitor crosses the main route from the southern entrance of the site.

Expo Park South

The difference between the garden and the park is underlined by a canal which runs along the entrance area from the Kalsaune Spring. The canal conjures familiar associations of a park, affording visitors an unimpeded view of the open landscape from the southern entrance. Their curiosity is aroused for what is to come. The canal, a water garden, a quay, a rainwater catchment and an artificial mound form the main elements of the Expo Park South. Here, visitors can experience the dimensions of these grounds in all their dramatic breadth. Looking back, they can also see the Evolving Gardens. An embankment with pyramidal trees and scarecrow sculptures forms the setting for the artificially created landscape of woodland and meadows in the background. Tall towers (Himmelstürme) on the landscaped mound, in conjunction with clearings, visual axes and dense thickets, allow a view of the exposition and the Parc Agricole. The linear element formed by the canal is contrasted with the natural outflow of water from the Kalsaune Spring and the ditches issuing from it. This traditional form of field drainage also serves to resaturate certain areas and create wet meadows. Here, the artificial and the natural meet.

The Expo Park South has a dual character: it is both a natural landscape and one evidently shaped by human hand. The dominant features are the artificial mound, the rainwater catchment basin to the side, and the structure of the vegetation, designed about a network of visual axes. In view of the topographic and hydrological character of the site, water and its different forms of treatment have been made a central theme of the South Park – a theme that has been subjected to various technical and design strategies.

Perhaps the main element of the Expo Park South is the innovative rainwater catchment lake naturally embedded in the landscape. It includes a shallow-water zone and an area with a filter bed. The water garden with aquatic plants and banks of gravel is accessible via timber walkways as far as the rainwater catchment basin. The straight, linear shoreline to the north and east underlines the man-made aspect of the design. The artificial mound screens off the areas to the south. The rainwater catchment basin is embedded in a hollow between the Kalsaune Spring and the hills. The shaping of the ground in this part of the site extends as far as the area around the southern entrance. After ascending the wooded hill via a peripheral path, the activities of the World Exposition can be viewed from the top. From here, removed from the immediacy of events, visitors may reflect on them at greater leisure.

The three sections of the park are linked by the flowing transitions between the various gardens. At the same time, the design facilitates the creation of different garden types and the presentation during the exposition of the various ways in which nature and technology may be exploited.

Das Sandhaus, Modell
The Sandhouse, Model

Das Teehaus, Modell
The Teehouse, Model

Parc Agricolé

At the end of the millennium, the Parc Agricolé, in its model setting, is intended as an undogmatic demonstration of the conflict between nature conservation on the one hand and land use for recreation and agriculture on the other. The design also seeks to stimulate landscape planning solutions that will allow a »coexistence« between the two. The various claims made on the land will be reflected in the design of the park.

The concentration of the design on only a few elements from the total repertoire of landscape architecture is seen as a means of uniting the many different demands made of the park into a coherent concept. The potential of the Parc Agricolé was explored in the form of plants, spatial perspectives and installations. The site merges at its edges with the surrounding landscape. By connecting up individual sections of the park and specific installations and by orienting the planting plan to the creation of visual axes, city and country are interwoven into a palpable reality. The network of routes and the various kinds of trees that are proposed tie together the Parc Agricolé, the Expo Park South and the surrounding landscape areas.

In the areas where there is built development, deciduous trees are used as in an urban context. These are succeeded by species that are more rural in nature. The various kinds of trees on the common land north-east of the earth mound continue into the Jardin des Murs. The attention of visitors is attracted by special points of emphasis. The permanent and temporary installations form an additional design layer. They accentuate the topography and serve as a means of spatial articulation. Individual elements of the site that already existed in rudimentary form are highlighted. The agricultural character of the land is underlined and given a new interpretation by the retention of arable areas and the incorporation in the design of traditional elements of a cultivated landscape. In the Jardin des Murs, the topography is brought out by the use of dry walling, which is also related to other salient features of the site. The trees to the east of the exhibition pavilions are used as veiling elements, half-masking, half-revealing the planned visual links. During the EXPO 2000, fields of colour are foreseen in which scarecrow sculptures will stand. The latter will be set out in a row and related to each other and to the curving line of the path. This will result in a perspective foreshortening of the space between the entrance areas to the north and the south. Along the curving path, various art objects will be visible through frames that will be erected in the fields for the duration of the EXPO 2000. Scarecrows are the »eternal witnesses of agriculture«. They have had their place in the landscape since time immemorial and in all cultures, and they will continue to exist in various

zügen entwickelte Vegetationsstruktur. Aufgrund der topografischen und hydrologischen Gegebenheiten wird der Umgang mit Wasser im Expo-Park Süd zum zentralen Thema, das mit diversen technischen und gestalterischen Mitteln aufgegriffen wird.

Gezeigt wird im Expo-Park Süd jedoch vor allem die innovative Version eines landschaftlich eingepaßten Regenrückhaltebeckens mit Flachwasserzone und integriertem Bodenfilterbecken. Der Wassergarten mit Wasserpflanzen und Kieseln ist über Holzstege bis zum Regenrückhaltebecken begehbar.

Die geradlinige Uferbegrenzung im Norden und Osten verdeutlicht das Artifizielle dieses Bauwerkes. Die künstliche Anhöhe hingegen schirmt das nach Süden auslaufende Gelände ab, so daß zwischen Kalsaunequelle und Hügelkuppen eine Mulde entsteht, in welche das Regenrückhaltebecken eingebettet ist. Die Modellierung faßt zugleich das Umfeld des Eingangs Süd. Auf der bewaldeten Anhöhe kann über einen Randwanderweg das gerade verlassene Geschehen der Weltausstellung wieder gelassener betrachtet und verarbeitet werden.

Durch den fließenden Übergang der unterschiedlichen Gärten sind die drei Parkteile gestalterisch miteinander verbunden. Gleichzeitig können auf diese Weise verschiedene Formen von Gärten und Möglichkeiten des Umgangs mit Natur und Technik während der Weltausstellung präsentiert werden.

Parc Agricole

Mit dem Parc Agricole sollen zum Ende dieses Jahrtausends an einem Beispielort undogmatisch die Konfrontation Naturschutz gegenüber Nutzungen (Erholung und Landwirtschaft) aufgezeigt und landschaftsplanerische

Gärten im Wandel, Modell
Evolving Gardens, Model

Lösungen angeregt werden, die eine »Cohabitation« ermöglichen. Die unterschiedlichen Ansprüche an das Gelände sollen in der Gestaltung des Parks berücksichtigt werden.

Die Konzentration auf einige wenige, der Landschaftsarchitektur zur Verfügung stehende Mittel wird als Möglichkeit angesehen, die Anforderungen an den Park in einem stimmigen Parkkonzept zu verbinden. Die Potentiale des Parc Agricole sind: Pflanzen, räumliche Perspektiven und Installationen. Das Gelände bildet den Übergang in die umgebende Landschaft. Die Verknüpfung der einzelnen Parkteile und Installationen und die Positionierung der Pflanzen auf der Basis der Sichtbeziehungen machen im Parc Agricole das Ineinandergreifen von Stadt und Land prägnant erlebbar. Die Wegeführung und die vorgesehenen Baumarten vernetzen den Parc Agricole mit dem Expo-Park Süd und den umliegenden Grünbereichen.

Ausgehend von der Bebauung gehen die Laubbaumarten in Arten, die ländliche Impressionen vermitteln, über. Die Baumarten der Allmende nordöstlich des Erdhügels werden bis in den Jardin des Murs fortgeführt. Einzelne Akzente ziehen die Aufmerksamkeit auf sich. Die dauerhaften und temporären Installationen bilden eine ergänzende gestalterische Schicht, verdeutlichen die Topografie und tragen zur räumlichen Gliederung bei. Einzelne, in Ansätzen schon vorhandene Komponenten des Geländes werden erlebbar gemacht. Der Charakter einer landwirtschaftlichen Nutzung wird durch den Erhalt von Ackerflächen und den gestalterischen Einsatz von traditionellen Elementen der Kulturlandschaft betont und interpretiert. Im »Jardin des Murs« werden Trockenmauern zur Verdeutlichung der Topografie und in bezug zu den übrigen Gegebenheiten des Geländes installiert. Östlich der Ausstellungspavillons sind Baumschleier und während der EXPO 2000 Farbfelder vorgesehen, in denen Vogelscheuchen-Skulpturen stehen. Sie bilden eine Reihe, in der sie zueinander und zum gebogenen Weg im Verhältnis stehen. Dadurch ergibt sich eine perspektivische Verkürzung zwischen den Eingangsbereichen im Norden und im Süden. Über den gebogenen Weg sind die künstlerischen Objekte durch Rahmen zu sehen, die während der EXPO 2000 in den Feldern aufgestellt werden.

Vogelscheuchen sind die »ewigen Zeugen der Landwirtschaft«. Sie existieren seit Menschengedenken und in allen Kulturen in der Landschaft und werden die Menschen auch im 21. Jahrhundert in unterschiedlichen Formen durch ihre Geschichte begleiten. Diese speziellen Exemplare sollen von Künstlern aus verschiedenen Ländern gestaltet werden und bleiben als ein Relikt nach der Weltausstellung erhalten. 2000 Lichtpunkte entlang der 90 Meter Höhenlinie dokumentieren während der EXPO 2000 das Millennium, weitere temporäre Installationen ergänzen das Konzept. Mit der Positionierung der Bäume auf der Basis der Sichtbeziehungen, dem Pflanzkonzept und den Installationen wird so das Gerüst eines Parks angelegt, auf dessen Basis er im Laufe der Zeit weiterentwickelt werden kann.

Der Parc Agricole wurde bewußt extensiv gestaltet, das offene Gelände wird neu gefaßt. Ziel ist es, einen prägnanten Landschaftsraum zu schaffen, der dauerhaft einen interessanten Übergang vom Stadtrand in die angrenzende Landschaft bildet. Bewußt werden in diesem Konzept die vorgefundenen Potentiale herausgearbeitet und durch die Integration künstlerischer und technischer Elemente der offene Charakter der Landschaft entwickelt. Im Parc Agricole gilt die Devise, daß »weniger mehr ist«.

Kamel Louafi ist Landschaftsarchitekt für die Grünbereiche auf dem Pavillongelände Ost.

Parc Agricole, Modell
Parc Agricolé, Model

forms and accompany human progress through the 21st century. These special models are to be created by artists from various countries and will remain as a remembrance of this event after the World Exposition has ended. Two thousand points of light laid out along the 90-metre contour line will document the millennium during the EXPO 2000. The concept will be complemented by other temporary installations. The planning of the park's structure was based on a number of factors: the layout of the trees to establish visual axes, the overall planting concept and the inclusion of various installations. The planning structure provides scope for further development in the course of time.

The Parc Agricolé was quite deliberately designed in an extensive form, resulting in a redefinition of the open landscape. The aim is to create a striking outdoor space that will form a permanent and interesting transition from the peripheral urban areas to the adjoining landscape. The existing potential was expressly articulated as part of this concept, and the open character of the landscape was brought out through the integration of artistic and technical elements. The slogan that »less is more« really does apply in the Parc Agricolé.

Kamel Louafi is a landscape architect for the East Pavilion Area.

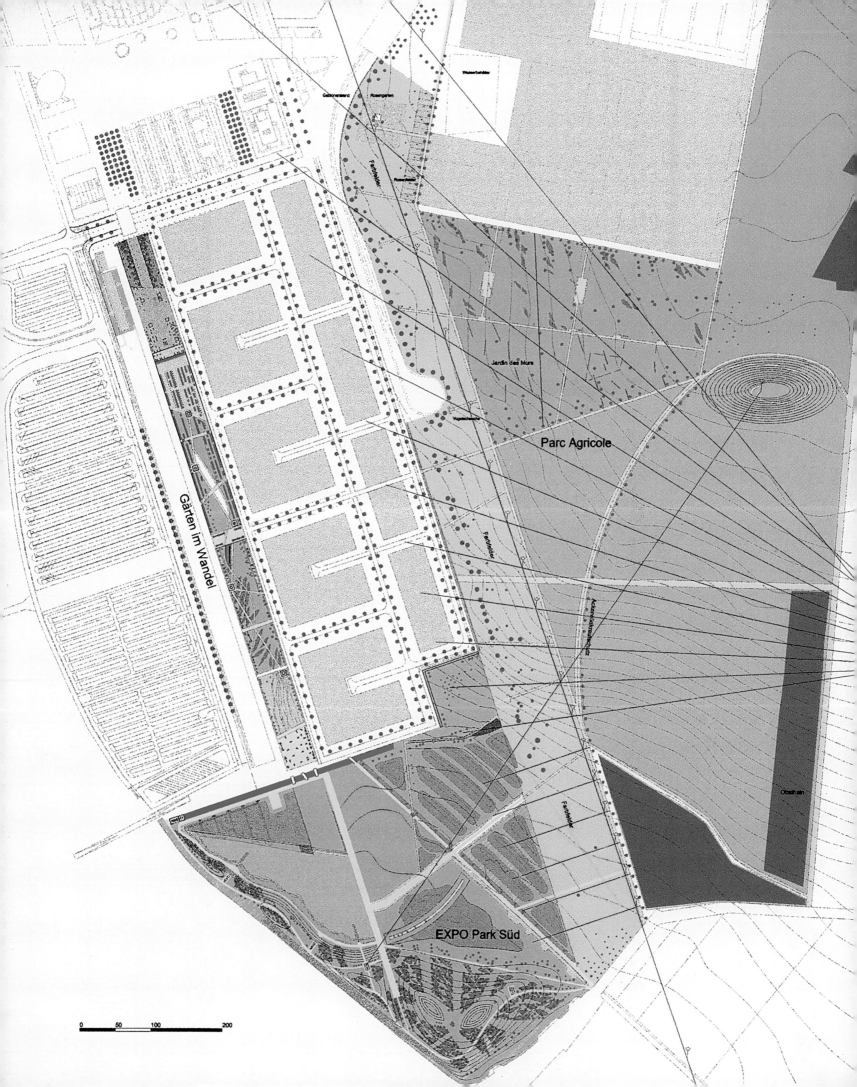

Gärten im Wandel

Parc Agricole

EXPO Park Süd

Rosengarten
Wasserbehälter
Rosenfelder
Jardin des Murs
Vogelschneise
Farbfelder
Ackerwildkrautschutz
Farbfelder
Obsthain

0   50   100   200

Eberhard Stauß, Ursula Wangler

Landschaft, Freiräume, Verkehrsbauwerke.
Aus den Gestaltungsrichtlinien der EXPO 2000

Landscape, Open-air Zones, Traffic Structures.
From the EXPO 2000 Design Guidelines

Leitbilder und Wirklichkeit

Wir machen alle die Erfahrung, daß das »Gedachte« und das »Wirkliche« selten zusammenpassen. In der Organisation dieser Abstimmung sind wir aktiv, tauschen wir uns aus, leben wir. Gehen wir einmal davon aus – ohne jegliche Überkritik –, daß die präsentierten oder initiierten Inhalte in den Nationenpavillons eher »unwirklich« sind (das hängt auch mit der notwendigen Verdichtung von Raum und Information zusammen), sind die Außenräume, die Wege, die Transportlinien, die Landschaft, die »Stadt«, die Region schon eher wirklich.

Setzen wir des weiteren voraus, daß wir in den Pavillons und Messehallen mehr »konsumieren« und in den anderen Bereichen mehr »kommunizieren« (passiv »mitgeführt« oder aktiv »mitgestaltend«), könnte daraus der Schluß gezogen werden, daß es für die EXPO 2000 zwei Leitbilder geben müßte, eines für die Präsentation der Exponate, ein anderes für die »Weg-Räume«. Es wäre sinnvoll, dafür eine mehrdeutige Zuordnung zu suchen.

Leitbilder haben Theorie-Charakter, es ist offen, ob ihre Übersetzung ins Formale gelingt. Deshalb ist es wichtig, ihnen ein regulatives Prinzip zur kritischen Bewertung ihrer Planung und Umsetzung beiseite zu stellen, auch um konkurrierende Ideen aufnehmen oder ausschließen zu können.

Ideals and Reality

We all know how rarely that which was intended coincides with what actually emerges in life. Striving for this match provides the framework within which we act, interact and, ultimately, live. If we accept – without any exaggerated criticism – that the content presented or initiated in the national pavilions tends to be »unreal« (which is also due to the need to compress information and space), then the outdoor areas, the paths, the transport lines, the landscaping, the »city«, the region are certainly real enough.

If we go on to consider that we are »consumers« in the pavilions and exhibition halls and »communicators« in the other areas (the difference between being passively guided and actively helping to shape our environment), we could conclude that EXPO 2000 needs two ideals, one for presenting the exhibits, and another for the »traffic spaces«. It would make sense, then, to look for one of an ambiguous nature.

Ideals have a theoretical nature, and there is no guarantee that their implementation will be successful. Thus, a guiding principle for critical evaluation of planning and implementation becomes very important, with the additional possibility for adopting or rejecting competing ideas.

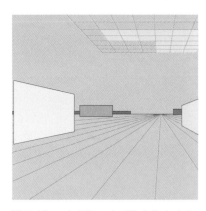
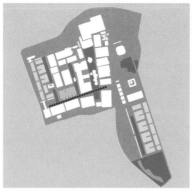
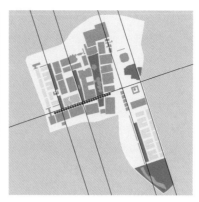
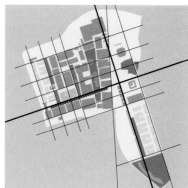

Die Freiräume sind Räume der Offenheit, sie sind weit gefaßt und übersichtlich.
The open spaces are areas of openness and are clearly defined.

Das Weltausstellungsgelände ist als Raum im städtebaulichen Kontext zu sehen, eine Landschaft, in der raumbildende »Körper« Freiräume schaffen.
The exposition site should be seen in urban terms, a landscape in which objects form open spaces.

Die linearen Strukturen, West-Ost-Allee und orthogonal angeordnete »Grünfinger«, sind geprägt durch Baumreihen und gestaffelte Grünelemente.
The linear structures, West-East-Avenue and the orthogonal »green fingers«, are characterized by rows of trees and formations of green elements.

In allen Bereichen des »freien Raumes« ist ein orthogonales Ordnungsprinzip spürbar.
In all the open spaces an orthogonal principle of order can be felt.

Leitbilder

Das Leitbild beziehungsweise das Leitthema für die EXPO 2000 ist bereits definiert und lautet:

Mensch – Natur – Technik

Den Titeln lassen sich weitere innovative Begriffe zuordnen wie:

Mensch	Natur	Technik
Identität	Allgegenwärtigkeit	Leistung
Information	Evolution	Verfügbarkeit
Argumentation	räumliche Ausdehnung	Entwicklung
Sinnlichkeit	materialisierte Zeit	totale Präsenz
Kommunikation	Unabgeschlossenheit	Rationalität
Poesie	Struktur	Konstruktion
Kreativität	Substanz	Funktion

Das Leitthema für den »Weg zwischen den Nationen« könnte in Entsprechung zum ersten Leitthema lauten:

Raum	Mensch	Gemeinschaft
Endlichkeit	Identität	Selbstbewußtsein
Zeitlichkeit	Information	Austausch
Raumort-Bildung	Argumentation	Unverfügbarkeit
»Da-Sein«	Sinnlichkeit	Solidarität
	Kommunikation	Initiativverantwortung
	Poesie	Offenheit
	Kreativität	Geselligkeit
		Aufgehobensein
		Vertrauen

Ideals proposed

The ideal – or, rather, the key theme – for EXPO 2000 has been defined as:

Humankind – Nature – Technology

The headings can have further innovative terms assigned to them, such as:

Humankind	Nature	Technology
Identity	Universality	Performance
Information	Evolution	Availability
Debate	Spatial Extension	Development
Senses	Materialized Time	Total Presence
Communication	Incompleteness	Rationality
Poetry	Structure	Design
Creativity	Substance	Function

The key theme for the »Path between the Nations« could accordingly be based on the first key theme as follows:

Space	Humankind	Community
Finiteness	Identity	Confidence
Duration	Information	Exchange
Spatial Formation	Debate	Unavailability
«Presence»	Senses	Solidarity
	Communication	Responsibility for Initiative
	Poetry	Openness
	Creativity	Sociability
		Security
		Trust

 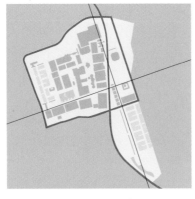 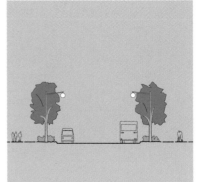 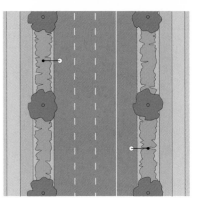

Das Weltausstellungsgelände ist als Raum im städtebaulichen Kontext zu sehen, eine Landschaft, in der raumbildende »Körper« wie Straßen, Straßenkreuzungen, Über- und Unterführungen lineare Räume schaffen.
The exposition site should be seen in urban terms, a landscape in which streets, street crossings, over- and underpasses form linear spaces.

Das übergeordnete Straßennetz, der Messering, folgt im wesentlichen der Geometrie des EXPO-/Messegeländes. Der Messeschnellweg folgt in seiner Raumorientierung den Messehallen.
The overriding street system, the trade fair ring road follows on an whole the geometry of the EXPO/trade fair site. The trade fair/dual carriage way follows the orientation of the trade halls.

Für das Ringstraßensystem des Ausstellungsgeländes wird ein einheitliches Straßenprofil erstellt, das die verkehrstechnischen Anforderungen erfüllt und eine gestalterische Linie vorgibt.
For the ring road system of the exposition site an uniform street profile will be used which will comply with necessary traffic requirements and postulate a line of design.

Regulative Prinzipien für die Konzeptbewertung des Leitbildes und seine Weiterentwicklung in einem Entwurf:

Draft of regulatory principles of the ideals proposed and their further developments:

Einfachheit

Einfachheit, der »leere«, sich anbietende Raum, weit gefaßt, übersichtlich, ohne enge perspektivische (auf einen Fluchtpunkt bezogene) Ausrichtung, kein Raumkanal, sondern ein »Raumort« mit fließenden Grenzen, seitlicher Ausweitung in die Raumtiefe und klarer, wenig unterbrochener Horizontausrichtung, mit geringer Informationsmenge und minimierter Ausstattung

Simplicity

Simplicity, the »empty« space offering itself, extensive, clearly visible, without any tight focus (tied to an exit point), not a spatial channel but rather a location with fluid boundaries, a lateral extension into space and a clear horizon with few interruptions, low volume of information and minimal fittings

Klugheit

Erzielung größtmöglicher Raumwirkung (Führung, Entlassung, Spannung, Dehnung, Rhythmisierung mit einfachsten, intelligent eingesetzten Mitteln)

Cleverness

Achieving maximum possible spatial impact (direction, release, tension, expansion, rhythm using the simplest means intelligently employed)

Natürlichkeit

Bewußte Verwendung von Materialien (Stein, Keramik, Holz, Edelmetalle), die bei den Hallen und Pavillons nicht vorkommen

Naturalness

Awareness with respect to use of materials (stone, ceramics, wood, precious metals) not found in the halls and pavilions

Redlichkeit

Keine appellativen »Angebote« im »leeren Raum« wie Werbung, keine stimulativen Angebote und Begleitungen durch Ton beziehungsweise Bildunterstützung zur Milieu-Prägung, keine »manipulierten« Details, die zu Erscheinungen führen, die nicht nachvollziehbar sind (Steinwände aus dünnen Platten, versteckte Hilfskonstruktionen, indirektes Licht et cetera) und keine »Hierarchisierung« der Raumfolgen

Integrity

No appeals in the »empty« space such as advertising, no stimulating prompts through sound or visual input to shape the environment, no manipulation of detail creating appearances which cannot be tested (stone walls using thin slabs, concealed supports, indirect lighting etc.) and no hierarchy in the spatial sequence

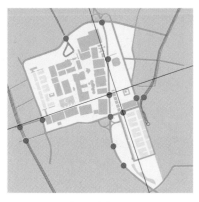 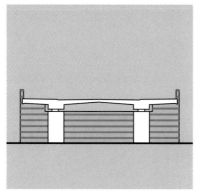 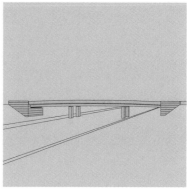

Für eine reibungslose Verkehrsabwicklung ist eine große Zahl von Brückenbauten zu erstellen, die sich in die Kategorien Straßenbrücke, Fußgängerbrücke und Gleisüberbrückung einordnen lassen. Neben ihrer Verkehrsfunktion haben diese Brücken eine wichtige Gestaltfunktion im Gesamterscheinungsbild.
For easy traffic flow a variety of bridges was necessary: street bridges, pedestrian bridges and railway bridges. Apart from their traffic-related functions, these bridges also play an important role in the overall visual impression.

Die charakteristischen Merkmale der Konstruktion – einfache bzw. geteilte Plattenbalken – und der Gestaltung – horizontale Bänderung – können entsprechend spezifischen Bedingungen innerhalb des gegebenen Systems abgewandelt werden.
The characteristics of these constructions – simple yet split T-beams – and the design – horizontal lines – can be changed within the system.

Der Typen-Entwurf (Architekten Pax und Hadamczik, Niedersächsisches Landesamt für Straßenbau, Tiefbauamt der Landeshauptstadt Hannover) bildet nach konstruktivem Prinzip und formaler Ausbildung die Norm für alle Brückenbauten des Messerings und des Messe-Schnellwegs.
This design (Architects Pax and Hadamczik, Niedersächsische Landesamt für Straßenbau, Tiefbauamt der Landeshauptstadt Hannover) forms the constructive principle for all bridge buildings on the trade fair ring road and the trade fair dual expressway.

Gestaltungskreis

Im Gestaltungskreis der EXPO 2000 werden alle für die EXPO 2000 und die Messe relevanten Gestaltungsfragen des Städtebaus, der Architektur, der Landschaftsplanung, des Designs, der Kunst und der visuellen Kommunikation behandelt.

Ziel ist es, dieser einmaligen, international ausstrahlenden Veranstaltung einen eindrucksvollen Rahmen mit höchster gestalterischer Qualität zu geben.

Der Gestaltungskreis entwirft nicht, er koordiniert, begutachtet, bewertet, entwickelt Alternativen und spricht einvernehmlich Empfehlungen aus. Nach Behandlung eines Gestaltungsthemas werden verbindliche Grundsätze formuliert und verabschiedet.

Der Gestaltungskreis repräsentiert ein Gremium fachkompetenter Persönlichkeiten:

Uta Boockhoff-Gries, Stadt Hannover
Dr. Wilfried Dickhoff, Berater EXPO 2000 GmbH
Prof. Meinhard von Gerkan, Architekt BDA
Sepp D. Heckmann, Deutsche Messe AG und EXPO 2000 GmbH
Prof. Thomas Herzog, Architekt BDA
Prof. Dieter Kienast, Landschaftsarchitekt (verstorben am 23. Dezember 1998)
Prof. Albert Speer, Architekt BDA
Prof. Eberhard Stauß, Büro für Gestaltung (verstorben am 28. Juni 1998)
Ursula Wangler, Büro für Gestaltung

Aus der großen Anzahl von entwickelten Leitlinien werden exemplarisch die Bereiche Landschaft, Freiräume und Verkehrsbauwerke vorgestellt.

Design circle

The EXPO 2000 design circle deals with all the design issues relevant to EXPO 2000 and the trade fair in the fields of urban engineering, architecture, landscaping, design, art and visual communication.

The goal is to ensure an impressive setting with the highest quality of design for this unique event with its international dimensions.

The design circle is not involved in designing, it coordinates, appraises, evaluates, develops alternatives and issues unanimous recommendations. After a design issue has been fully reviewed, binding principles are formulated and agreed on.

The design circle consists of leading individuals in their special fields:

Uta Boockhoff-Gries, City of Hanover
Dr Wilfried Dickhoff, consultant to EXPO 2000 GmbH
Prof. Meinhard von Gerkan, architect BDA
Sepp D. Heckmann, Deutsche Messe AG and EXPO 2000 GmbH
Prof. Thomas Herzog, architect BDA
Prof. Dieter Kienast, Landscape architect (dec. 23 December 1998)
Prof. Albert Speer, architect BDA
Prof. Eberhard Stauß, Design Office (dec. 28 June 1998)
Ursula Wangler, Design Office

The guidelines for landscape, open-air zones and traffic structures are presented as examples of the many guidelines which have been developed.

Martin Roth

Der EXPO 2000-Themenpark: authentische Architektur als inszenierte Ausstellung

The EXPO 2000 Thematic Area: Authentic Architecture as a Staged Exhibition

Die zentralen Menschheitsfragen, wie aus Ideen Realität wird, wie Hoffnungen sich zu Handlungen entwickeln und aus Visionen sich der Fortschritt ableitet, sind auch die inhaltlichen Schwerpunkte der Themenausstellung der EXPO 2000 – im Arbeitstitel »Themenpark« genannt. Es ist das Angebot des Gastgeberlandes Deutschland, die sinnliche, dreidimensionale Darstellung des Mottos »Mensch – Natur – Technik«.

Die Attraktivität des Mediums Großausstellung wird verwendet, um die Lösungsansätze für globale Probleme von morgen zu zeigen. Es sind aber nicht ausschließlich die großen Lösungen, die hierbei von Interesse sind, sondern auch gerade die mannigfaltigen Lösungsversuche in den verschiedenen Bereichen unserer Civil Societies.

Der Themenpark ist mehr als das riesige Fernrohr, mit dem wir in die Zukunft schauen wollen. Es ist eine Reise aus dem Heute in das Morgen, mit der wir zeigen, daß unsere gemeinsamen Ideen die Zukunft bestimmen werden. Die Zukunft ist nicht Science-fiction, nicht einmal Fiktion, sondern sie wird aus unseren Ideen gemacht. Aus dieser Reise in die Zukunft wollen wir mit Lösungen in die Gegenwart zurückkehren, um das Morgen entsprechend menschenwürdiger gestalten zu können.

Große Themenausstellungen haben in hundertfünfzig Jahren Weltausstellungsgeschichte immer dazu beigetragen, daß das Neue in die Welt kam. Bekannt sind Industrieprodukte vom Automobil bis zur ersten Zahnpasta in der Tube, von Aspirin bis zum Zeppelin. Ein Schaufenster in die Zukunft: Die Multivision ist beispielsweise ein Zauberwort der Weltausstellungen seit den sechziger Jahren, heute gehört sie zur allgemeinen Anwendung. Aber auch der Wissenschafts- und Forschungsbereich hat die Weltausstellungen stets als Motor genützt, um zu demonstrieren, wozu die angewandte Forschung fähig ist. Und ohne einen gewissen Wettbewerb der Nationen auch im sozialen Bereich hätte sich manche Errungenschaft nur

The central human questions – how do ideas become reality, how do hopes become action, how do visions become progress – are also key elements in the Thematic Area at EXPO 2000. This is the contribution of the Federal Republic of Germany as the host country, a concrete, three-dimensional presentation of the motto »Humankind – Nature – Technology«.

The appeal of a large-scale exhibition is used to show possible solutions for the global problems of the future. The focus is not restricted to global approaches, however, but embraces widely diverse schemes in a variety of areas within our societies.

The Thematic Area will be more than a giant telescope for us to peer into the future. It will be a journey from the present to the world of tomorrow, showing how our ideas will shape the future. And the future is not science fiction, not even fiction – it is the product of our ideas. Our purpose in this journey is to return to the present with solutions for shaping our future to be more compatible with human dignity.

Over a century and a half of world expositions, major thematic exhibitions have always helped to bring something new into the world. Familiar examples are industrial products from the automobile to the first tube of toothpaste, from aspirin to the zeppelin: a showcase for the future. Multivision, for example, has been a term to conjure with in world expositions since the sixties. Today, it is in general use. Science and research have also used world expositions as a platform to show what applied research is capable of. And without an element of international competition in the social area, many achievements would have been slow to catch on – house building, industrial safety and insurance plans have always been issues for world expositions. Themes that moved the world were natural subjects to be found at such expositions. This places the Thematic Area into the context of a certain tradition that includes not only the major social exhibi-

54

langsam durchgesetzt: Wohnungsbau, Arbeitsschutz, Versicherungssysteme waren stets Themen von Weltausstellungen – alle Themen, die die Welt bewegten, waren auf einer solchen Ausstellung zu finden. Der Themenpark hat somit Vorläufer. Dazu zählen neben den großen Sozialausstellungen, die stets ein Massenpublikum angezogen haben, auch ethnografische Ausstellungen: Ganze Dörfer, Kleinstädte, architektonische Besonderheiten wurden aus der ganzen Welt zusammengetragen und möglichst authentisch nachgestellt. Ein faszinierendes Unterfangen, an das wir gern anknüpfen würden, indem wir beispielsweise die Welt vor eintausend Jahren wiederbeleben.

Wir haben die Möglichkeit, sämtliche Techniken der modernen Kommunikation und der Bildprojektion mit dem dreidimensionalen Reiz einer Ausstellung zu mischen – Illusion und Realität werden im Zusammenklang dazu beitragen, den Besucher in die Brisanz und Spannung der Themen hineinzuziehen und zugleich Freude an ihnen zu wecken. Die Ausstellungen werden wie dreidimensionale Filme sein, in denen sich die Besucher wie Schauspieler, Akteure bewegen und hautnah die Zukunft erleben und mitgestalten.

»Mitgestalten« ist das Grundprinzip des Themenparks. Aufgrund dieses Prinzips unterscheidet sich der Themenpark von allen bisher konzipierten Großausstellungen. Die EXPO 2000 lädt weltweit Wirtschaftsunternehmen, Institutionen aus Wissenschaft und Forschung, Nichtregierungsorganisationen und Privatpersonen dazu ein, sich mit Fragen an die Zukunft und Lösungsvorschlägen für konkrete Vorhaben zu beteiligen. Sie stellt den Präsentationsrahmen und die aufregende Gestaltung, die zukunftsorientierten Lösungen kommen von den Partnern. Der Themenpark ist eine nie dagewesene Mitmach-Ausstellung für internationale Partner aus allen gesellschaftlichen Bereichen.

Zentrales Thema ist der »Mensch« im Gleichklang des Mottos mit Natur und Technik. Die einzelnen Ausstellungen – auf einer Gesamtfläche von 100.000 Quadratmetern – bilden eine inhaltliche Einheit und zeigen die Querbeziehungen zwischen »Umwelt: Landschaft, Klima« (es handelt sich um Arbeitstitel), den »Basic Needs«, der »Energie«, den Life Sciences »Gesundheit« und »Ernährung«. Wir zeigen die »Mobilität« der Zukunft, auch die Mobility of the Mind, die wir alle benötigen, um eine neue »Zukunft der Arbeit« zu kreieren, die die Selbständigkeit des einzelnen fördert. Alle Einzelausstellungen werden durch das Thema »Wissen, Information, Kommunikation« verbunden. Es zeigt, wie wir mit dem Schatz des angehäuften Wissens umgehen, wie es die Welt neu belebt, verbindet, kleiner, aber im Detail wiederum größer macht – und vielleicht eine neue Chancengleichheit der Zukunft ermöglicht. Der Prolog, »Planet of Visions«, besteht in Form einer Ausstellung, die zeigt, wie über Jahrhunderte hinweg Träume, Utopien, Visionen, Ideen unsere Wirklichkeit von heute gestaltet haben und in Zukunft gestalten werden. Der Epilog, die Ausstellung »Das 21. Jahrhundert«, ermöglicht einen weiten Blick in das dritte Millennium: eine Reise zurück aus der Zukunft.

Weltausstellungen sind nicht mehr dazu da, neue Erdteile zu entdecken. Unsere Entdeckungsreise geht tief in die unentdeckte Welt des Gehirns, der vernetzten Kommunikation, der Gentechnologie, der Ressourcenforschung, des kulturellen Erbes, der Kernfusion oder auch der Menschenrechte. Das magische Jahr 2000 verlangt von uns, über uns selbst nachzudenken, die spannende Welt der Gedanken, Ideen und Visionen für eine bessere Zukunft zu erforschen. Verbindliches Grundthema – darin unterscheidet sich die EXPO 2000 von allen anderen Weltausstellungen – ist die populäre Darstellung der Inhalte und Ziele der Agenda 21 und insbe-

tions (which have always attracted a mass audience) but also ethnographic exhibitions. Entire villages, small towns, architectural curiosities have been brought together from all over the world and recreated as authentically as possible. A fascinating venture, which we would like to build on, by reviving the world of a thousand years ago, for instance.

We have the opportunity to combine all the technologies of modern communications and of image projection with the three-dimensional appeal of an exhibition – illusion and reality working together to help draw visitors into the excitement and suspense of the themes, while at the same time stimulating their enjoyment of them. The exhibits will be like three-dimensional films in which visitors will be actors, experiencing and helping to shape the future first hand.

»Shaping« is the basic principle of the Thematic Area, and the thing that sets the Thematic Area apart from all previous major expositions. EXPO 2000 is inviting commercial companies, scientific and research institutions, non-governmental organizations and private individuals all over the world to join in tackling questions of the future and proposals for concrete projects. It is providing the setting, while its partners supply the exciting designs and future-oriented solutions. The Thematic Area is a totally new interactive exhibition for international partners from all sections of society.

The central theme is »Humankind«, and in the motto it is flanked by nature and technology. The individual exhibits – on a total area covering 100,000 sqare meters – will form a coherent whole with respect ot content, pointing out links between »Environment: Landscape, Climate«, »Basic Needs«, »Energy«, the life sciences »Health« and »Nutrition» (all these are working titles). We will present the »Mobility« of the future, including the »Mobility of the Mind« we all need to create a new »Future of Work« which promotes individual empowerment. All the individual exhibits are linked by the theme »Knowledge, Information, Communication« which deals with how we handle the wealth of accumulated knowledge, how this knowledge stimulates and connects the world and thus makes it shrink – but, at another, more detailed level, grow again – and which may provide new equality of opportunity in the future. The prologue »Planet of Visions« consists of an exhibition showing how dreams, utopias, visions and ideas over the centuries have shaped today's reality and will continue to shape future realities. The epilogue, the exhibition »The 21st Century«, provides a broad view of the third millennium – a journey back from the future.

World expositions are no longer there to discover new continents: our journeys of exploration take us deep into the undiscovered world of the brain, of networked communication, genetic engineering, resource research, cultural heritage, nuclear fusion and even human rights. The magic year 2000 calls on us to look in the mirror and research the exciting world of thoughts, ideas and visions for a better future. The binding basic theme – and this is where EXPO 2000 is different from all other world expositions – is the popular presentation of the content and goals of Agenda 21, and specifically the programme for sustainable development. The themes described above have been taken from Agenda 21.

Partner contributions are fitted into this concept: integrated traffic/transport concepts for megacities, the social and economic consequences of fuel cell development, their everyday effects, everyday life in the year 2030 – what will work be like? How will we eat? Will neurotechnology give blind people a chance to learn to see? Our partners have answers to these and many other questions, and together we are trans-

sondere des Programms der nachhaltigen Entwicklung. Die obengenannten Themen sind der Agenda 21 entnommen.

Entsprechend gestalten sich auch die Beiträge der Partner: integrierte Verkehrskonzepte für die Mega-Cities, die sozialen und ökonomischen Folgen der Entwicklung der Brennstoffzelle, ihre Auswirkungen im Alltag, ein normaler Tag im Jahre 2030 – wie werden wir arbeiten? Wie uns ernähren? Bringt die Neurotechnologie manchen Blinden die Möglichkeit, sehen zu lernen? Auf diese und viele andere Fragen haben unsere Partner bereits Antworten parat, gemeinsam sind wir dabei, diese in eine publikumsorientierte, informative Ausstellung zu übersetzen.

Sehr viel ist in den letzten fünf Vorbereitungsjahren geschehen. Fachinstitutionen (externe Projektleiter), die sowohl wissenschaftliche als auch ausstellungstechnische Erfahrung haben, erarbeiten gemeinsam mit der EXPO 2000 den inhaltlichen Rahmen. Für »Mobilität« zeichnet das Fraunhofer Institut für Materialfluß und Logistik verantwortlich. »Wissen, Information, Kommunikation« wurde vom Zentrum für Kunst und Medientechnologie in Karlsruhe erarbeitet, die »Zukunft der Arbeit« von einer eigens dafür gegründeten GmbH, »Energie« vom World Energy Council, »Ernährung« vom Heureka Science Center in Helsinki gemeinsam mit IFPRI in Washington, »Gesundheit« von der Weltgesundheitsorganisation, »Basic Needs« vom Royal Tropical Institute in Amsterdam, »Umwelt: Landschaft, Klima« von der Bundesanstalt für Geowissenschaften und Rohstoffe in Hannover und der »Mensch« schließlich vom Deutschen Hygiene-Museum in Dresden. Für den großen Prolog und Epilog wurde eigens ein Fachbeirat einberufen. Stets standen beratend und konstruktiv kritisierend das Kuratorium unter Leitung von Professor Richard Schröder und das International Advisory Board unter dem Vorsitz von Ricardo Diez Hochleitner zur Seite. Um den wirklichen Charakter des Themenparks, eine Beteiligung von möglichst vielen Ideengebern zu sichern, wurde ein offizieller Einladungsprozeß gestartet. Arbeitsgruppen, zusammengesetzt aus allen gesellschaftlichen Bereichen, standen den externen Projektleitern zur Seite und jurierten die Ergebnisse des Einladungsverfahrens.

Wir haben eine sehr lebendige und geradezu explosiv mit Ideen umgehende Crew von Gestaltern gewinnen können – Architekten, Filmemacher, Designer, Künstler, Bühnenbildner: Jean Nouvel baut eine mobile Architektur aus Bildern; Toyo Ito inszeniert Wasser als fließende Architektur; Wolfram Wöhr wendet zum ersten Mal seine bekannte Formensprache in einer Ausstellung an, François Schuiten, dem es durch den Umbau der Metro-Station »Arts et Metiers« in Paris gelang, Menschen für einige Sekunden in eine surreale Welt zu versetzen, nimmt in seiner Ausstellung den Besucher gänzlich aus den vertrauten Raum- und Zeitvorstellungen; Antoni Miralda kreiert einen Kunstraum und transformiert ihn in eine Prozession; Rajeev Sethi gestaltet als »Basic Needs« die Einfachheit im Überfluß; die Filmakademie Ludwigsburg experimentiert mit dem begehbaren Film; das Zentrum für Kunst- und Medientechnologie in Karlsruhe lehrt Robotern die Gesetze der Bionik, und am Grundthema »Mensch« haben wir die Einflüsse vieler unter der Ägide des Deutschen Hygiene-Museums gebündelt: Durs Grünbein, Via Lewandowsky und Sasha Waltz gehörten dazu, und auch die Meinungen der Altmeister Volker Schlöndorff und Harald Szeemann wurden eingeholt. Die Gestalter unterscheiden sich in bezug auf ihre Disziplinen, aber ebenso auf den kulturellen Hintergrund. Es sind erfahrene Ausstellungsmacher und junge, experimentierfreudige Kreative, die in besonderem Maße die Bildwelten des kommenden Jahrhunderts mitprägen werden. »Forever young« soll für den Themenpark nicht gelten, deshalb haben wir bewußt auf die stets gleichen großen Namen verzichtet. Es scheint generell

forming them into an informative exhibition aimed at the general public.

A great deal has happened during the past five years of preparation. Specialist institutions (external project managers) with scientific and exhibition experience are working together with EXPO 2000 on its content. The Fraunhofer Institut für Materialfluß und Logistik (Fraunhofer Institute for Material Flow and Logistics) is responsible for »Mobility«, the Zentrum für Kunst und Medientechnologie (Art and Media Technology Center) at Karlsruhe for »Knowledge, Information, Communication«. A company has been specially formed for »Future of Work«, the World Energy Council is handling »Energy«, the Heureka Science Center in Helsinki is collaborating with IFPRI in Washington on »Nutrition«. The World Health Organisation has taken on »Health«, the Royal Tropical Institute in Amsterdam »Basic Needs«, the Bundesanstalt für Geowissenschaften und Rohstoffe (Federal Institute for Geosciences and Natural Resources) in Hanover is spearheading »Environment: Landscape, Climate«, and Deutsches Hygiene-Museum (German Hygiene Museum) in Dresden is responsible for »Humankind«. A specialist advisory board was assembled for the Prologue and Epilogue. The Board of Trustees chaired by Professor Richard Schröder and the International Advisory Board chaired by Ricardo Diez Hochleitner have been constantly available for advice and constructive criticism. To ensure as many sources of ideas as possible, an official invitation process was launched. Working groups formed from all walks of life assisted external project managers and served as juries in reviewing the results of the process.

We have succeeded in attracting a very lively and explosively creative crew of designers – architects, film makers, designers, artists, set designers: Jean Nouvel is building a mobile architecture out of images; Toyo Ito is creating a setting which uses water as architecture in flux; Wolfram Wöhr is bringing his well-known style to an exhibition for the first time; François Schutten (whose remodelling of the Paris Métro station »Arts et Métiers« transported people briefly into a surreal world) is creating an exhibition which will free visitors from their habitual ideas of space and time; Antoni Miralda is creating an artistic space transformed into a procession; Rajeev Sethi generates simplicity in abundance in his treatment of »Basic Needs«, the Filmakademie Ludwigsburg (Ludwigsburg Film Academy) is experimenting with walk-through film, the Art and Media Technology Center at Karlsruhe is teaching robots the laws of bionics. Finally, for the central theme of »Humankind« we have drawn together influences from many under the aegis of the German Hygiene Museum: Durs Grünbein, Via Lewandowsky and Sasha Waltz (to name but three), with advice from veteran creatives Volker Schlöndorff and Harald Szeemann. The designers differ in their disciplines and also in their cultural backgrounds – there are experienced exhibition designers and young, experimental creatives who will play a special role in shaping the imagery of the coming century. »Forever young« is not a goal for the Thematic Area, which is why we have deliberately avoided using the same great names. It looks generally as if this is the EXPO of the young generation, as illustrated by the Netherlands pavilion. I admire the courage shown in the directness of this pavilion and recall all the debate in the Federal Republic of Germany over the supposed impossibility of giving concrete reality to the motto »Humankind – Nature – Technology«. The Netherlands pavilion teaches us the courage to aim for simplicity. One level for technology, one level for nature, one level for humankind. A pavilion which could be a symbol for EXPO 2000. I am happy that this World Exposition will above all else be a major architectural exhibition.

The Thematic Area is one side of a coin whose reverse is the »Worldwide Projects«. A unique competition for functioning, successful projects in

die EXPO der Jungen zu werden, der holländische Pavillon ist ein Beweis dafür. Ich bewundere den Mut zur Direktheit dieses Pavillons und erinnere mich an all die Diskussionen, die es in Deutschland gab in bezug auf die vermeintliche Nicht-Umsetzbarkeit des Mottos »Mensch – Natur – Technik«. Der holländische Pavillon lehrt uns den Mut zur Einfachheit: eine Etage Technik, eine Etage Natur, eine Etage Menschen. Ein Pavillon, der EXPO 2000-symbolverdächtig ist. Ich freue mich darauf, daß auch diese Weltausstellung vor allen Dingen eine große Architektur-Ausstellung sein wird.

Der Themenpark bildet die eine Seite der Medaille, auf deren komplementärer anderer Seite sich die »Weltweiten Projekte« finden. Ein erstmals durchgeführter Wettbewerb von funktionierenden, erfolgreichen Projekten aus allen Teilen dieser Erde zu den obengenannten Themen. Diese Projekte werden selbstverständlich vor allem an ihrem Ursprungsort präsentiert, eine Vielzahl davon wird aber auch die Möglichkeit erhalten, sich im Themenpark zu zeigen: Bildungsprogramme für Kinder, Nebelfänger zu Wassergewinnung in Trockengebieten, Bionikforschung, um aus der Natur zu lernen. Dieses und vieles mehr wird dazu dienen, daß der Themenpark ein Schauplatz wird, an dem sich Ideen, Visionen und die Realität vereinigen. Im Jahre 2000, während der Dauer der EXPO 2000, soll schließlich ein »Global Dialogue«, ein Diskussionsforum für Betroffene und Entscheidungsträger, diese beiden Seiten der Medaille verbinden.

Der Themenpark selbst ist durch seine Existenz eine Beweisführung für Zukunftsideen. Die Finanzierung erfolgt zu einem erheblichen Maß frei, gemeinsam mit den erwähnten Partnern. Die Grundfinanzierung und die Garantiesumme, daß eine attraktive Ausstellung entstehen kann, sind vorhanden. Die Durchführung muß nicht nur konzeptionell, sondern auch finanziell erarbeitet werden. Auf diese Weise ist der Themenpark sicherlich das größte temporäre Unternehmen in Sachen Public Private Partnership – einer adäquaten Organisationsform für eine Civil Society der Zukunft. Und für uns, das verantwortliche Team der Ausstellungsmacher, ist der Themenpark ein Kraftwerk der Kulturen und eine Kathedrale der Zivilisation.

Dr. Martin Roth ist Bereichsleiter Themenpark und Weltweite Projekte der EXPO 2000 Hannover GmbH.

all parts of the world on the above themes. These projects will naturally be primarily exhibited at their original locations, but many will also have a chance to exhibit in the Thematic Area: educational programmes for children, dew traps for obtaining water in arid zones, bionic research to learn from nature. These and many others will help make the Thematic Area a showplace bringing together ideas, visions and reality. In the year 2000, for the duration of EXPO 2000, there will also be a »Global Dialogue«, a discussion forum for people affected and decision-makers, linking the two sides of the coin.

The very existence of the Thematic Area is itself a demonstration of ideas about the future. It is largely self-financed, with partners. Basic funds and the obligatory sums that can make an attractive exhibition are on hand. Both the concept and also the financial aspects of implementation had to be worked out. Consequently, there is no doubt that the Thematic Area is the largest limited-term public private partnership enterprise – indeed a very appropriate form of organization for civil society of the future. And for us, the team of exhibition creators responsible for it all, the Thematic Area constitutes a power-station of the cultures, and a cathedral of civilization.

Dr. Martin Roth is the director of Thematic Area and Projects around the world of the EXPO 2000 Hannover GmbH.

Plant of Visions, François Schuiten

EXPO 2000-Architektur

EXPO 2000 Architecture

Halle 13: Offenheit und Dialektik

Hall 13: Openness and Dialectics

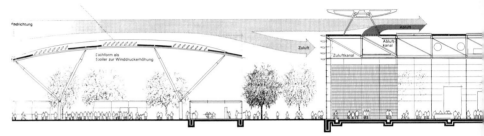

Schnitt durch den Eingang West und die Halle 13 mit der natürlichen Be- und Entlüftung
Section trough Western Entrance and Hall 13, Showing the Natural Ventilation System

Der sogenannte »Skywalk«, ein glasüberdachtes 320 Meter langes Rollband, verbindet den EXPO 2000- und Messebahnhof Hannover/Laatzen mit dem Eingang West der Weltausstellung. Besonders Flugreisende sollten diese Verbindung unbedingt nutzen; vom Airport Langenhagen aus gibt es dann eine direkte S-Bahn-Verbindung; die Fahrt dauert nur circa zwanzig Minuten. Der »Skywalk« mündet vor der Halle 13 in einem Stahl-Glas-überkuppelten Eingangsbauwerk, dessen Formen einen erkennbaren Gegensatz zur Architektur der Halle bilden. Der ursprünglich Plan, hier einen wesentlich eleganteren, wellenförmigen »Spoiler« einladend anzubieten, scheiterte an der nachträglichen massiven Erhöhung der erwarteten Besucherzahl von 12.000 auf 18.000 Personen; die Lüftungstechnik der Großhalle wäre von der Aerodynamik eines solchen »Entrees« zu sehr beeinträchtigt worden.

Entlang des Eingangsbauwerks verläuft die vierreihige Allee der Vereinigten Bäume, die aus 467 Solitären unterschiedlichster Arten besteht. Flankiert wird diese »Magistrale« durch eine Reihe voluminöser Ausstellungshallen, deren Defilee die Halle 13 eröffnet: Mit ihren Außenmaßen von 225 x 120 Metern und einer Grundfläche von 27.400 Quadratmetern ist sie eine der größten auf dem Gelände.

Über den Entwurf, der 1995 aus einem Wettbewerb als 1. Preis hervorging, schrieb die Jury: »Die Halle selbst fügt sich harmonisch in das Gesamtbild der Messe ein. Die Fassade der Halle ermöglicht einen intensiven Wechsel zwischen dem Innen- und Außenraum …. Durch die sechs Technikkerne erhält die Halle eine hohe Funktionalität und klare räumliche Qualität. Diese räumliche Qualität wird durch das Tageslichtkonzept von Fassade und Dach deutlich verstärkt.«

Das fertiggestellte Gebäude bestätigt diese Urteile. Die doch sehr große Baumasse erhält durch fast 4.000 Glasflächenelemente eine spürbare »entschwerende« Transparenz; hinzu kommt, daß das liegende Format

The »Skywalk«, as it is known, a glass-covered moving walkway 320 metres long, links the Laatzen EXPO station in Hanover with the western entrance to the World Exposition. Air passengers in particular should use this link. From Langenhagen Airport, there is then a direct rapid suburban rail connection. The journey takes only about 20 minutes. The Skywalk ends at Hall 13 in a steel and glass vaulted entrance structure, the forms of which are clearly contrasted with the architecture of the hall itself. The original plan to place a much more elegant, inviting, wave-like »spoiler« here was abandoned after predictions for the numbers of visitors to the hall had been revised from 12,000 to 18,000 per day. The ventilation technology for the large hall would have been adversely influenced by the aerodynamic effects of an entry structure in this form.

The four-row United Trees Avenue running along the side of the entrance structure consists of 467 individual specimens. This thoroughfare is flanked by a series of large exhibition halls, at the beginning of which stands Hall 13. With external dimensions of 225 x 120 metres and an area of 27,400 square metres, it is one of the largest halls on the site.

The design won first prize in the competition held in 1995. In the words of the jury: »The hall itself fits harmoniously into the overall picture of the trade fair site. The hall façade allows an intense interaction between inside and outside… The six service cores ensure that the hall has a high functional quality and a clear spatial articulation. The spatial quality is accentuated by the daylighting concept for the façade and roof.«

The completed building confirms this verdict. The 4,000 planar glass facade elements lend the hall a transparency that relieves this very large volume of much of its weight. In addition, the horizontal format (2.50 x 1.25 metres) of these elements visually reduces the considerable height of the building (17 metres). On the south side of the hall, the glazed skin is

dieser Elemente (2,5 x 1,25 Meter) die nicht unbeträchtliche Gebäudehöhe von 17 Metern optisch zu vermindern hilft. Auf der Südseite der Halle wird die gläserne Fassadenhaut zusätzlich durch feststehende, vorgesetzte Sonnenschutzlamellen filigran gegliedert: Es entsteht eine zweite Schicht.

Die Auflagerzonen der Dachkonstruktion sind in der Fassade durch opake, transluzente Glaselemente abgebildet; besonders die Eckbereiche werden dadurch gestalterisch gefestigt und prägnant. Da aber die Auflagerkerne nicht die ganze Fassadenhöhe beanspruchen, umläuft die Glasfassade die Gebäudeecken in schwebender Leichtigkeit.

Die spannungsvolle Dialektik dieser eher ungewöhnlichen Ecklösung bleibt bemerkenswert, ebenso wie die – mit Ausnahme der abgeblendeten Südfassade – gläserne Offenheit der Halle, welche die gesamte Konstruktion und deren Logik verständlich werden läßt. Neben der schmalseitigen Eingangsfront verspricht besonders die zur Allee der Vereinigten Bäume orientierte Nordseite der Halle ein höchst attraktives »Schaufenster« zu werden.

Der Konzeption der Gebäudetechnik entstammen die auf dem Hallendach im Bereich der Kerne installierten Venturi-Flügel. Durch den beständigen Hannoverschen Westwind wird hier ein Unterdruck erzeugt, der die verbrauchte Hallenluft über die Fluchttunnel und Abluftkanäle an den Fassaden absaugt und über das Dach führt. Diese eleganten, technogenen Objekte – als Aufbauten mag man sie gar nicht bezeichnen – akzentuieren das Gebäude zusätzlich und erzeugen seine charakteristische Fernwirkung.

Im Inneren der Halle verspürt man eine ganz eigenartige, inspirierende Atmosphäre. Sie verdankt sich vor allem den unterschiedlichen Dimensionen der massiven Auflagerblöcke aus Beton und dem wiederum fast filigran zu nennenden offenen Stahlträgerrost der Decke. Sechs dreigeschossige Kerne mit je 15 x 15 Metern Grundfläche, welche auch die Servicebereiche enthalten, nehmen das Dachtragwerk auf. Es besteht aus einem Trägerrost mit Systemachsen von 7,5 x 7,5 Metern und einer Systemhöhe von 4,5 Metern. Ober- und Untergurte, Druckstäbe und Zugdiagonalen sind als Stahlrundrohre mit Gußknoten verbunden. Zusätzlich zu den Kernen liegt der Trägerrost im Randbereich auf vertikalen, druck- und zugbeanspruchten Stahlrundrohren im Abstand von 7,5 Metern. Mit diesen Fassadenrohren ist die selbsttragende Fassade punktuell verbunden. Sie besteht aus thermisch getrennten Stahlprofilen mit Isolierverglasung. Vorgefertigte Holzkassettenelemente bilden die Dachdecke (Aufbau: Mineralwolledämmung, Dampfsperre, UV-beständige Folie).

Louis Kahn sagte einmal: »Architektur ist es dann, wenn man sieht, wie es gemacht ist.« Das strenge, geometrisch konstruierte, nach Kraftfluß dimensionierte Tragwerk ist hier ebenso deutlich lesbar wie die Ortbetonwände der Kerne mit ihren typischen, durch Zufall schönen Schütt-Ornamenten. Auch sie zeigen dem Besucher, »wie es gemacht ist.«

Autor: Dietmar Brandenburger; er ist Architekt und Architekturkritiker.

further articulated by a finely dimensioned outer layer of fixed, projecting sunscreen louvres.

The supporting zones for the roof structure are marked in the façade by translucent glass elements. As a result, the corner areas in particular stand out through the impression of solidity they convey. Since the structural cores do not extend over the full height of the façade, however, the transparent glass skin continues round the corners of the building at the top, lending the structure a sense of hovering lightness.

The exciting dialectic of this unusual corner solution is one of the striking features of the building, as is the open quality of the glazed hall as a whole (with the exception of the south face), which allows the entire structure and logic of the system to be comprehended. In addition to the narrower entrance front, the north face of the hall – oriented to the United Trees Avenue – promises to become a most attractive »shop window«.

The Venturi structures over the cores on the hall roof form part of the overall concept for the service installations. The prevailing wind in Hanover is from the west. When wind flows around the Venturi elements, a vacuum is created that sucks exhaust air out of the hall. The air is drawn, via the escape tunnels and ventilation ducts in the facades, up to roof level where it is extracted. These elegant, aerodynamic objects, which bear no comparison to conventional roof structures, accentuate the building and give it its distinctive appearance when viewed from a distance.

Inside the hall, visitors experience a unique and stimulating atmosphere. This is attributable in the first instance to the dimensional contrast between the massive, block-like concrete supporting cores and the almost filigree-like open grid of steel girders forming the roof structure. The six three-storey cores are 15 x 15 metres on plan. In addition to bearing the loads of the roof, they also accommodate the mechanical services for the hall. The roof consists of a steel girder grid laid out to a structural module of 7.5 x 7.5 metres and with a system height of 4.5 metres. The tubular steel upper and lower chords, compression members and diagonal tension members are jointed with cast node elements. Along the edges of the hall, the roof is also supported by vertical tubular steel columns in addition to the cores. Laid out at 7.5-metre centres, the columns are subject to both compression and tension loads. They also serve as a means of stabilizing the self-supporting façade construction, which is point fixed to them. The façade consists of thermally divided steel sections with double glazing. The roof is covered with prefabricated timber coffer elements, which include mineral-wool insulation, a vapour barrier and a UV-resistent membrane.

Louis Kahn once said that architecture comes about when one can see how it is made. The construction of the hall is clearly legible both in the strict, geometrically designed load-bearing roof grid, dimensioned according to the flow of forces in the members, and in the in-situ concrete walls of the cores. The latter are attractively ornamented with the typical random patterns resulting from the casting and formwork. In this way, the hall also shows the visitor »how it is made«.

Author: Dietmar Brandenburger; he is an architect and architectural critic.

Halle 14: Zurückhaltung und Inspiration
Hall 14: Restraint and Inspiration

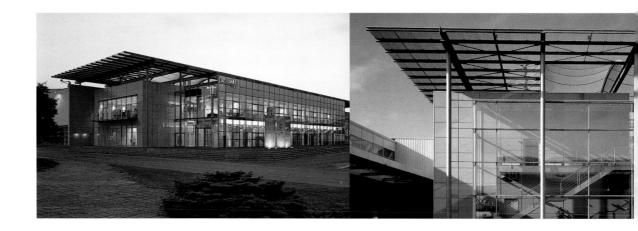

Das Gebäude bildet die Fortsetzung des bereits bestehenden Ensembles mit den Hallen 15, 16 und 17 und schiebt sich – von Norden kommend – als eine Art »Kopfbau« an die Allee der Vereinigten Bäume heran. Damit erhält die neue Halle eine wichtige städtebauliche Funktion zwischen dem Expo-See im Westen und dem Vorbereich am Tagungszentrum (TCM) im Osten; beide Freibereiche werden durch die Verengung, die die Halle 14 an der Allee erzeugt, spannungsvoll herausgearbeitet. Hinzu kommt, daß ihre Westfassade im direkten optischen »Zielbereich« der von der Expo-Plaza heranströmenden Besucher liegt und sie damit eine zusätzliche wichtige Orientierungsfunktion übernimmt. Auch von der Seilbahn, die während der EXPO 2000 in 40 Metern Höhe das Gelände quert und direkt am Gebäude vorbeiführt, wird man – neben seiner ungewöhnlichen Konstruktion – auch die Prominenz seiner Lage erkennen. Besonders auffallen wird dabei der Übergang zwischen den Hallen, der sich als eine passagenartige, hohe gläserne Fuge zeigt.

Das Gebäude umfaßt eine Fläche von circa 11.000 Quadratmetern; die Südfassade hat eine Länge von 170 Metern, die stützenfreie Spannweite verringert sich infolge der Trapezform des Baukörpers von 70 Metern im Westen bis auf 50 Meter im Osten. Ein »Haus-im-Haus«-Effekt entsteht zusätzlich durch die Überspannung der bereits vorhandenen Fernmeldezentrale (MFA) der Messe Hannover. Um dieses Gebäude herum, also im Inneren der Halle, gruppieren sich ein Restaurant im Osten, im Süden und Westen befinden sich Büro- und Ladenflächen.

Das architektonisch-konstruktive Hauptmerkmal des Gebäudes bezeichnet den Übergang zwischen altem und neuem Hallenraum: die gläserne Passage, die von beiden Seiten gleichzeitig und formal unübersehbar Haupteingänge ausbildet. Die Idee, dieses Thema im Zwischenbereich aufzugreifen, kann als gelungen bezeichnet werden, und

The building forms the continuation of an existing ensemble, consisting of Halls 15, 16 and 17. To visitors approaching from the north, Hall 14 appears as a salient structure facing on to the United Trees Avenue. Situated between the Expo Lake to the west and the approach area to the Congress Centre (TCM) to the east, the new hall thus fulfils an important urban function. Both open areas are excitingly articulated through the constriction Hall 14 causes in the avenue at this point. In addition, the west façade of the hall lies in the direct line of view of visitors coming from the Expo-Plaza, thereby serving as a point of orientation as well. From the cable cars that will traverse the site at a height of 40 metres during the EXPO 2000 - travelling immediately past this building - visitors will become aware of the hall's prominent location and its unusual form of construction. A specially striking feature will be the transition between the halls in the form of a tall arcade-like glazed seam.

The building covers an area of roughly 11,000 square metres. Its south face is 170 metres long. As a result of the trapezoidal shape of the hall, the column-free span diminishes from 70 metres at the western end to 50 metres at the eastern end. A »house within a house« effect is created by the fact that the new structure spans the Hanover Fair telecommunications centre (MFA). Laid out around this building in the interior of the hall are a restaurant to the east and offices and shops to the south and west.

The main architectural and constructional feature of the building is the transition between the old and new hall space in the form of a glass arcade, which introduces formally conspicuous main entrances on both sides. The concept of adopting this theme in the intermediate zone may be regarded as a most successful idea - and not only because it repeats an element that occurs twice in the northern parts of the building.

In structural terms, the old hall is hung on to - one might say, hooked

dies nicht nur, weil es in nördlichen Gebäudeteilen bereits zweimal durchgespielt wurde.

Konstruktiv betrachtet, hängt sich die alte Halle an die neue an, oder – auch so kann man es sehen – die neue nimmt die alte an den Haken: Die Außenstützen der Halle 15 wurden entfernt und der alte Hallenrand wurde über ein Zugpendel an den kranartigen Stützen des neuentstandenen Gebäudes aufgehängt.

Diese Reihe von »Kranstützen«, die im Winkel von circa 45 Grad nach oben streben, erzeugen in der 8 Meter breiten Passage zusammen mit ihrer fast völligen Durchlichtung ein äußerst dynamisches Innenleben. Die Leichtigkeit, auch Eleganz dieser konstruktiven Lösung wird unterstützt durch die »Entschwerung« des himmelwärts strebenden Stützenkragarms: Mit Hilfe von Aussparungen werden hier die Kraftflüsse verdeutlicht.

Die sich daran anschließende, auf Konsolen gelegte Tragkonstruktion der neuen Halle besteht aus unterspannten Stahl-Kastenträgern, darüber Stahlpfetten und aufliegenden Trapezblechen; die Last der Dachbinder an der Südseite nehmen Stahl-Pendelstützen auf. Der Binderabstand von 15 Metern bezieht sich auf den im Altgebäude vorhandenen, erzeugt so, über die Passage hinweg, eine gewisse »Durchlaufwirkung«.

Seitenfassaden und Südfassade sind konstruktiv wie gestalterisch unterschiedlich durchgebildet. Die der Allee zugewandte Südfassade wirkt in ihrer Filigranität fast urban; sie besteht aus einer kittlosen Isolierverglasung mit thermisch getrennten Profilen. Aus dem Dach springt ein ausladender, feststehender Lamellen-Sonnenschutz hervor, in den unteren Fassadenbereichen findet man bedrucktes Glas. Die Seitenfassaden sind zu den jeweiligen Außenbereichen kräftig aufgefächert, auch um blendfreies Nordlicht einzufangen. Hier sind der Tragkonstruktion großflächige, wärmegedämmte Fassadenplatten aus Aluminium im Wechsel mit horizontal strukturierten Glasschlitzen vorgesetzt.

Angenehm wirkt eine umlaufende, circa 2,5 Meter hohe gläserne Sockelzone, die den Maßstab der die Halle ansteuernden Besucher direkt anspricht und auch auf die umgebenden Freibereiche hinauswirkt.

Die Halle 14 gehört eher zu den kleineren Hallen auf dem Gelände; ihre Tragwerkskonstruktion ist im Gegensatz zu angrenzenden Hallen wenig spektakulär, eher zurückhaltend, mit Ausnahme der wirklich inspirierenden »Passage«. Und dennoch, trotz ihrer in einen großen Hallenkomplex eingebundenen Lage und ihrer Funktion als dessen Kopfbau, vermag sie eine eigenständige, sogar autonome gestalterische Aussage zu formulieren. Hinzu kommt ihre wichtige städtebauliche Aufgabe im Rahmen der sie umgebenden Freiräume und der Allee der Vereinigten Bäume.

Autor: Dietmar Brandenburger; er ist Architekt und Architekturkritiker.

up by - the new one: the outer columns of Hall 15 were removed, and the edge of the old hall was suspended by means of a hinged tension member from the crane-like columns of the new building.

This row of raking columns, inclined at an angle of roughly 45 degrees, results in an extremely dynamic interior in the 8-metres-wide arcade, which allows an ample amount of light to enter the hall. The feeling of lightness, the elegance of this structural solution, is accentuated by relieving the cantilevered column arms of any sense of weight as they aspire upwards towards the sky. Openings in the structural members indicate the flow of forces.

The load-bearing structure of the new hall adjoining this consists of steel box girders trussed on the underside and supported on brackets, with steel purlins on top covered with trapezoidal-section ribbed metal sheeting. The loads of the roof girders along the southern edge are borne by hinged steel columns. The spacing of the girders - at 15-metre centres - is related to that in the existing building, so that a certain continuity is established across the arcade.

The side and south façades are treated in different ways in respect of their construction and their design. The south face overlooking the avenue has a filigree composition that radiates an almost urbane quality. It consists of dry-fixed double glazing in thermally divided supporting members. A broad sunscreen canopy of fixed louvre elements, is raised above the roof and projects out at the sides. In the lower zones of the façade, printed glass was also used. The side faces of the hall are splayed out in a fan-like form to allow non-glare north light to enter the building. At these points, large thermally insulated aluminium façade panels are set on the outside of the load-bearing structure, alternating with horizontally articulated strips of glass.

The roughly 2.5-metre-high continuous glazed plinth zone is a feature that is pleasantly related to the scale of visitors approaching the hall and to the surrounding external spaces.

Hall 14 is one of the smaller halls on the site. The load-bearing structure is relatively restrained and less spectacular in design than those in the adjoining halls. The only exception to this is the truly inspiring arcade. In spite of the location of the building, integrated into a large ensemble of halls in which it forms the salient structure, it has an independent, even autonomous design identity. What is more, it plays an important urban role in the context of the surrounding open spaces and the United Trees Avenue.

Author: Dietmar Brandenburger; he is an architect and architectural critic.

Halle 12: Integration und Komposition
Hall 12: Integration and Composition

Die meisten Besucher der EXPO 2000 werden am Eingang West erwartet, täglich circa 90.000 Personen innerhalb von sechs Stunden. Die Halle 12 befindet sich ganz in der Nähe dieses Eingangs in exponierter Lage: unmittelbar an der Allee der Vereinigten Bäume, aber auch darüber hinaus direkt am Expo-See, einem der zentralen Plätze für Veranstaltungen (zum Beispiel wird dort jeden Abend das sogenannte Flambee stattfinden, eine internationale Feuerwerk-Show); das Gebäude bildet mit seiner Nordfassade gewissermaßen die südliche Platzwand.

Die Bauaufgabe war für die Architekten eher ungewöhnlich und verlangte – unter Zeitdruck und laufendem Messebetrieb – eine intelligente, einfache Lösung: Gefordert war die »Erweiterung einer bestehenden Messehalle auf das Dreifache ihrer ursprünglichen Größe«, mithin vorhandene 10.000 Quadratmeter um circa 17.000 Quadratmeter zu ergänzen. »Aus alt mach neu«, so beschrieben die Architekten ihren Ansatz, der aber über die Komplexität des Vorhabens eigentlich wenig aussagt. Aus der Lage der bestehenden Halle und der Vorstellung von seiten der Messe und der EXPO 2000, eine einheitliche Hallenfront an der Allee der Vereinigten Bäume zu erhalten, ergab sich der Zwang, die alte Halle nach beiden Seiten erweitern zu müssen, und dies in nur neun Monaten!

»Der architektonische Reiz der Aufgabe lag darin, für die neuen Hallenteile ein Konstruktionssystem zu finden, das zusammen mit dem Tragwerk der alten Halle eine technische und gestalterische Einheit bildet«, so die selbstformulierte Vorgabe der Architekten.

Die Integration der drei Hallenteile fand in mehreren baulich-konstruktiven Schritten statt:
– Das neue Primärtragwerk wurde von beiden Seiten an die bestehende Halle herangeführt; dieses Primärtragwerk besteht aus stählernen Dreigurtträgern auf stählernen Rundstützen.

Most visitors to the EXPO 2000 - roughly 90,000 persons a day within a period of six hours - are expected to arrive at the western entrance of the site. Occupying a prominent position close to this entrance, Hall 12 is also situated on the United Trees Avenue and immediately next to the Expo Lake, which is a central location for various events. Every evening, for example, an international firework display, the so-called »flambee«, will take place there. The north face of the building forms the southern enclosing wall to this space in a sense.

The design brief was an unusual one for the architects. Subject to time pressures and ongoing trade fair operations, they were required to find an intelligent yet simple solution for »the enlargement of an existing trade fair hall to three times its original size«: the addition of 17,000 square metres to the existing 10,000 square metres. »Making something new out of something old« was the way the architects described their approach, although this reveals little of the complexity of the task. In view of the position of the existing hall and the wishes of the Hanover Fair and EXPO 2000 organizers to ensure a uniform front along the United Trees Avenue, there was no alternative but to extend the old hall on both sides - and within a period of only nine months!

»The architectural attraction of the project lay in finding a structural system for the new sections of the hall that, in conjunction with the load-bearing structure of the old building, would form a technical and formal unity.« That was how the architects formulated their concept.

The integration of the three sections of the hall took place in a number of constructional steps:
– The new primary structure, consisting of triangular steel girders and round steel columns, was erected on both sides of the existing hall. The architects refer to the pairs of columns as »pylons«.

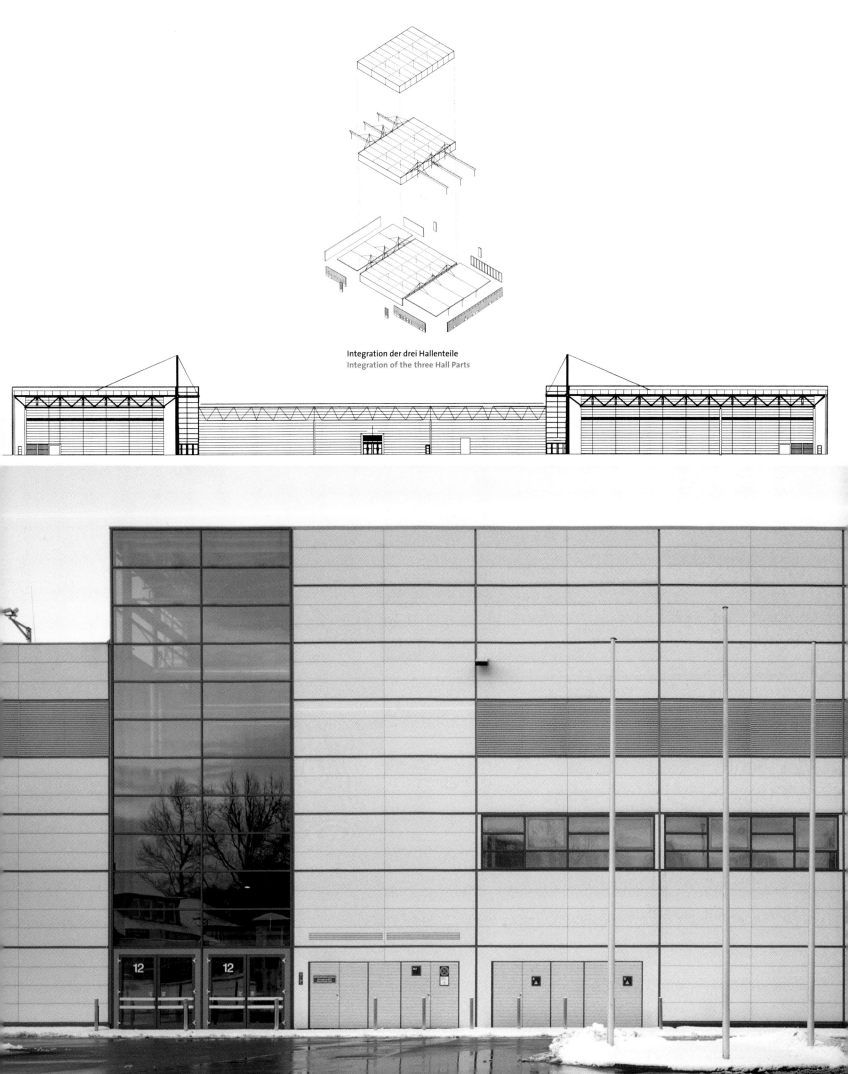

Integration der drei Hallenteile
Integration of the three Hall Parts

– Die dem alten Gebäude – mit Abstand – am nächsten zur Seite stehende Rundstützenreihe (die Stützenpaare werden von den Architekten Pylone genannt) übernimmt mehrere statische Aufgaben:

– Durch eine Zugseilkonstruktion werden die Binder der alten Halle mit den Dreigurtträgern der neuen Anbauten elegant verbunden.

– Nach Beseitigung der Seitenfassaden mit ihren Stützen »hängt« die alte Konstruktion beidseitig in der neuen.

– Das »hängende« Gewicht entlastet die Tragwerke der beiden neuen Hallenteile und gestattet eine Minimierung der Höhen der Dreigurtbinder.

Die operativen Zonen dieser beidseitigen Anbauten sind als breite gläserne Zäsuren in der Fassade ablesbar; da die Zubauten höher sind als die alte Halle, ergibt sich so ein recht spannungsvoller Verlauf der Längsfassaden.

Neue Wege wurden bei der Konstruktion des Sekundärtragwerks begangen: Holzkastenträger (2 Meter breit, 1 Meter hoch) aus Brettschichtbindern und Multiplex-Platten. Diese Träger sind multifunktional; ihre Spannweite beträgt 30 Meter, sie enthalten im Inneren die Dachentwässerung, die Elektroinstallationen sowie die Belüftungskanäle. Außerdem gestatten ihre Querschnittsdimensionen problemlose Revisionen und Reparaturen. Die eng aneinanderliegenden, weiß lasierten Holzkästen bewirken eine glatte Deckenuntersicht, die Tragwirkung der darunter verlaufenden Dreigurtbinder wird so herausgearbeitet und erläutert.

In der Fassade werden die alte Halle und die beiden Anbauten durch einen gemeinsamen Modul zusammengebunden: Eine gestalterische Einheit, die Großhalle, entsteht. Der Vorgang der Zusammenfügung dreier Baukörper wird nur durch die beiden breiten gläsernen »Fugen« erinnerlich, und dies auch nur den Eingeweihten.

Das Kleinmodul von jeweils sechs Blechpaneelen mit den Abmessungen 3 x 0,6 Meter addiert sich – strukturiert durch die Fassadenpfosten – zu einem Großmodul von 6 x 1,8 Metern. Das Großmodul wird auch in den Bereichen der Glasfassade fortgeführt, die horizontale Teilung allerdings durch eine zurückhaltende Vertikalstruktur ersetzt. Die Sockelzone der Halle weicht – ohne die gestalterische Grundstruktur zu verlassen – von der Grundmodulierung ab, hier mußten Hubtore, Türen und Eingänge eingebaut werden. Die gläsernen »Fugen« integrieren sich in dieses Fassadenspiel mit einem eigenen, allerdings kompatiblen Modul, sie zeigen so ihre Sonderstellung.

Ähnlich wie schon bei der Halle 14 mußten sich die Architekten auch hier mit vorhandener Bausubstanz auseinandersetzen. Auch ihnen ist es gelungen, über ein sehr differenziertes statisches System zu einer architektonischen Gesamtaussage zu gelangen: Eine neue Großhalle (210 x 120 Meter) ist so entstanden, das »Missing link« ist eingepaßt, die Enfilade der Hallen an der Allee der Vereinigten Bäume komplettiert.

Das Äußere des Gebäudes machte den Synthese-Vorgang der Bauaufgabe kaum deutlich: Die neue Halle wirkt komponiert; auch die von weitem sichtbaren Abspannungen, die das Dach durchstoßen, verraten nicht ihre Nachträglichkeit, die modulierte »Verpackung« zieht ohnehin zur Einheit zusammen. Das Gebäude gibt sich eher zurückhaltend und unangestrengt, bei den vielen Aufgeregtheiten ringsum ein eher angenehmer Zug. Beim Durchschreiten des Inneren werden sich (möglicherweise) Fragen einstellen nach der so differenzierten Raumstruktur; die Antwort, daß diese großformatige Halle das Ergebnis zweier Zubauten ist, wird vielleicht dann nicht überraschen.

Autor: Dietmar Brandenburger; er ist Architekt und Architekturkritiker.

– The rows of columns closest to the existing building - though set back slightly from the edge - have a number of structural functions.

– The trusses in the existing hall are elegantly linked with the triangular girders of the extensions by a tension cable construction.

– After the side faces and their supporting columns had been removed from the existing hall, the old structure was suspended on both edges from the new.

– The suspended weight relieves the structures of both new sections of the hall of some of their loading and thus allowed the depths of the triangular trusses to be kept to a minimum.

The structurally operative zones of these two side extensions are legible in the façade in the form of broad glazed dividing strips. The long faces of the hall are enlivened by the fact that the new sections of the building are higher than the existing structure.

New paths were explored in the design of the secondary load-bearing structure. An example of this may be found in the timber box girders, which span a distance of 30 metres. These multifunctional elements, two metres wide and one metre high, are constructed of laminated timber beams and multiplex sheets. Housed within these hollow girders are the roof drainage system, the electrical installation and the ventilation ducts. In addition, the dimensions of the hollow cross-sections facilitate inspection and maintenance. The closely spaced white-varnished timber box girders lend the soffit a smooth appearance that helps to set off the triangular girders beneath and clarify their structural effect.

The old hall and the two extension tracts are united into a single large-scale hall by the use of a common modular dimension in the façades. The integration of the three volumes of the building into a unified whole is indicated solely by the two broad glazed »joints« - and even then, only to those aware of the history of the project.

The smaller modular units, consisting of groups of six sheet metal panels with dimensions of 3.0 x 0.6 metres - structured by the façade posts - form a larger modular unit 6.0 x 1.8 metres in size. The larger module is continued in the glazed areas of the façade, where the horizontal divisions are replaced by a restrained vertical structuring. The plinth zone of the hall deviates from this basic modular layout, but without abandoning the overall design concept. At this level, it was necessary to incorporate lifting gates, doors and entrance openings. The glazed vertical strips - the «joints» between the sections - have their own compatible modular dimensions and are integrated into the rhythm of the facade elements, yet in a way that demonstrates their special function.

Here, as in Hall 14, the architects had to come to terms with an existing building. They, too, succeeded in achieving a unified overall architectural statement by using a sophisticated structural system. The outcome is a new large-scale hall 210 x 120 metres on plan. It is the missing link that closes the gap in the chain of halls along the United Trees Avenue.

The exterior of the building scarcely reveals the process of synthesis underlying this project. The new hall seems to form a single entity. Even the stay members projecting through the roof and visible from afar, do not betray the fact that they were a later addition to a building already existing in part. The modular outer skin «wraps» everything together into a unified whole. The building appears pleasingly calm, restrained and unlaboured among all the excitement and activity going on around it. Questions may arise concerning the varied nature of the internal spaces. In that case, the reply that this large hall came about through the addition of two extension structures will not be surprising.

Author: Dietmar Brandenburger; he is an architect and architectural critic.

Halle 8/9: Ästhetik und Dauerhaftigkeit

Halls 8/9: Aesthetics and Permanence

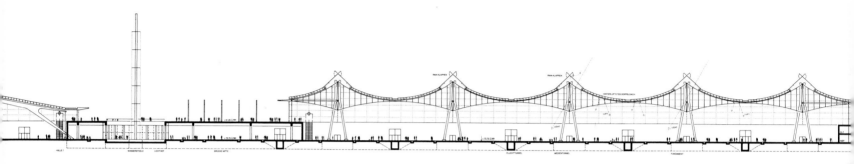

Wenn der künftige Expo-Besucher, von der One-World-Plaza kommend, das Pavillongelände West ansteuert, muß er den dazwischenliegenden sogenannten Messeschnellweg überqueren. Er wird dies über eine 130 Meter lange und 30 Meter breite Stahlbrücke tun, die von 170 im Raster eingesetzten Stahlstelen rhythmisiert ist; noch bevor er die andere Seite erreicht, wird ihm ein langgestrecktes Gebäude mit wellenförmigem Dachprofil auffallen. Die Halle 9, die er dann erreicht, hat die schönste Lage auf dem Expo-Gelände: Sie hat eine ganz wichtige Torwirkung. Die Halle 8 sucht man hier vergebens; sie befindet sich im Basement des Brückenkopfes, und der Besucher, der bis hierher gelangt ist, steht sozusagen auf ihrem Dach. Von hier oben, 8,7 Meter über dem Bodenniveau, hat man einen großzügigen Panoramablick über das Westgelände und in die hier anlandende Allee der Vereinigten Bäume.

Schon im Wettbewerb 1997 erwies sich dieser Entwurf, der Tragwerk-Raffinesse und städtebauliches Denken so einleuchtend miteinander zu verbinden wußte, als die mit Abstand beste Lösung. Eine zusätzliche, innenräumlich höchst wirksame Besonderheit findet sich in der Halle 9: Das Dachplateau der Halle 8, der bereits erwähnte Brückenkopf, läuft niveaugleich in die große Halle hinein und – mit Ausnahme der Westseite – als »Galerie« an ihren Innenwänden entlang, bevor diese mit Treppen und Fahrtreppen in das untere Hallengeschoß einmündet: ein fast szenografischer Einfall und Effekt! Der »Hallenhimmel« mit seinen dem Besucher entgegendrängenden konvexen Ausformungen evoziert eine durchaus heitere, fast circensische Stimmung; manchem eher nüchternen Ausstellungsereignis wird ein solches »Flair« sicherlich willkommen sein.

Die Abmessungen beider Hallen sind beeindruckend (Halle 8 umfaßt 100 x 120 Meter, Halle 9 sogar 137 x 240 Meter). Die gemeinsame Ausstellungsfläche beträgt 31.000 Quadratmeter; die Halle 9, die – man hat es errechnet – 3,5

Visitors to the future EXPO 2000, approaching from the One World Plaza and heading in the direction of the western pavilion, will have to cross the expressway of the fair, which lies between the two. They will do so via a 130-metre-long and 30-metre-wide steel bridge, articulated by 170 rhythmically spaced steel stelae. Before reaching the other side of the bridge, visitors will see an elongated structure with a wave-like roof. Hall 9 enjoys the finest position on the Expo site and has an important gateway function. Hall 8, in contrast, may be sought in vain. It is located in the basement of the bridgehead, so that the visitor is actually standing on its roof at this point. From this elevated position, 8.70 metres above ground level, there is a magnificent panoramic view over the western area of the fair site and along the United Trees Avenue, which ends here.

In the competition held in 1997, this scheme provided by far the best solution for the situation. The design was distinguished by the cogent way it combined structural refinement with urban concepts. A further highly effective feature can be found in the interior of Hall 9. The plateau formed by the roof of Hall 8 - the bridgehead mentioned above - continues into the large hall at the same level and runs round the walls, with the exception of the west side, in the form of a gallery, before descending via stairs and escalators to the lower hall level. The idea and the effect achieved is almost scenographic. The »sky« over the hall, with its convex curves billowing down towards the visitor, evokes a happy, almost circus-like atmosphere that will certainly provide a welcome relief to some of the more sober events to be held here.

The dimensions of both halls are impressive: Hall 8 is 100 x 120 metres in extent; Hall 9 is even larger at 137 x 240 metres. Together they offer an exhibition area of 31,000 square metres. Hall 9, which could accommodate

three and a half football fields, is thus the largest free-spanning trade fair hall in Europe.

The two halls are based on quite different structural principles. Hall 8, with a clear height of 6.7 metres, is articulated by a grid of reinforced concrete columns at 15-metre centres in both directions. These support a barrel-vaulted concrete roof with downstand beams. Fixed to the underside are plywood »soffit sails«. In contrast to this solid form of construction, Hall 9 has a suspended roof with extremely large spans and a clear height of 12.5 metres to the underside of the supporting structure.

The primary load-bearing structure in steel is based on the principle of a suspension bridge. Five main beams at 45-metre centres are supported along the inside edges of the hall by pairs of masts and stabilized along the principal bearing side by tension cable stays anchored in external foundations.

Sheet metal and cable trusses at 15-metre centres across the width of the hall function as secondary girders. These support the timber roof, which consists of load-bearing timber box sections. The box beams are

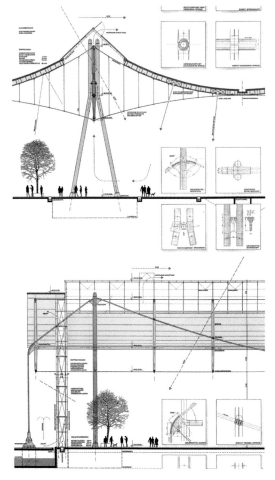

Schema des konstruktiven Systems
Scheme of the Constructive System

Fußballfelder aufnehmen könnte, ist damit die größte freitragende Messehalle Europas.

Die Konstruktionsprinzipien beider Hallen unterscheiden sich grundsätzlich. Die Halle 8 mit einer lichten Höhe von 6,7 Metern wird von Stahlbetonstützen im Raster von 15 x 15 Metern strukturiert; sie tragen eine tonnengewölbeartige Unterzugsbetondecke, an der sogenannte Sperrholz-Deckensegel befestigt sind. Solcher Massivbauweise steht die über extreme Spannweiten freitragende Konstruktion der Halle 9 mit einer lichten Höhe von 12,5 Metern (unterhalb der Tragkonstruktion) entgegen.

Das stählerne Haupttragwerk verwendet das Prinzip der Hängebrücke: Fünf Hauptträger im Abstand von 45 Metern werden in den jeweiligen innenseitigen Randbereichen der Halle von Zwillingsstützenmasten aufgenommen und über eine Rückverankerung der Haupttragseite in außenliegenden Zugseilfundamenten stabilisiert.

Eine dazu über die Breite der Halle im Abstand von 15 Metern verlaufende Blech-Seil-Binderkonstruktion als Nebenträger nimmt die Holzdecken aus tragenden, hölzernen Kastenquerschnitten auf. Diese Kästen sind untereinander gelenkig verbunden, so daß die Bewegungen des Hängedachs aufgenommen und kompensiert werden können. In der Holzkastenkonstruktion finden sich die Installationen der Raumlufttechnik, der Beleuchtung, Elektrotechnik, Kommunikations- und Brandmeldetechnik. Die Fassade der Halle 8 ist als Sandwichbauweise ausgebildet (Stahlbeton-Fertigteilelemente, tragende Schale, Wärmedämmung, Sichtbetonschale), die der Halle 9 als stählerne, thermisch getrennte Pfosten-Riegel-Konstruktion.

Fast über die gesamte Gebäudebreite tragen die jeweiligen »Wellenfirste« Glasoberlichter mit Entlüftungsklappen. Die weitere Dachkonstruktion

besteht aus einer Folieneindeckung auf einer Wärmedämmung und Dampfsperre.

Im Süden der Halle wird sich während der EXPO 2000 das International
Broadcasting Centre (IBC) etablieren und Fernseh- und Hörfunk betreiben;
auch ARD und ZDF werden von hier aus auf einer Fläche von circa 500 Quadratmetern berichten.

Die Architektur deutscher Messehallen ist in der Nachkriegszeit oft
nicht als »weicher« Standortfaktor begriffen worden. Erst in jüngerer Zeit
sind Begriffe wie räumliche Anmutung, konstruktive Eleganz und designeri-
sche Durchformung ins Bewußtsein gelangt. Gerade weil die bauliche Nachhaltigkeit derzeit so oft und laut gefordert wird und die »Schönheit des
Nichtdauerhaften« (Bergius) nicht mehr aufrechtzuerhalten sein wird, muß
sich die »Schönheit des Dauerhaften« erweisen, auch im Ausstellungsbau.
Zumindest die Halle 9 geht hier weit über die bloße Erfüllung funktionaler
Anforderungen hinaus: Ökologisch bestimmte Materialwahl, Energiespar-
konzepte, aber auch architektonisch formale Qualitäten machen sie anre-
gend und deswegen wichtig. Wenn die EXPO 2000 sie zur Spielstätte für
den Themenpark vorgeschlagen hat, dann auch aufgrund ihrer architektonischen Aussage: Unbeschwertheit, Heiterkeit, Einprägsamkeit. Hier wird man
dann etwas über das 21. Jahrhundert erfahren, über Entwicklungen der
Städte Shanghai, Sao Paulo, Dakar, Aachen.

Autor: Dietmar Brandenburger; er ist Architekt und Architekturkritiker.

flexibly fixed to each other to absorb and balance out any movement in
the suspended roof. Various service installations are accommodated in the
timber box sections, including air-conditioning, lighting, electrical, communications and fire-alarm technology. The façade to Hall 8 is in a sandwich
form of construction with precast concrete elements, comprising thermal
insulation between a load-bearing skin and an exposed concrete facing
skin. The façade to Hall 9 is in a thermally divided steel post-and-rail construction. Glass skylights with ventilation flaps were installed along the
crests of the roof »waves« over almost the entire width of the building.
The roof covering consists of a sheet membrane on thermal insulation and
a vapour barrier.

During the EXPO 2000, the southern part of the hall will house the
International Broadcasting Centre (IBC), which will be responsible for both
television and radio transmissions. The two German public TV channels,
ARD and ZDF, will also have a transmission area of roughly 500 square
metres here.

For a long time in the post-war period, the architecture of German
trade fair halls reflected mainly »hard« functional requirements. Only in
recent times has an awareness of so-called »soft« factors manifested itself
- qualities such as »spatial atmosphere«, »structural elegance« and a »fully
articulated design«. Since ecological sustainability is so much in demand in
construction nowadays and so vociferously advocated, the »beauty of tran-
sient things« (Bergius) has almost disappeared, especially in exhibition
buildings. A new beauty has to be sought, therefore, in permanence. Hall 9,
at least, goes much further than simply fulfilling functional needs. The
choice of materials based on ecological considerations, the energy-saving
concepts implemented in its construction, and the formal qualities of its
architecture make this an exciting and important building. If the EXPO
2000 has proposed it as the venue for various events within the theme
park, that is certainly because of its architectural expression of lightness
and serenity and its memorable form. Here, it will be possible to learn
something about the 21st century - and about developments in the cities of
Shanghai, Sao Paulo, Dakar and Aachen.

Author: Dietmar Brandenburger; he is an architect and architectural critic.

Landschaftsarchitekten/Landscape architects: Kienast, Vogt und Partner

Natur und Gestalt:
Freianlagen von Messe und EXPO 2000

Nature and Form:
External Areas of the Trade Fair and Expo Site

Als ordnende Elemente greifen die Grünräume in die unüberschaubare Struktur des Messegeländes ein, sie bilden, ähnlich der Struktur einer modernen amerikanischen Stadt, ein orthogonales Rastersystem, das eine leichte Orientierung ermöglicht. Von West nach Ost verläuft die Allee der Vereinigten Bäume. Sie bildet das Rückgrat des Freiraumkonzepts und verbindet zwei Haupteingänge der Weltausstellung, während die Nordallee einige 100 Meter weiter nördlich vom Erdgarten zum IC-Gebäude im schon bestehenden Grünraum führt.

Durch die unregelmäßigen Pflanzabstände entstehen wechselhafte Raumsequenzen. Sichtbar die Aufenthaltsqualität betonend, erweisen sie sich als Antipode einer regelmäßigen barocken Allee. Die Artenvielfalt der Baumbepflanzung und das unmittelbare Nebeneinander von einheimischen und fremdländischen Baumarten verweisen auf die EXPO 2000 und die Messe als internationale Ereignisse, können aber auch als Metapher für das friedliche Miteinander unterschiedlichster Menschen interpretiert werden.

Rechtwinklig zu den Alleen verlaufen die Parkwelle und der Erdgarten, erstere anscheinend Ausschnitt aus einem großen Landschaftsgarten und von ihrer Grundthematik her nach außen orientiert, letzterer ein in sich abgeschlossener Raum, eine Insel der Ruhe inmitten der Betriebsamkeit von Messe und EXPO 2000, durch Topografie, Bepflanzung, Bodenbeläge und in den Boden eingelassene Schriften auf den Garten als alle Sinne ansprechendes Paradies verweisend.

Der Expo-See, der mit seiner großen und kleinen Wasserfläche im Gegensatz zur Dynamik der langgezogenen Räume Ruhe ausstrahlt und Weite schafft, bildet entlang der Allee der Vereinigten Bäume das Zentrum des Expo-Westgeländes.

Als Grünräume zwischen alten und neuen Messehallen sind die ver-

The landscaped spaces function as ordering elements in the complex layout of the trade fair and Expo site. Like the structure of a modern American city, they follow an orthogonal grid that facilitates easy orientation. The United Trees Avenue runs from west to east, forming the spine of the concept for the external spaces and linking two of the main entrances to the World Exposition. A few hundred metres further north, the North Avenue runs from the Earth Garden to the IC building in the existing landscaped open space.

The irregular layout of the plantings results in a varied sequence of spaces. In view of the visible emphasis placed on leisure qualities, the planting programme at this point is the very opposite of a regular, symmetrical Baroque avenue. The great variety of trees and the juxtaposition of native and foreign species make specific reference to the international nature of the EXPO 2000 and the trade fairs to be held here. The variety of the vegetation can also be seen as a metaphor for the peaceful coexistence of people of quite different origins.

Set at right angles to the avenues are the undulating park waves and the Earth Garden. The former area, which seems like a detail or section of a larger landscaped park, is distinguished by the outward orientation of its basic thematic content. The Earth Garden, in contrast, is a self-contained, introverted space, a peaceful oasis amid the bustle of trade fairs and the EXPO 2000. In view of the topography, plantings, pavings and the inscriptions in the pavings, this space may be seen to allude to the garden as a paradise that appeals to all the senses.

The Expo Lake, with its larger and smaller areas of water, radiates a sense of calm and expansiveness in comparison with the dynamics of the elongated spaces. Laid out parallel to the United Trees Avenue, it is the focus of the western part of the Expo site.

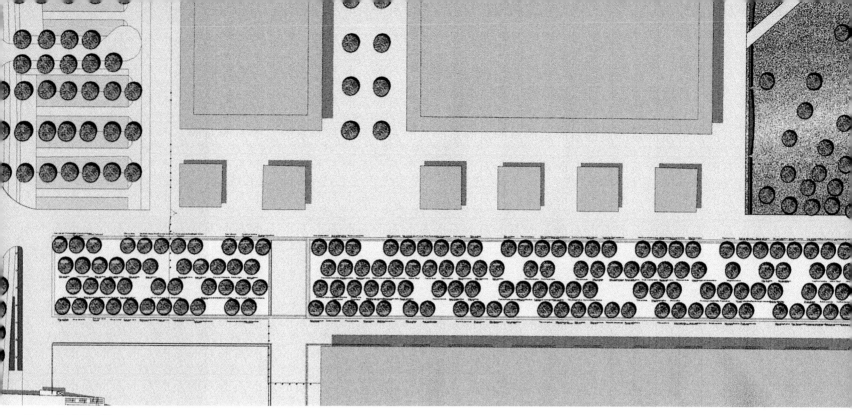

Allee der Vereinigten Bäume
United Trees Avenue

schiedenen Parkbereiche das wichtigste ordnende Element im zukünftigen Messe- und Expo-Westgelände.

Elemente der Parkwelle

Treppenstufen 10 Millimeter starke rohe Stahlprofile mit 32 Zentimeter tiefen begrünten Auftritten.

Pavillon Eine Holzständerkonstruktion mit gehobelter Holzlattung ist als hochgestellter Quader oben vierfach eingeschnitten und auseinanderge-klappt. Durch die verglasten Schlitze fallen Lichtstreifen an die Wände. Eine Betonplatte bildet den Boden. Nachts leuchten große Kerzen den Innen-raum aus und werfen den Lichtschein durch die Glasschlitze nach außen. Ein in sich gekehrter, stiller Ort an exponierter Lage, dramatisch inszeniert.

Stahltreppen im Wald Treppen aus rohem Stahl, seitlich gefaßt, schneiden in die bewaldete 2 : 3-Böschung ein und führen zum Pavillon.

Sitzstufen 15 Millimeter starke rohe Stahlplatten unterstreichen mit ihrem bogenförmigen Verlauf die Bewegung der Parkwelle. Die 80 Zentimeter tiefen Auftritte sind als Rasen ausgebildet.

Landschaftsliegestühle Leichte, transparente Liegestühle aus Metall bieten auf dem Wellenrücken Erholungsmöglichkeiten. In der Form der Liegestühle geschnittene, 50 Zentimeter breite Buchshecken geben den Liegen seitlichen Halt.

See In einer mit Trauerweiden bepflanzten Rasenmulde liegt mit einer

The various areas of parkland that form the landscaped spaces between the old and new halls are the most important ordering element in the future western site for the trade fair and EXPO.

Elements of the Park Waves

Steps Ten-millimetre-thick untreated steel sections with planted treads 32 centimetres wide.

Pavilion Consisting of a timber post construction with wrought timber slats, the cubic vertical volume of the pavilion is cut away at four points at the top and opened up. Light entering through the glazed slits casts bright strips on the walls. The floor consists of a concrete slab. At night, large candles illuminate the interior and cast their light outside through the glass slits. A quiet, introverted, but dramatically staged space in a busy location.

Steel stairs in the woods Leading up to the pavilion are untreated steel steps cut into the wooded slope (2:3 gradient) and restrained at the sides.

Steps for sitting With their curved form, the 15-millimetre-thick untreated steel plates accentuate the sense of movement of the grass slope. The 80-centimetre-wide "treads" are grassed.

Landscape deckchairs Lightweight, transparent metal deckchairs situated on the crests of the waves offer scope for relaxation. Trimmed box hedges 50 centimetres wide enclose the deckchairs at the sides.

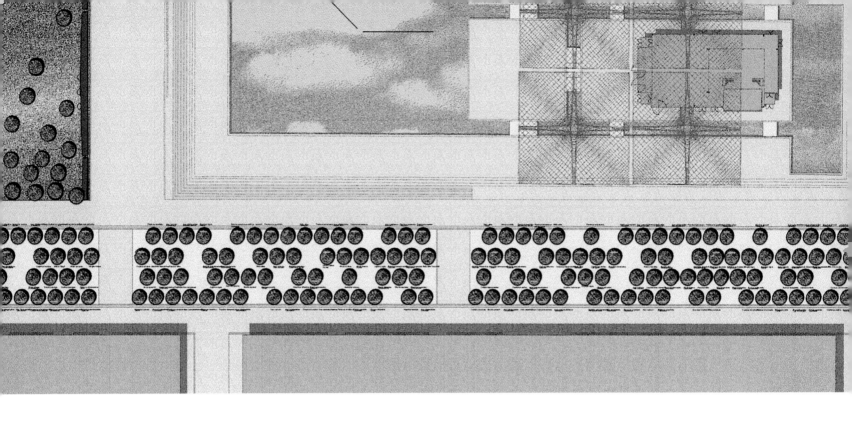

Wassertiefe von 10 bis 50 Zentimetern der See, dessen Wasserspiegel durch einen Wasserzufluß und ein Ablauf- und Überlaufrohr reguliert wird. Der Schotterrasen wird bis ans Ufer geführt. Acht UNP-Stahlprofile liegen nebeneinander auf fünf Stützen auf und bilden so die Fußgängerbrücke. Über die verbreiterte Schotterrasenbrücke gelangt man – vorbei an Pappelpflanzungen und der Wirtschaftszentrale, die noch um 10 Meter nach Norden verbreitert werden soll und deren Dach künstlerisch gestaltet wird – in den südlichen Abschnitt der Parkwelle.

Lindenoval Zehn hochstämmige Linden umrahmen eine geschliffene, ovale Betonplatte. Da sie gefällelos ausgeführt ist, bildet liegenbleibendes Regenwasser einen feinen Film, der ihre Oberfläche zum Glänzen bringt.

Holzstangen 5 Meter hohe, schlanke Stangen aus verschiedenfarbig gestrichenem Lärchenholz werden von blühenden und duftenden Kletterpflanzen berankt und begleiten so das Thema der Sonnenblumenpflanzungen.

Sonnenblumenbeete Linsenförmige Pflanzflächen, 7 Meter lang und bis 2 Meter breit, von rohen Stahlbändern belagsbündig eingefaßt, akzentuieren die ersten 150 Meter der Gartenwelle. Zusammen mit dem provisorischen Charakter der berankten Holzstangen verweisen sie auf ihre kurzes, durch die Dauer der Weltausstellung begrenztes Dasein.

Böschungen Die Steilböschungen am Ostrand der Welle werden mit geotextilen Stützkonstruktionen mit Neigungswinkeln von 60 Grad ausgeführt und mit Efeu bepflanzt.

Die nach oben führenden Böschungen am Westrand mit Neigungsverhältnissen von 2 : 3 werden mit rohen, genau zugeschnittenen, 25 Millimeter starken Stahlplatten verkleidet. Die von oben nach unten verlaufenden,

Lake Situated in a grassy hollow planted with weeping willows, the lake has a depth of between 10 and 50 centimetres. The water level is regulated by a stream flowing into the lake and by an overflow and drainage pipe. The areas of coarse gravel with vegetation growing through it extend down to the water's edge. A pedestrian bridge is formed by eight steel channel sections set next to each other on five columns. Visitors reach the southern section of the park waves across a wider bridge of planted gravel. On the way, they pass newly planted poplars and the services centre, which is to be extended to the north by 10 metres. The roof of the centre will also be subject to an artistic form of design.

Oval of lime trees Ten tall lime trees are set out round a smooth-finished oval concrete slab. Since the slab was laid without inclination, rainwater covers the surface with a thin shiny film.

Timber posts 5-metres-high slender larch posts, painted in various colours, provide support for fragrant, flowering climbing plants which complement the theme of the sunflower plantings.

Sunflower beds The first 150 metres of the garden waves are articulated by planting beds in lenticular form. The beds, 7 metres long and up to 2 metres wide, are enclosed by untreated steel strips set flush with the pavings. Like the provisional character of the wood posts with the climbing plants, the sunflower beds are an expression of the limited life of these measures - designed only for the duration of the World Exposition.

Embankments The steep embankments at the eastern edge of the wave area are executed with geo-textile supporting structures. They have a 60-degree gradient and are planted with ivy. The embankments at the

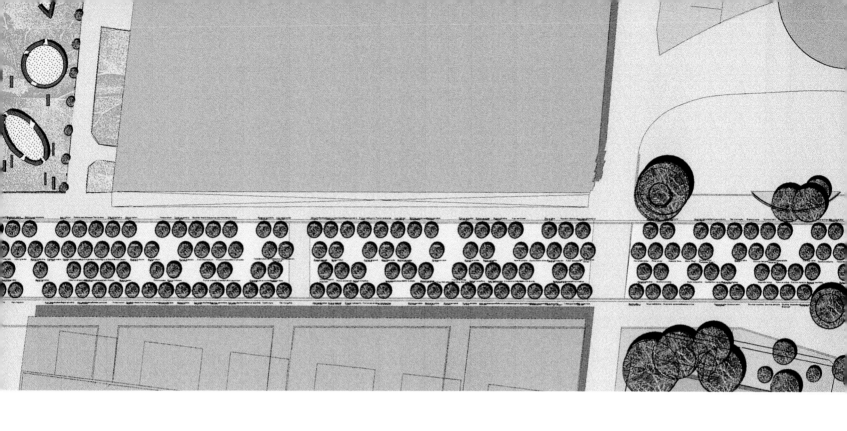

Allee der Vereinigten Bäume
United Trees Avenue

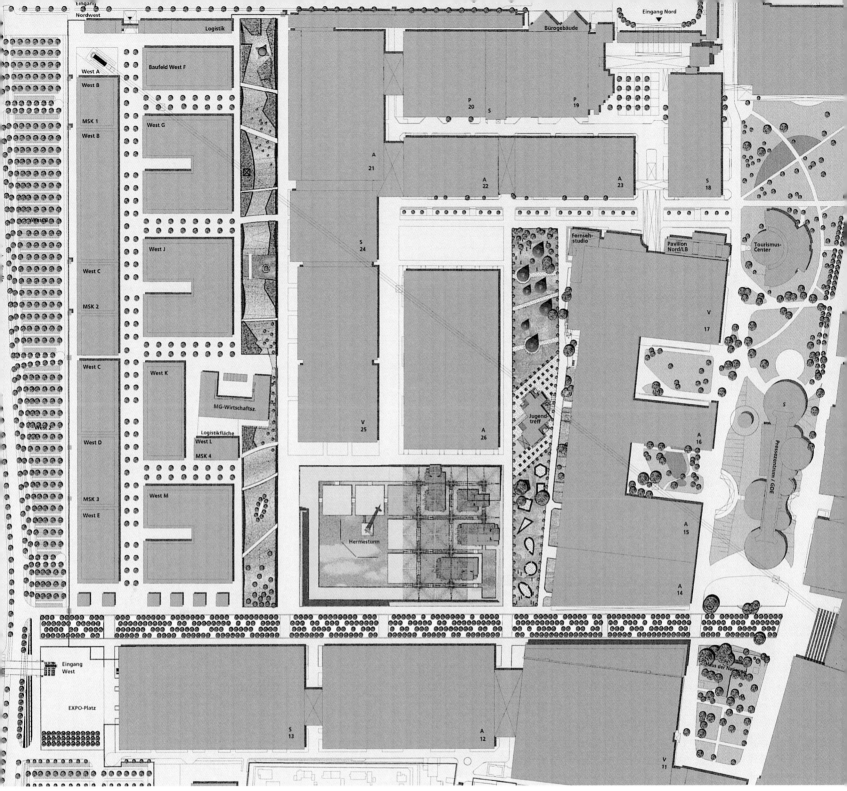

Grundriß Gesamtübersicht
Total Groundplan

5 Zentimeter breiten offenen Fugen werden mit Thymian und anderen trockenheitsverträglichen, duftenden Pflanzen eingesät beziehungsweise ausgepflanzt. Anfallendes Hangwasser wird in einem 30 Zentimeter breiten Versickerungsstreifen am Böschungsfuß gefaßt. Die Böschungen am Westrand, die nach unten in die Rasenmulden führen, weisen Neigungswinkel von 1 : 1 auf und sind immer mit 2,5 Meter breiten Hecken bepflanzt.

In den 100 Zentimeter hohen geschnittenen Hecken, die auf den Böschungskronen verlaufen, schützt ein 90 Zentimeter hoher Zaun gegen Abstürze.

western edge, with a gradient of 2:3, are covered with untreated, precisely cut steel plates 25 millimetres thick. The five-centimetre-wide open joints running from top to bottom of the slope will be planted or sown with thyme and other aromatic plants that can endure dry conditions.
A 30-centimetre-wide soakaway trench at the foot of the slopes collects rainwater from the embankments. At the western edge, the embankments, with grassy hollows at their base, have a slope of 1:1 and are all planted with 2.5-metre-wide hedges. Within the one-metre-high hedges along the crests of the embankments are 90-centimetre fences, designed to prevent people falling down the slope.

Allee der Vereinigten Bäume
United Trees Avenue

Platz und grüne Orte: die Expo-Plaza

External Areas and Landscaped Spaces: The Expo-Plaza

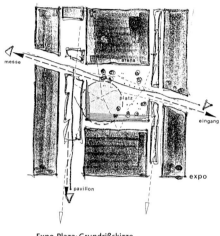

Expo-Plaza: Grundrißskizze
Expo-Plaza: Groundplan

Die vorgefundene Situation war eine schwach von Ost nach West geneigte Fläche. Die Planung stellt die Plaza gleichsam auf ein Podest mit der Grundhöhe NN circa 81,5 Meter. Auf diese Weise entsteht zur westlichen Umgehung hin ein Höhenunterschied von etwa 5 Metern. Die ermittelten Höhenunterschiede nach Norden sowie nach Süden zur Kronsbergstraße werden durch leicht geneigte Rampen überwunden. Der östliche Anschluß an die Neue Laatzener Straße erfolgt annähernd höhengleich.

Die Expo-Plaza setzt sich aus einem Rahmen und einer von diesem gebildeten Fläche zusammen. Der Rahmen wird im Osten durch eine fünfreihige Baumallee artikuliert. Die Plaza ist von Norden – dem Ort der Arena – nach Süden – dem Ort des Deutschen Pavillons – mit einem Gefälle von 2 Prozent flach geneigt.

Der Platz ist der eigentliche Veranstaltungsbereich. Vor dem Deutschen Pavillon befinden sich eine große Stufenanlage, die eine Höhe von 1,5 Metern überwindet, sowie – im Südwestbereich – eine Bühne.

Die raumbildenden Baumalleen aus Platanen – Hochstammsolitärbäumen – bilden eine grüne Platzkante. Die Strenge dieser Alleen wird gelegentlich gebrochen: Bestandsbäume, darunter Apfelbäume, Ahorn und Linde, lockern die Figur auf.

Das Grün der inneren Plaza ist wesentlich charakterisiert durch die Erhaltung einiger Bestandsbäume – Pappeln und Linden im ausgewachsenen Zustand. Ihnen werden einige neu zu pflanzende Großbäume zugesellt. Sie bilden die Maßstäblichkeit auf der Plaza. Die Entscheidung, die Bestandsbäume zu erhalten, führte zu eigenen Gestaltungselementen. Die Fußpunkthöhen bleiben unverändert. Die Veränderung der Topografie macht es erforderlich, daß die Bäume von eigenen »Bauwerken« umgeben sind: Die Bäume stehen in Arenen aus Sitzstufen – entweder abgesenkt oder zu Sitzpyramiden erhöht.

The existing site slopes gently from east to west. The design sets the plaza on a platform at a reference level of approximately 81.5 metres above sea level. This results in a difference in height of roughly 5 metres between the platform and the peripheral route to the west. Gently sloping ramps overcome the differences in height to the north and to Kronsbergstrasse to the south. To the east, the platform is at roughly the same level as Neue Laatzener Strasse.

The Expo-Plaza consists of a supporting framework and the top surface. The frame is articulated to the east by a five-row avenue of trees. The plaza slopes down gently (with a two per cent gradient) from the north - the location of the arena - to the south, where the German Pavilion is situated.

This open public space is a venue for various events. Outside the German Pavilion is a broad flight of steps 1.5 metres high, and to the south-west is a stage area.

The space-enclosing avenue of plane trees, planted as tall individual specimens, forms a green edge to the plaza. The strict lines of these rows of trees are interrupted at certain points. Existing trees, including apple, maple and lime, relieve the rigid order.

The vegetation within the area of the plaza consists mainly of existing trees that have been retained - mature poplars and limes. These will be complemented by additional plantings of mature trees. Together they will help to create a sense of scale within this space. The decision to preserve the existing trees imposed certain design constraints. The ground level at their feet remains unaltered, but in view of the changes in the topography, the trees have to be surrounded with special »structures«. These take the form of »arenas« with the trees at their centres and with steps around the edges on which people may sit. The arenas are

Expo-Plaza mit Überdachung
Expo-Plaza with Roofing

Expo-Plaza im Bau
Expo-Plaza under Construction

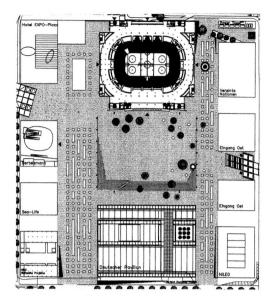

Bestandsbäume
Existing Trees

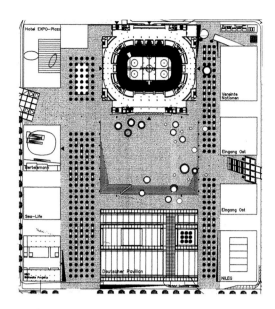

Neupflanzungen
New Plantings

Abends werden diese grünen Orte zu einem besonderen Ereignis, wenn einige Stufenringe aus dem Grund heraus leuchten. Das Licht läßt die Baumkronen gleichsam über der Plaza schweben.

Für die Beläge wurden nach längeren Experimenten Betonvorsatzsteine gewählt.

Die Randbereiche werden mit 25 x 25 Zentimeter messenden Platten, die innere Plaza mit Steinen von 75 x 75 Zentimetern belegt. Das Oberflächenmaterial besteht aus einem Vorsatz, dem Glimmerplättchen und Edelstahlsplitter beigemischt sind.

Das Wasser ist ein weiteres prägendes Element der Konzeption. Es wird in drei Bewegungsformen inszeniert:

Die Fontänen 98 Fontänen sind den Stufen vorgelagert. Sie können tanzen und bewirken ein angenehm erfrischendes Klima.

Nebel Nebeldüsen in den tiefen Baum-Arenen sorgen für eine besondere Stimmung und an heißen Sommertagen für Abkühlung. Der Nebel ist still und wirkt abends zusammen mit dem Licht geheimnisvoll.

Das Wasserauge Das Wasserauge ist ein Spiegel – es liegt unter den Bestandsbäumen und steht für Ruhe und Besinnung.

Insgesamt wird ein Platz geschaffen, der viele Menschen anziehen wird und zugleich Orte anbietet, die zum Verweilen einladen.

either sunk below the general level of the plaza or raised in pyramidal form.

In the evening, these verdant locations become an event in their own right, when some of the rings of steps are illuminated from beneath and appear to radiate from the earth. The light also makes the crowns of the trees seem to float above the plaza.

After extensive trials, concrete blocks with a fine granular surface were chosen for the pavings.

The peripheral areas will be finished with 25 x 25 centimetre slabs and the inner areas of the plaza with 75 x 75 centimetre slabs. The surface is finished with a layer containing mica flakes and stainless-steel particles.

Water is a further distinctive element of the design. It is used in three forms of movement:

Fountains In front of the steps are 98 fountains, which can play in various forms and create a pleasantly refreshing atmosphere.

Mist Mist issuing from outlets in the sunken arenas around the trees evokes a special mood and has a cooling effect on hot summer days. In combination with the lighting in the evening, the scarcely moving mist creates a mysterious ambience.

Water eye The »water eye«, a mirror beneath the existing trees, evokes a mood of silence and contemplation.

The design of the plaza will create a location that will attract large numbers of people and at the same time provide oases that will invite visitors to linger a while.

Entwurf/**Design**: Jörg Schlaich und Volkwin Marg

Verbinden und Verweilen: die EXPO 2000-Fußgängerbrücken

Linking and Lingering: EXPO 2000 Pedestrian Bridges

Ein Entwurf für die geforderten vielseitigen Gestaltungsanforderungen muß ein Inszenierungskonzept für weiträumige Überbrückungen mit jeweils ortsbezogenen Varianten als Ausstellungsinstallation zum Ziel haben. Und so bemüht das angebotene Konzept für die Markierung der Ein- und Übergänge zur EXPO 2000 nicht die konventionelle Figur des festen Stadttors, sondern empfiehlt für den Empfang der Gäste eine dieser offenen Situation angemessene Figur: die des Begrüßungsspaliers – masthohe Stangen mit wehenden Flaggen oder Spruchbändern sowie Zeltdächer, in der Dämmerung und abends Spaliere von Leuchtstäben.

Die Stangen tragen Stege, wie man es von Stegen an Seen und Flüssen kennt. Hier werden die Stege zu Brücken.

Die horizontale Überhöhung gibt dem »Dickicht« der Masten eine wirkungsvolle Dimension in der Vertikalen, die sie beim Durchschreiten zum Raumerlebnis werden lassen: Die Überquerung der Hindernisse und Höhendifferenzen wird – gemessen am räumlichen Erlebnis, das die Installationen vermitteln – zur angenehmen Nebensache.

Die Begrüßungsspaliere lassen sich durch die Gäste der EXPO 2000 auf die unterschiedlichste Art wahrnehmen, interpretieren und nutzen: Die Allee der Vereinigten Bäume läßt sich ebenso assoziieren wie eine festliche Flaggenparade, Zelte zwischen Baumstämmen ebenso wie imaginäre Zwischenräume in den Nagelbrett-Skulpturen des Künstlers Günther Uecker. Auch ein Vergleich mit Pfahlbauten bietet sich an.

Brücken verbinden nicht nur, sie laden auch zum Verweilen ein. Stege an Seen haben diese Qualität – nicht anders übrigens als Brücken über Flüsse in den Metropolen der Welt. Charakter und Ausstattung der Expo 2000-Brücken – Bänke, Nischen und vor der Sonne schützende Zeltdächer – machen aus Ortsverbindungen Aufenthaltsorte, gleich ob es sich um Stege im eigentlichen Sinne handelt oder um Brücken von Autobahnbreite (30 Meter).

A design that seeks to embrace the whole range of formal needs must necessarily include a concept for a system of broad bridging structures capable of variation to meet local situations and having the form of an exhibition installation. The concept proposed for the entrances to the EXPO 2000 and the points of transition within the site does not adopt the conventional form of a four-square urban gateway. To welcome visitors, a concept was sought that would be appropriate to this open situation. A guard of honour was proposed to greet the public: a line of masts with flags or banners fluttering in the wind – together with tent roofs – transformed at dawn and dusk into rows of illuminated staves.

The masts support walkways resembling jetties on lakes and rivers. Here, the walkways become bridges.

The horizontal elevation lends the labyrinth of masts an effective vertical dimension. On passing between them, visitors have an experience of space, so that overcoming the obstacles and the changes of level becomes a pleasant incidental occurrence compared with the spatial experience derived from the installations.

The rows of welcoming masts may be perceived, interpreted and used by visitors to the EXPO 2000 in many different ways, evoking a whole range of images and associations: the United Trees Avenue, a festive parade with banners, tents between the trunks of the trees, the conceptual spaces in the nailed-plank sculptures by the artist Günther Uecker, or even the form of pile structures.

Bridges are not just links between different points. They are also places that invite people to linger on them for a while. Walkways on lakes have this quality, as do the bridges spanning the rivers that flow through the cities of the world. The character of the EXPO 2000 bridges and the facilities they offer – seating, recesses and tent roofs that provide shade from

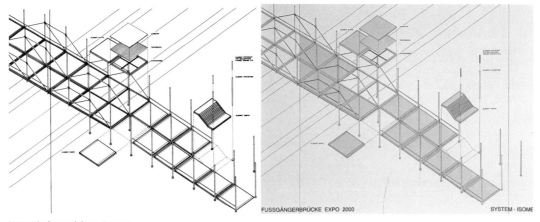

Isometrie des modularen Systems
Isometrics of the Modular System

Ein extrem einfaches, aber gleichermaßen signifikantes, streng modular aufgebautes System: Im Raster von 7,5 x 7,5 Metern werden Stützenstäbe zu einem »Mastenwald« zusammengestellt. Bei größeren Spannweiten – etwa bei der Überbrückung von Straßen – werden die Stützenstäbe in ein abgespanntes Tragwerk eingehängt, das konstruktive und zeichenhafte Funktionen vereint. Je nach Bedarf werden in das Raster Platten, Rampen oder Treppen eingefügt.
An extremely simple but yet significant strictly modular constructive system in grid system 7.5 x 7.5 metres column bars make up a »mast forest«. All larger ranges – i. e. the crossing of a street – the columns BSS go to form past of a three dimensional framework which combines constructed and designed functions. According to need slabs, tamps or stemps are integrated.

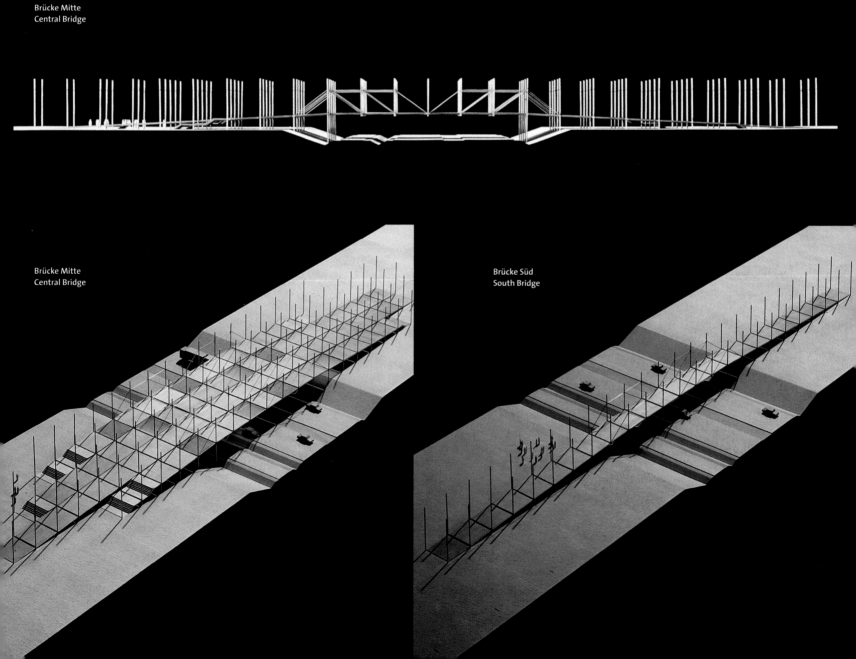

Brücke Mitte
Central Bridge

Brücke Mitte
Central Bridge

Brücke Süd
South Bridge

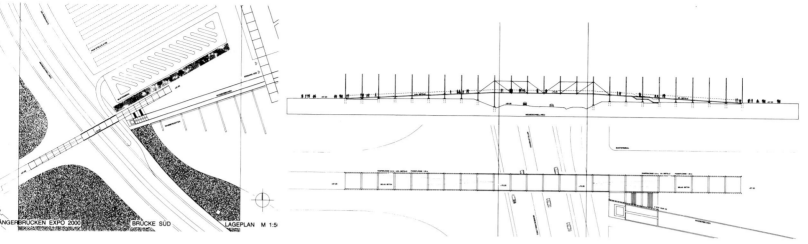

Brücke Süd
South Bridge

Das Raster des Stangenspaliers erlaubt den Wechsel
– von massiven Platten zu offenen Rosten,
– von geschlossenen Betonflächen zu gestreiften Holzbohlen und gerasterten Stahlrosten,
– von Podesten, Treppen, Rampen,
– von transparenten Lichtfugen aus Metallgittern oder Glasplatten im Bandraster zu den großen quadratischen Flächen der Gehflächen.

Den unterschiedlichen Nutzungsmöglichkeiten während und nach der EXPO 2000 entspricht die Möglichkeit des Umbaus oder Abbaus der Module. Als dauerhafte Module sind die stählernen und massiven Versatzelemente konzipiert; die der Verwitterung ausgesetzten hölzernen Elemente lassen sich temporär entfernen und zwischenlagern.

Das Projekt geht mit den eingesetzten Mitteln ökonomisch und ökologisch um: Das Baukastensystem ist hoch flexibel, sparsam in bezug auf Material und Energie. Und nicht zuletzt sind die Elemente wiederverwendbar.

the sun - make these links places where people may relax and spend more time. This applies no matter whether the links are narrow walkways or bridges wide as a motorway (30 metres).

The grid spacing of the rows of masts allows a change
– from solid slab pavings to open gratings;
– from continuous areas of concrete to timber strip paving and gridded steel gratings;
– from platforms to stairs and ramps;
– from transparent joints, consisting of metal gratings or glass in a strip-like grid, to the large quadratic areas of the pavings.

The scope for modifying or removing the modules is reflected in the different uses to which these structures may be put during and after the EXPO 2000. The steel and solid elements are conceived as permanent modules. The timber elements, which are exposed to the weather, can be removed temporarily and stored till needed again.

The project conserves resources and uses them in an ecologically friendly manner. The modular construction system is extremely flexible and economical in the use of materials and energy. Last, but not least, the individual elements can be reused.

Architekten/Architects: Architekten Gössler

Mobilität und Architektur:
der EXPO 2000- und Messebahnhof Hannover Messe/Laatze

Mobility and Architecture:
The Hanover Fair/Laatzen Station for the EXPO 2000

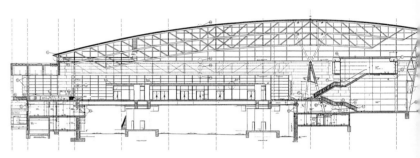

Bahnhofshalle, Längsschnitt
Station, Longitudinal Section

Der EXPO 2000- und Messebahnhof Hannover Messe/Laatzen ist in ost-westlicher Richtung quer über die Gleistraße Hannover-Kassel im Bereich des heutigen Haltepunktes Laatzen gelegt. Der Baukörper findet seine Fortsetzung nach Osten in Richtung EXPO 2000/Messe-Westeingang durch die »Stadtloggia« und das »Dienstleistungszentrum«. Der Bahnhof ist etwa 36 Meter breit und rund 208 Meter lang. Die durchschnittliche Höhe beträgt etwa 12 Meter.

Insgesamt handelt es sich um eine streng axial aufgebaute Struktur, in die die einzelnen Nutzungen als eigenständige geometrische Körper eingestellt sind.

Die etwa 55 Meter breite und rund 32 Meter lange Bahnhofshalle überspannt die Gleise der Fernbahn. Der westliche Gebäudekopf ist der Bahnhofseingang Laatzen. Dieser Teil besitzt ein Tiefgeschoß auf der Höhe des S-Bahnsteigs, der als Kopfbahnhof ausgebildet ist und nicht unter dem Empfangsgebäude mit der sogenannten Verteilplatte liegt (Treppenansatz auch für die Rolltreppen zum S-Bahnsteig, unterster Halt des Bahnsteiglifts, Zentrale für die Steuerungstechnik des Bahnhofs et cetera).

Die Bahnhofshalle zwischen den Achsen eins bis neun ist über die Verteilplatte als Brückenbauwerk über die Fernbahngleise gespannt. Die Verteilebene ist auf vier Rundstützen sowie auf seitlichen Stützbauwerken gelagert. Sie liegt um etwa 3 Meter höher als der Bahnhofsvorplatz (»Stadtloggia«) auf der Messeseite. Im nächsttieferen Bereich dieses Geschosses befinden sich die geforderten Sozialeinrichtungen sowie Lagerräume für die verschiedenen Fachdienste und die gewerblichen Einheiten des Bahnhofs. In die Verteilebene münden die doppelgeschossigen Bahnsteiganlagen sowie der S-Bahnsteig; die Aufzüge befinden sich in den Rundstützen, die des S-Bahnsteiges unmittelbar vor der Bahnhofshalle im Bereich des Bahnhofseingangs Laatzen.

The Hanover Fair/Laatzen Station for the EXPO 2000 is laid out in an east-west direction across the Hanover-Kassel railway line in the area of the present Laatzen Station. The structure is continued eastward - in the direction of the western entrance to the EXPO 2000 and trade fair site - in the form of an »Urban Loggia« and »Service Centre«. The station is roughly 36 metres wide and approximately 208 metres long. It has an average height of about 12 metres.

The structure has a strictly axial layout in which the individual functional elements are inserted as independent geometric volumes.

The station hall, roughly 55 metres wide and 32 metres in length, straddles the long-distance railway lines. At the western end of the building is the entrance to Laatzen Station. This section of the development has a basement storey in the area of the rapid suburban railway (S-Bahn) platforms. The S-Bahn terminal station does not extend beneath the reception building with the so-called »junction area« (staircase and escalator access to the S-Bahn platform; the lowest level of the platform lift; and the technical control centre for the station, etc.)

Between axes one and nine, the station hall bridges the long-distance railway platforms. The distribution level is supported by four circular columns and by load-bearing structures at the sides. On the trade fair side, it lies roughly 3 metres above the level of the station square (Urban Loggia). On the next level down within the same storey are the requisite social facilities for the staff, as well as stores for of the various special services and the commercial areas of the station. The two-storey platform areas are linked with the S-Bahn platform via the distribution area. Lifts are located in the circular columns. Those serving the S-Bahn platform are immediately in front of the station hall near the Laatzen Station entrance.

The primary structure of the two-storey platform tract is in a solid

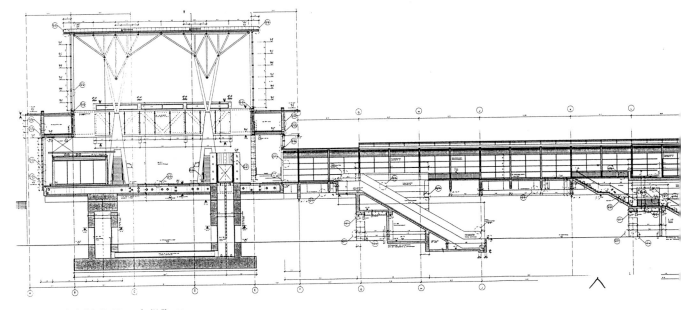

Querschnitt Bahnhofshalle, Längsschnitt Finger
Cross Section Station, Longitudinal Cross Section

Bahnhofshalle, Modell
Station, Model

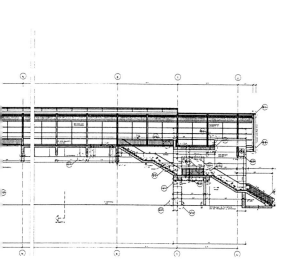

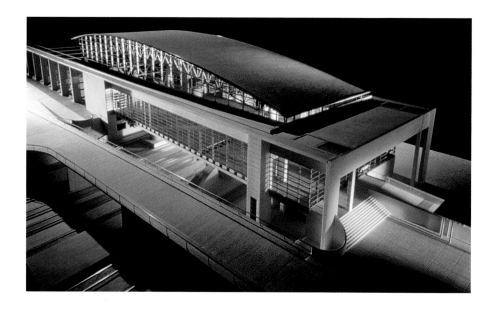

Die zweigeschossigen Bahnsteiganlagen in der Form begehbarer Bahnsteig-dächer haben eine massive Primärkonstruktion, die wetterschützenden Aufbauten sind als Stahl-Glas-Aufbauten konzipiert. Bis auf die eigentlichen Tragbauwerke, die zwischen zwei Scheiben in Längsrichtung die Treppenanlagen aufnehmen, sind die Bahnsteige stützenfrei gehalten. Das Dach des S-Bahnsteiges ist als Stahlkonstruktion vorgesehen.

Die Bahnhofshalle ist eingefaßt durch eine massive Struktur, die drei »Schiffe« in Längsrichtung bildet. Die Seitenschiffe sind rund 6 Meter breit, das Mittelschiff hat eine Breite von 24 Metern. In Längsrichtung haben die Joche einen Achsabstand von 12 Metern. Das Bauwerk ist in diesem Bereich etwa 9 Meter hoch. Das Hauptschiff ist mit einer leichten, an vier Punkten gelagerten Dachkonstruktion aus Stahl und Holz überspannt. Der Sockel des Bauwerks ist aus Beton und Naturstein, das Hallendach aus Stahl und Holz, die Fassaden sind aus Stahl und Glas.

In Längsrichtung vor der Nordfassade der Halle befinden sich vier Positionen für Läden in variabler Größenteilung. Die Shops sind als temporär nutzbare Einbauten konzipiert. Innerhalb der Bahnhofshalle – etwa 6 Meter oberhalb der Verteilebene im Bereich des Messeeingangs – ist ein separater Nutzungsbereich (Café-Bistro, Veranstaltungs- und Konferenzbereich) eingehängt, der über eine Treppenanlage und ein Treppenhaus an die Bahnhofshalle angeschlossen ist.

Im Bereich des Messe-/EXPO 2000-Eingangs finden sich die Angebote der Telekommunikation, der Briefpost und der Postbank. Eine weitere gewerbliche Einheit, etwa für touristische Einrichtungen, läßt sich hier mit direkter Orientierung zum Bahnhofshallenvorplatz plazieren.

form of construction. The structures on top, which provide protection against the weather, are in steel and glass. Apart from the load-bearing elements which support the staircases between two longitudinal slabs, the platforms are column-free. The roof over the S-Bahn platform consists of a steel structure.

The station hall is enclosed by a solid structure comprising three longitudinal bays. The outer bays are 6 metres wide, the middle bay 24 metres wide. In the longitudinal direction, the structural axes are at 12-metre centres. In this area, the building is approximately 9 metres high. The central bay is covered with a lightweight steel and timber roof structure, supported at four points. The plinth at the base of the building is in concrete and stone. Over the hall is a steel-and-timber roof construction, while the façades are in steel and glass.

Along the north face of the hall are four locations for shops. These can be flexibly divided into units of different sizes. The shops are conceived as elements that can be installed separately and used on a temporary basis. Suspended within the station hall, roughly 6 metres above the distribution level in the entrance zone to the trade fair, is a separate functional area containing a café-bistro and facilities for conferences and various other events. These areas can be reached from the station hall via an open flight of stairs and an enclosed staircase.

Near the fair and EXPO 2000 entrance are various telecommunications, mail and post-office banking facilities. A further commercial element - for tourist services, for example - can be located here, directly oriented to the station hall and forecourt.

Architekten/Architects: Pax und Hadamczik

Zentraler Ort: Expo Café

Central Location: Expo Café

Die Figur des Baukörpers bezieht sich auf die stadträumliche Geometrie ebenso wie auf diejenige des Hannoverschen »Cafés am Kröpcke«, das zu einem Expo Café erweitert wird. Ein hochgesetzter, transparenter Glasschirm in der Flucht der Ständehausstraße ist das Fenster der EXPO 2000 in der Innenstadtfassade, Darstellung und Raumbildung zugleich. Lichtobjekte und Informationsträger bilden die lineare Fortsetzung des Glasschirms.

Als hoher, verglaster Raum setzt das Expo Café den Cafégarten fort. Innen und Außen gehen bis ins Obergeschoß ineinander über. Die großzügige Treppenführung macht diese Raumidee erfahrbar.

Im Erdgeschoß bestimmen Bar und EXPO 2000-Info-Shop das Geschehen. Im Veranstaltungsbereich im Obergeschoß bietet die Expo-Gesellschaft ein vielseitiges Programm an: Ausstellungen, Lesungen, Parties und so weiter.

Die »Unterwelt« der Warenanlieferung mit Rampen-, Lüftungs- und Fluchtweg-Bauwerk bildet den Sockel, auf dem das Expo Café sitzt: schwarzer Granit mit Lichtfugen zur Stadt – die Rampenausfahrt wird zwar respektiert, gerät aber in der Konzeption in den Hintergrund.

Das aus schwarzen Emailelementen bestehende, dreieckige aufgesetzte und unterlüftete Dach ist als gestalterisch prägende Ansichtsfläche konzipiert. Im Sommer dient es durch Ventilation als Sonnenschutz.

Der Eingang befindet sich, dem Opernhaus zugewandt, an der Ständehausstraße. Der sich entlang einer Bar beziehungsweise eines Selbstbedienungstresens entwickelnde Caféraum bezieht sich linear auf das Opernfoyer und öffnet sich frontal zum Cafégarten.

Der Aufgang ins Obergeschoß wahrt den Blick auf das Café – der Weg teilt sich und führt zum Veranstaltungsbereich beziehungsweise zur Galerie mit Buffet. Die Nebenräume sind von der Galerie abgeschirmt. Der Veranstaltungsraum ist über Schiebewände in Einheiten zwischen 100 und 250

The shape of the building reflects the spatial geometry of the urban surroundings and that of the Café am Kröpcke in Hanover, which will be extended to create an Expo Café. An elevated transparent glass screen aligned with Ständehausstrasse forms the EXPO 2000 window in the façade oriented to the city centre – self-portrayal and spatial enclosure in one. The line of the screen is continued by lighting objects and signs.

The tall glazed space of the Expo Café forms an extension of the café garden. Internal and external space flow into each other from ground to upper floor level, and the sweeping staircase allows visitors to experience this sense of spatial continuity.

The ground floor is dominated by the bar and the EXPO 2000 information shop. On the upper floor, with areas for various events, the Expo organization will mount an extensive programme of exhibitions, readings, parties, etc.

Deliveries take place in the »netherworld«, with its ramps, ventilation installation and escape routes. The Expo Café is set on top of this plinth zone. It is finished in black granite, with lighting strips in the side facing the city. The concept takes account of the exit ramp, although this plays only a subordinate role.

The triangular roof, consisting of black enamel elements, is conceived as a visible surface – a fifth façade – that plays an important role in the formal design. In summer, its ventilated construction serves as a buffer against insolation.

The entrance is located in Ständehausstrasse, in the side facing the opera house. In its linear form, the café space, extending along the length of a bar and self-service counter, is in fact related to the opera foyer. At the front, it opens on to a café garden.

The stairs to the upper floor afford a view over the café. The route

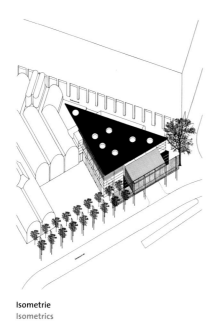

Isometrie
Isometrics

Expo Café (vorn), Café am Kröpcke (hinten)
Expo Café (Front View), Café am Kröpcke (Background)

Quadratmeter teilbar. Ein kleines Studio ist ebenso vorgesehen wie ein Lagerbereich. Der gläserne Aufzug ist rollstuhlgerecht.

Der Sonnenschutz der Glasfassaden erfolgt im oberen Bereich über verstellbare Aluminium-Lamellen, im unteren Bereich über außenliegende Raffstores. Der verglaste Wandschirm wirkt thermisch als Puffer.

Einfache Projektionen mittels Videokanonen erfolgen auf Wandschirmen; am reizvollsten ist ein offenes Bespielen der Raumskulptur, hinzu kommen Projektionen im Cafébereich. Projektionen auf Fassadenflächen lassen sich gleichermaßen vom Café wie von der Stadt aus verfolgen.

Insbesondere die Tag-Nacht-Wirkung ist bei der Planung von Bedeutung gewesen: ein gläserner Wandschirm, eine regelbare Lichtdecke unter dem übergreifenden Dachschirm sowie eine Lichtinszenierung durch Bodenstrahler.

divides and leads to the events area and to a gallery with buffet facilities. The ancillary spaces are screened from the gallery. The events space can be divided up by means of sliding walls into units of between 100 and 250 square metres. A small studio and storage facilities are also provided. The glazed lift is designed for wheelchair use.

Sunshading to the glazed façades at the upper level is in the form of adjustable aluminium louvres. At the lower level, it is provided by external louvre blinds. The glazed wall screen functions as a thermal buffer.

Simple video projections can be made onto wall screens. One of the most attractive features of the café is the possibility for animation of this sculptural space in the form of live activities and other events. In addition, projections can be made in the café area. Those on the areas of the façade can be viewed both from the café and from the city.

Creating an effective day and night contrast was an important part of the planning. This was achieved by means of a glass screen, an adjustable lighting soffit beneath the projecting area of the roof and the dramatic lighting effects created by light spots in the floor.

Klaus Wenzel

EXPO 2000-Geländeplanung:
Phase 1 – Architekturwettbewerbe für komplexe Aufgabenstellungen

EXPO 2000 Site Planning:
Phase I – Architectural Competition for Complex Functions

Die Grundlage des Masterplans aus dem Jahr 1994 war bewußt nicht als unveränderbare Planungsgrundlage konzipiert. Vielmehr bildete sie die Basis für nachfolgende Konkretisierungsschritte, die Basis einer prozeßhaften Fortschreibung – des »Masterplannings«. In dieser ersten Phase der Entwicklungsplanung des Weltausstellungsgeländes galt es nun folgerichtig, den konzeptionellen Ansätzen des Masterplans allseits tragfähige planerische Lösungen zu hinterlegen.

Dieser Entwicklungsprozeß setzt eine strenge terminlich-inhaltliche Disziplin voraus. Wesentlich ist das frühzeitige Erkennen der »Verflechtungsbereiche«, deren Grad an Komplexität wohl jeden herkömmlichen Planungsprozeß zum Scheitern verurteilt hätte. Die zeitliche Priorisierung der Aktivitäten und die frühzeitige Thematisierung besonders komplexer Aufgaben sind ein wesentlicher Verdienst der frühen Masterpläne. Eine der Hauptaufgaben bei der Vorbereitung der Architekturwettbewerbe im Zuge des Masterplannings war die Koordination der im Umfeld befindlichen weiteren Maßnahmenträger, der Deutschen Messe AG, der Stadt Hannover/ EXPO-GRUND GmbH und der Stadt Laatzen.

Im Sinne der Nachhaltigkeit gebauter Umwelt galt es, die auf Langzeit konzipierten Anforderungen dieser Maßnahmenträger mit den verkehrstechnischen, betrieblichen und funktionalen Anforderungen einer Weltausstellung, die ja nur für einen begrenzten Zeitraum von 153 Tagen Spitzenbelastung bedeutet, in Deckung zu bringen. Dank der Kooperationsbereitschaft aller Beteiligten war es möglich, viele zunächst divergierende Anforderungen auf ein Maß allseitiger Verträglichkeit zu bringen. Durch die Formulierung eindeutiger Rahmenbedingungen konnten, ohne den Zeitverlust mehrstufiger Verfahren in Kauf nehmen zu müssen, Realisierungswettbewerbe weitestgehend zielgerichtet ausgelobt werden. Bei den Verfahren wurden Planungsbereiche so weitläufig gefaßt, daß die Verflechtungen

The master plan from 1994 was deliberately not structured as an immutable basis for planning. Instead it was designed as the basis for subsequent phases of concretization, an ongoing process of master planning. In this first phase of development planning for the World Exposition site, the logical step was to buttress the conceptional approaches in the masterplan with viable planning solutions.

This development process requires strict discipline on deadlines and content. A key factor is early recognition of the realms of interdependence, whose level of complexity would have doomed any conventional planning process from the start. Scheduling prioritization of activities and early identification of particularly complex tasks are major benefits of the earlier masterplans. One of the main tasks in preparations for architectural competitions in the course of master planning was coordination of the other organizations and authorities involved in measures (Deutsche Messe AG, the State capital of Hannover/EXPO GRUND GmbH and the town of Laatzen).

The sustainability of the developed environment required congruence between the requirements of the other organizations with their long-term orientation and the transportational, operational and functional requirements of a world exposition – which involves peak capacity for a limited period of only 153 days. The willingness of all parties to co-operate made it possible to bring the multitude of initially divergent requirements together in a generally acceptable manner. Thanks to the formulation of a clear framework it was possible to organize the implementation of competitions without losing time on multi-step procedures. In the procedure used, areas for planning were defined broadly to ensure that interdependencies on the site could be reviewed at the earliest possible stage and in the most comprehensive manner.

innerhalb des Geländes einer möglichst frühzeitigen und umfassenden Betrachtung unterzogen werden konnten.

Zwischen den Jahren 1995 und 1997 wurden unter Federführung der EXPO 2000 Hannover GmbH insgesamt sechs Architekturwettbewerbe durchgeführt. Dabei handelte es sich um Themenstellungen des Städtebaus und der Architektur ebenso wie der Landschaftsarchitektur und des Ingenieurbauwesens.

Der erste Wettbewerb unter Federführung der EXPO 2000 Hannover GmbH wurde 1995 initiiert und hatte als weitere Maßnahmenträger die Deutsche Messe AG, die Stadt Laatzen und maßgeblich die Deutsche Bahn AG. Gegenstand des Wettbewerbs war der für das Gelingen der Weltausstellung heute noch wichtigste Parameter – der Bahnhof Laatzen. Die Bedeutung des Bahnhofs war und ist heute noch elementar – ein Drittel der prognostizierten Weltausstellungsbesucher wird über ihn und den Partner Deutsche Bahn AG das Weltausstellungsgelände erreichen.

Zeitliche Priorisierung war angesagt, da Bahnkapazitäten und Netzplanungen aufeinander abzustimmen waren und Gleisbau und Bau des Bahnhofsgeländes einen verhältnismäßig langen Vorlauf benötigen. Darüber hinaus waren erhebliche Eingriffe im Umfeld des Bahnhofs vorzunehmen. Die Münchener Straße, der Zubringer zum Eingang West, mußte für die benötigten Personenkapazitäten vorbereitet werden; Grundstücksankäufe und Gebäudeabrisse wurden vorgenommen. Ziel des ausgelobten Architektenwettbewerbs war der Realisierungsteil des Bahnhofsareals. Gleichzeitig war das Verfahren aber auch städtebaulicher Ideenwettbewerb für die Erschließung des Eingangs West und für das marode Laatzener Umfeld. Auf Grundlage des Preisträgerentwurfes der Architekten Gössler, Gössler & Döring wurde der Bebauungsplan anschließend rechtskräftig entwickelt, um auf Laatzener Hoheitsgebiet die Basis für ein mittel- und langfristiges Entwicklungspotential darstellen zu können.

Seit Anfang 1998 sind die Gleise des Bahnhofs Laatzen in Betrieb, und die Münchener Straße ist mit einem Lichtraumprofil von 24 Metern Breite fertiggestellt. Ebenfalls realisiert ist das »Highlight« in der Münchener Straße, der »Skywalk« – eine auf der +1-Ebene befindliche gläserne Röhre der Architekten Schulitz + Partner, die circa 20.000 Personen pro Stunde die Gelegenheit gibt, mittels Rollbändern den Haupteingang West des Weltausstellungsgeländes witterungsgeschützt zu erreichen. Das Bahnhofsgelände selbst wird im Jahr 2000 rechtzeitig fertiggestellt werden. Der Bahnhof Laatzen wird dann in der Lage sein, mit dem Fernbahnverkehr, dem vom Flughafen Hannover ankommenden S-Bahn-Verkehr und der Erweiterung des B-Terminals circa 130.000 Besucher täglich zum Weltausstellungsgelände zu bringen.

Annähernd parallel wurde die größte Eingangssituation des Weltausstellungsgeländes – der Eingang West und die Halle 13 – als Realisierungswettbewerb von der Deutsche Messe AG und der EXPO 2000 Hannover GmbH ausgelobt. Der Preisträgerentwurf der Architekten Ackermann und Partner aus dem Jahr 1995 wurde hinsichtlich der Halle 13 nahezu unverändert realisiert. Das Eingangsgebäude hingegen hatte erhebliche Modifikationen erfahren und wurde, nach anhaltender Diskussion, mit großer gestalterischer Distanz zur Klarheit der Halle 13 im Frühjahr 1999 zur CeBIT durch die Deutsche Messe AG fertiggestellt.

Einer der wesentlichsten Bausteine der Entwicklungsplanung für das Weltausstellungsgelände waren die Fußgängerbrücken. Aufgrund der Heterogenität des Geländes haben die Brücken eine elementare verbindende Funktion. Immerhin wird der Zugang zu drei von sechs Weltausstellungseingängen über Fußgängerbrücken gewährleistet. Die wohl wesentlichste

Between 1995 and 1997 six architectural competitions were held under the leadership of EXPO 2000 Hannover GmbH. These involved central issues of town planning and architecture and landscaping and engineering.

The first competition was held under the leadership of the EXPO 2000 Hannover GmbH, together with the other implementing organisations Deutsche Messe AG, the town of Laatzen and as a key player Deutsche Bahn AG (German Federal Railways). The subject of the competition was the object that is still the most important parameter determining the success of the World Exposition – the Laatzen station. The role of the railway station was – and still is – of fundamental importance, given that one-third of the predicted number of World Exposition visitors will come to the World Exposition site through the station and its partner Deutsche Bahn AG.

Scheduling prioritization was crucial, as rail capacity and network planning had to be coordinated and platform construction and development of the station site have relatively long lead times. In addition, extensive work was required in the area around the station. The Münchener Strasse, as the road serving the west entrance, had to be upgraded to handle the number of people, sites had to be acquired and buildings demolished. The goal of the architectural competition was the implementation phase of the station site. At the same time the process was also an urban planning concept competition for the development of the west entrance and the derelict Laatzen area. Based on the winning design by the architects Gössler, Gössler & Döring, the development plan was subsequently given legal force to make it the basis for medium and long term development potential in the Laatzen administrative area.

The platforms of the Laatzen station have been in operation since the start of 1998, and Münchener Straße has been completed with a 24 metres wide clearance. Another completed feature is the highlight of the Münchener Straße scheme, the »Skywalk«, a glass tube one storey up designed by the architects Schulitz + Partner, which protects visitors from the elements as moving walkways carry c. 20,000 people an hour to the west main entrance to the World Exposition site. The station building itself will be completed on schedule in 2000, after which the Laatzen station will have the capacity to transport approximately . 130,000 visitors a day via the railways, the rapid transit link with Hannover airport, its terminal extension and the expansion of the B-terminal.

The second logical step was also held as an implementation competition, this time for the largest entrance complex on the World Exposition site, Entrance West and Hall 13. The 1995 winning design by architects Ackermann und Partner was implemented virtually unmodified as far as Hall 13 is concerned.

One of the most important elements in the development planning for the World Exposition site was the pedestrian bridges. Given the heterogeneity of the site, the bridges have a central integrating function. The bridges provide access to three of the six World Exposition entrances, and the most important link between the west and east site areas is the central bridge from the trade fair grounds to the Plaza, an umbilical link.

Preparations for the competition involved a joint effort by all the organizing bodies of almost unparalleled complexity. A balance had to be struck for dimensions (bridge width) and functionality (ramps or stairs and lifts) between the needs of the World Exposition and the maintenance costs in subsequent use. In addition, besides the organizations and authorities whose participation was already recognized as essential for measures in

Verbindung der Geländeteile West und Ost ist durch die Brücke Mitte vom Messegelände zur Plaza sichergestellt – eine Brücke mit Nabelschnurfunktion.

Die Vorbereitung des Wettbewerbs war eine an Komplexität wohl kaum zu steigernde Gemeinschaftsleistung aller im Umfeld zuständigen Maßnahmenträger. So mußten Dimensionen – die Brückenbreite – und Funktionalität – Rampen oder Aufzüge/Treppen – als Anforderungen für die Weltausstellung gegen die Unterhaltungsaufwendungen in der Nachnutzung abgewogen werden. Über die schon bekannten Maßnahmenträger des Umfelds Deutsche Messe AG, Stadt Laatzen und Landeshauptstadt Hannover/EXPO-GRUND GmbH hinaus waren die Belange der öffentlichen Baulastträger für Bundesfernstraßen zu koordinieren.

Der Wettbewerb wurde im Jahr 1997 als Einladungswettbewerb für Planungsgemeinschaften zwischen Ingenieuren und Architekten ausgelobt. Im Sinne übergeordneter Gestaltungsqualität verlangte die Aufgabenstellung eine familiäre Zusammengehörigkeit aller seinerzeit konzipierten sechs Fußgängerbrücken. Das Ergebnis des Wettbewerbs, entwickelt von der Planungsgemeinschaft Schlaich, Bergermann & Partner und von Gerkan, Marg & Partner, war folgerichtig ein Baukastensystem mit einem hohen Maß an Flexibilität, sich an die unterschiedlichen topografischen Rahmenbedingungen anpassen zu können. Der Entwurf überzeugte vor allem deshalb, da er neben der Darstellung der Torsituation aus der Sicht des Autofahrers die wegbezogene Dimension beim Überqueren der Straße als gestalterisch bestimmendes Motiv entwickelte.

Übergeordnete Einsparungsmaßnahmen führten im Zuge des Masterplannings dazu, daß nur vier der ursprünglich sechs ausgelobten Fußgängerbrücken realisiert werden.

Die nachfolgenden Wettbewerbe beschäftigten sich mit der Konkretisierung der östlichen Geländebereiche.

Das Ergebnis des städtebaulichen Realisierungswettbewerbs zur Expo-Plaza von 1996 war eine der prägenden Entwicklungen des Weltausstellungsgeländes. Die Maßnahmenträger EXPO 2000 Hannover GmbH und Landeshauptstadt Hannover/EXPO-GRUND GmbH lobten diesen städtebaulichen Realisierungswettbewerb als Einladungswettbewerb mit internationaler Besetzung aus. Der Planungsbereich war auch an dieser Stelle größer, als es die eigentliche Aufgabe notwendig gemacht hätte. Einbezogen wurden der Vorplatz und die Eingangssituation Ost sowie die Fußgängerbrücken Ost und Mitte auf funktional-städtebaulicher Ebene. Das Programm des Wettbewerbs sah die Fläche des Deutschen Pavillons vor, der als ein eigenständiger Parallelwettbewerb unter Federführung des Generalkommissariats der EXPO 2000 ausgelobt wurde, sowie die zentrale Veranstaltungsstätte »Arena«. Darüber hinaus waren Flächen vorgesehen, die weitestgehend Investoren zur nachhaltigen Entwicklung der Plaza vorbehalten waren und interimsmäßig während der Weltausstellung verschiedene Programmbestandteile unter dem Thema One-World-Plaza beinhalten sollten. Der Schwierigkeitsgrad der Aufgabe war durch die städtebauliche Situierung dieser Programmbestandteile gegeben.

Das Ergebnis des Wettbewerb-Preisträgers Meinhard von Gerkan (von Gerkan, Marg & Partner) in Planungsgemeinschaft mit den Landschaftsarchitekten Wehberg, Eppinger, Schmidtke & Partner überzeugte insbesondere durch die Klarheit der städtebaulichen Grundfigur und der damit verbundenen genügend großen Robustheit und Flexibilität gegenüber der sich entwickelnden Investorenarchitektur.

Anschließende Rahmenplanungen qualifizierten das Ergebnis des Wettbewerbs zur B-Plan-Reife. Mittlerweile ist durch intensive Anstrengun-

the surrounding area – Deutsche Messe AG, the town of Laatzen and the State capital Hannover/EXPO GRUND GmbH – it was necessary to coordinate the needs of the state agencies involved in Federal railway construction funding.

The competition was held in 1997 as an invitation competition for planning consortia of engineers and architects. In the interests of overall design quality the specifications required identifiable common traits for the six bridges then in the concept. The result of the competition, won by the planning consortium Schlaich, Bergermann & Partner and Gerkan, Marg & Partner, was logically a modular system with a high degree of flexibility, enabling adaptation to the different topographical contexts. The design was particularly impressive in the way it not only showed the gate settings as seen by drivers but also developed the route-specific dimension on crossing the road as a dominant design motif.

Due to overarching austerity measures within the implementation of master planning, only four of the original six pedestrian bridges are being implemented.

The following competitions were then concerned with concrete aspects of the eastern area.

The result of the 1996 urban planning implementation competition for Expo-Plaza was one of the most striking developments of the World Exposition site. The implementing bodies EXPO 2000 Hannover GmbH and the State capital Hannover/EXPO GRUND GmbH organized the implementation competition as an international invitation competition. The planning area at this point was larger than the actual function would have required, including the boarding area for the D-line and the Eastern Entrance setting and East and Central pedestrian bridges at the functional and urban planning level. The competition programme covered the site for the German Pavilion, which was the subject of a parallel competition organized under the leadership of the Office of the Commissioner General of EXPO 2000, and the central location for events, the Arena. In addition there were sites largely reserved for investors for long-term development of the Plaza, which are to house temporary programme elements during the World Exposition under the theme One World Plaza. The difficulty of these specifications was determined by the urban planning positioning of these programme elements.

The result by competition winner Meinhard von Gerkan (von Gerkan, Marg & Partner) as a member of the planning consortium with landscape architects Wehberg, Eppinger, Schmidtke & Partner was particularly impressive by virtue of the clarity of the basic urban planning outline and the associated adequate level of robustness and flexibility for the needs of the developing investor architecture.

Subsequent framework planning advanced the result of the competition to the stage of construction planning. The resulting construction is an impressive justification of the urban planning concept, thanks to the intensive efforts by the implementing bodies and investors. The One World Plaza as a symbol of sustainable development policy will more than satisfy its central function in the World Exposition site.